WHAT SET ME FREE

A True Story of Wrongful Conviction, a Dream Deferred, and a Man Redeemed

Brian Banks
with Mark Dagostino

ATRIA PAPERBACK

New York   London   Toronto   Sydney   New Delhi

ATRIA
PAPERBACK

An Imprint of Simon & Schuster, Inc.
1230 Avenue of the Americas
New York, NY 10020

First Atria Paperback edition July 2019

ATRIA PAPERBACK and colophon are trademarks of Simon & Schuster, Inc.

For information about special discounts for bulk purchases, please contact Simon & Schuster Special Sales at
1-866-506-1949 or business@simonandschuster.com.

The Simon & Schuster Speakers Bureau can bring authors to your live event. For more information, or to book an event,
contact the Simon & Schuster Speakers Bureau at 1-866-248-3049 or visit our website at www.simonspeakers.com.

Interior design by *Wendy Blum*

Manufactured in the United States of America

10 9 8 7 6 5 4 3 2 1

Library of Congress Cataloging-in-Publication Data is available.

ISBN 978-1-9821-2131-0
ISBN 978-1-9821-2132-7 (ebook)

Author's Note

I have chosen in writing my book to name only the heroes. (In most instances, I've simply omitted the names. In the case of my accuser, I have changed her name—in part, I will admit, because I don't care to see her name in my book.) I did this because this is the story of what set me free, not who wronged me. And what's most important in my story is not the false accusation or the action of any individual in the criminal justice system. Even those who may have been trying to do the right thing couldn't, because of the deeply flawed American criminal justice system that was primed to convict me and destroy my life, even after I left prison. It is this system that deserves the blame, but more important is that we focus on the reforms that will ensure that it does provide justice for all those who are not yet free.

Thanks.

ONE

Just a Taste

Freedom.

I was just beginning to taste it.

In that summer of 2002, I was sixteen years old—and I was finally about to start driving.

I'd taken the driver's education course at my high school, and I'd just passed the test to get my learner's permit. I wanted it so bad that I kept checking the mailbox every day after school, just waiting for that permit to arrive so I could start driving for real.

It was more than that, though.

I was in summer school, like I was pretty much every summer, working hard to get my grades up so I would be ready to rise up and meet the possibilities that were right in front of me. I hadn't even started my senior year and I had already made an early commitment to the University of Southern California. *USC!* My dream school. My dream football team. Hell, I could hardly imagine something as big as playing for USC when I was a kid, but I'd worked hard and played my best and now here I was, ranked eleventh in the nation as a linebacker, getting personal calls from USC head coach Pete Carroll, and all kinds of attention from local media along the way. All I had to do was keep playing hard and keep my grades up and I'd be off to college. *Me! And who knows what could happen from there!* If I kept playing like I was playing, everybody told me I'd for sure be a top draft pick out of USC. I'd make it to the NFL. Make some money. Lift my mom and my brother and sister and our whole family up to a whole new *life*!

I still had a long way to go. I knew that. I *knew* that. But I couldn't help but feel as if everything was finally going right—and I wanted to celebrate.

July Fourth was coming up. I knew we had the day off from school, and I mentioned to my mom that I wished I could throw a party.

"Well, as long as you promise to be responsible, I don't see why not," my mom said.

"Are you serious right now?" I asked her. I could hardly believe those words came out of my mother's mouth.

"Yeah, why not? Just a few friends, though."

"Most definitely. But like, you're not gonna be here. You said you were going out of town that day. I mean, I was thinking of inviting some girls, too—"

"Brian," my mom said, looking me right in the eyes, "I trust you."

Whoa. That was something. My mom had never let me or my little brother have girls over to the house, especially if she wasn't going to be there. It's not that she *didn't* trust us; it was just that she's way too much of an old-school Southern Baptist to let anyone think there might be any kind of impropriety going on in her home. The only partying we did at home was for birthdays and Christmas—family parties—and she went all out for those. I remember she'd decorate the whole house, and our uncles and aunties would all show up carrying presents and all kinds of food, and my uncle Stanley would man the barbecue. The family parties my mom threw were always over-the-top. And I swear every year she told us she couldn't afford the presents we wanted. We knew she meant it, too, so we never got our hopes up, but somehow she managed to surprise us with exactly the gifts we wanted when the big day came. I still don't know how she did that on a schoolteacher's salary, but she did. She even did it before she started teaching, when us kids were real little and she'd just gotten divorced from our dad, and laid off from her job, and she was putting herself through school trying to get her degree so she could get a job teaching in the first place. Even then she did it. Every time.

I love my mom. Everybody loves my mom. But the overprotective thing could be frustrating sometimes. I know she did it for our own good. I knew it even then. I understood where she was coming from because I saw what happened to some of our neighbors and friends. I heard stories. I read the news.

Raising kids in a city like Long Beach, California, was challenging. There was temptation all over the place, and the dark side of the city was like a magnet that sometimes sucked kids in and trapped them. A lot of kids went in the wrong direction, got stuck right where they were and never saw anything beyond the city. My mom wasn't having that. She wanted more for her kids. She wanted us to get an education. To go places. She drilled it into our heads nonstop that we could accomplish whatever we wanted if we stayed on the right track. If we worked hard. And it looked like she was going to see her dreams for our possible futures come true.

Heading into that Fourth of July, all I saw was possibility.

I'm pretty sure I know why my mom said "yes" to me throwing a party at that exact moment in time: It was her way of easing up on me. Of letting me know that she realized how hard I'd worked.

Life hadn't gone easy on us those past few years. Just three years before this, my mom's partner of six years, my stepdad, passed away. It left us all reeling. This man, this good man, this kind man who always treated Mom right and who was always so good to us kids, a strong man who'd fought in the Korean War and who taught us kids tai chi—lung cancer took him in a matter of months. He was a lot older than my mom, but he was the most solid father figure my brother and sister and I ever knew. It was shocking. He died right there in the comfortable little home our family had made on the corner of Twenty-Eighth and Magnolia, in one of the safest neighborhoods in Long Beach, and we just couldn't stay there anymore after that. So my mom moved us outside the city, to a townhouse on a quiet cul-de-sac—and without saying a word about it, she asked me to grow up. Fast.

I was six foot one. She needed me to take on the role of protector to her and my older sister. That was clear. She also needed me to be responsible, to be the man of the house. I'd done it. And she had already rewarded me for that with a gift that absolutely blew me away. Now that I was almost old enough to drive, my mom went out and bought me a car— a 1995 Honda Civic, all white with a black stripe down the side—so I'd be able to drive my brother and myself to school now that we lived farther out. I could hardly believe it. But there it was, parked at the curb, waiting for me as I anxiously waited for that learner's permit to come in the mail.

The school we went to, Long Beach Polytechnic High School, is a school like no other. It's a public school with private-school level expectations. It ranks as one of the top high schools anywhere, by all sorts of measures. But its biggest achievement, the thing it's really known for, is producing more NFL players than any other high school in the country. More than sixty NFL players have come out of Poly through the years, and I was slated to be one more. So the pressure to perform at that school was intense.

Long Beach Poly is also world renowned in baseball, basketball, and track and field. In 2005, *Sports Illustrated* named it the "Sports School of the Century," out of all the schools in the whole country. But what's amazing is our school wasn't all about sports. It was all about *everything*. Even our music program was top-notch, producing more than one Grammy Award–winning artist.

I guess another way to put it is to say our school was mixed. Not just mixed race, but mixed interests. To give a little perspective, rappers Snoop Dogg and Nate Dogg both went to Long Beach Poly, but so did actress Cameron Diaz. So did a guy named Keith Kellogg Jr., a decorated army general who's serving as security advisor to the vice president of the United States as I write this book. There were all sorts of different groups and factions, like there are in any high school, I suppose, but no matter what group we were talking about, I got along with all of them.

That was a good thing, because it's a big school—4,400 students—and it's positioned smack in the middle of the 'hood. Our beautiful, fenced-in, multi-building campus was around the corner from car washes and liquor stores, adjacent to some of the most ghetto apartment buildings in the whole city, and near parks where gangs met up.

But the gangs in Long Beach weren't exactly what people think of when they think of gangs in some other cities. They weren't about destroying the city and terrorizing the community. In Long Beach, there are no Bloods. Only Crips. It's an all-Crips city. And while some of the individual gangs would sometimes go to war with each other, there weren't the sort of Bloods-versus-Crips gang wars like you'd see in other places. There were fights between the Hispanic gangs and the black gangs, and those could get ugly sometimes. But when I was growing up, most gangs were just a part of the culture here, a part of the city, a part of feeling like you belonged—whether you belonged to a gang or not.

Some of my friends' dads were in gangs. Even some moms were in gangs. It was no big thing. This was especially true in the 1990s. My first Pop Warner football coach was a respected OG (that's "original gangsta," for those who don't know), and my mom wasn't scared at all to put me in a car with him and send me off to football practice. It was like "Take care of Brian now. We'll see you later!" And off we went.

The Crips presence even affects our language in the way we call each other "cuz." As in, "What up, cuz?" "How you doin', cuz?" If you're from Long Beach, even if you're a white kid, that's pretty much how you say hello.

Gangbangers and those who weren't gangbangers hung out. We were friends. We were classmates. We all interacted together at school—and sometimes at parties, too.

• ◆ •

That Fourth of July, my mom left town just like she'd planned, and I kept the party small just like I'd promised. It was ten, maybe twelve kids total. Some of my teammates. A couple of girls I knew. A couple of girls I didn't know, whom my teammates invited. I manned the barbecue myself, and we turned up the music, and we danced. The community we were in had a shared pool, and late that afternoon we all went and jumped in it. We weren't supposed to have that many guests in the pool and we got a little too noisy before somebody finally kicked us out. I hoped that incident wouldn't get back to my mom, but we were having fun, and I didn't want the fun to stop. So instead of letting things get too rowdy at my mom's place, we all piled into a couple of cars, like teenagers do, and we drove back to Long Beach to a party at my friend's place.

This friend of mine was a gang member, and his party was *huge*. We could make as much noise as we wanted there.

After hanging for a while at that homey's party, full of mostly black teens nodding heads to blaring hip-hop, my friends and I piled into a couple of cars again and drove over to one of my white friends' parties. Now *that* was a whole different scene. It was a full-on frat party. We actually had fraternities at my high school. And this party was like what people describe parties looking like at colleges up in the Northeast or something—a bunch of guys, a bunch of girls, a couple of kegs of beer, all dancing around and hanging out with alternative rock and progressive jam-band music on the stereo. Some of these guys listened to far-out bands like Portishead, and I dug that sound as much as any hip-hop I'd ever heard.

Like I said, I got along with everybody. We had a great time at that party, too. But it was a school night, and we were definitely getting tired. So two of my best friends and I headed back to my mom's house, where we found my little brother messing around with some fireworks. He's just two years behind me. He was an amazing basketball player and apparently he needed to let off some steam that holiday, too: he'd gone and emptied the explosives from a whole bunch of smaller fireworks into big soda bottles, and then tied them all together in a crazy-looking contraption. I think he was waiting for me to get there and supervise before he dared to light the thing off.

After all, a big brother was the closest thing he had to a father figure in our home at that point.

So we took it out to the middle of the cul-de-sac and all gathered around as he lit the wick. Then we looked at each other—and *ran*. We jumped behind my little Honda parked at the curb and poked our heads up just enough to see it, watching that wick burn, waiting to see what would happen.

Then all of a sudden: *Boom!*

That contraption didn't shoot up in the air or pop all sorts of colors. It just plain *exploded*. Like a *bomb*. It set off car alarms for blocks. It was crazy! And it was probably a really stupid thing to do. But we were kids, man. Just kids. And kids sometimes do really stupid things.

Realizing there could be consequences for what we'd just done, we all ran inside as fast as we could and hid in the dark from the curious neighbors as they all turned their lights on and stepped out to see what had happened.

Lucky for us, no one got hurt—and no one came knocking.

The four of us stayed up real late, talking and laughing until we all fell asleep on the living room floor.

Yeah.

That was a good day.

A memorable day.

A momentous day full of friends, and family, and fun.

Freedom.

On that Independence Day of 2002, I could *taste* it.

TWO

Hitting the Spot

For some reason school was open again the very next day. It seemed like half the students were absent that Friday, and those of us who showed up were both tired and rowdy at the same time. A bunch of kids brought bottle rockets in with them and kept setting them off in the quad area. I honestly think the school would have been better off giving us a four-day weekend, because hardly any work got done on that fifth of July at all.

Monday morning, though, July 8, things got serious again. Classes moved like clockwork. Every classroom was full. We were right back to normal—pressure, possibilities, and all. And in the middle of my social studies class, I remembered that I needed to take care of something.

I didn't have a phone of my own. That's one of those things that my mom just couldn't justify paying for month after month. So I asked a friend if I could borrow hers, and I asked my teacher if I could step outside to make an important call.

"Sure, but while you're at it, take these papers down to the main office for me," my teacher said.

The main office was way over in the 100 building, in the middle of the school. I was in the 600 building, at the far end of the campus near the baseball fields, which meant I had to walk outside and across campus to get there. But running an errand seemed like a small price to pay for him letting me out of class to make a phone call. Especially since it was a call to a television producer. A crew had been filming a documentary about our football team. We had played in the first-ever high school football national championships at the beginning of our season, and the camera crew was profiling our whole team in anticipation of the rematch. The producer I was in touch with was planning to come film a segment on me that morning. Just on me! But I hadn't heard from him yet. It was now the last period of the shortened summer-school day, which ended at 12:40, and I knew I would have a couple of hours to kill before football practice started. I expected that we would meet during that time after school, but as the clock ticked down, I needed to know.

The producer didn't pick up the phone the first time I tried him, so I went and dropped the papers off in the office just like my teacher had asked, and I was just about to try him again as I made my way back to class.

That's when I saw Tiana.

Tiana Miller* was two grades below me, the younger sister of a girl I knew in the class just below mine. I'd seen her around the way, but I didn't know her all that well. There being upwards of four thousand students at Long Beach Poly, there are a lot of people you see around and recognize, that you might even talk to now and then, but that doesn't mean you know them. She was one of those people.

---

*This is not her real name. I prefer, for reasons that will soon be clear, not to see her real name in my book.

Tiana was walking right toward me. She was always friendly, and sometimes even a little bit flirty with me. And on this day, when we spotted each other on that empty walkway between the buildings, she said, "Hey, Brian," and she came right over and gave me a hug hello.

"Where you goin'?" I asked her.

"To the bathroom," she said.

"All right, well, I'll walk with you 'cause I'm trying to reach this guy and I don't want to go back to class yet," I said.

"Okay," she responded.

I tried the producer's number again a couple of times as we walked.

She was clearly headed over to the 700 building, a stand-alone building on our fenced-off campus that housed a separate group of classrooms. A building that was supposed to be off-limits to us regular high school kids. There were young-adult nursing classes held on the ground floor of that two-story building, and there were advanced classes for the accelerated programs held in the classrooms upstairs. And anyone caught going into that building who wasn't supposed to go into that building received an automatic suspension from school.

"Why you goin' over here?" I asked Tiana as we walked in the sunshine.

"I like this bathroom better," she said.

I was focused on trying to reach this producer, so I didn't think a whole lot about that. Students who weren't supposed to went into the 700 building all the time. As long as you were real quiet and didn't get caught, it was no big deal.

One of the reasons Long Beach Poly students risked going into the 700 building wasn't for the bathrooms. It was 'cause the

700 building had a private nook in it that everybody knew as a make-out spot—a spot where you could go to have some private time with the guy or the girl you were into at the moment.

I don't know what the culture is like at other high schools, but at Long Beach Poly, all that mixed-interests-intermingling stuff I talked about earlier carried over into relationships. Guys and girls at that school, they hooked up. I'm not talking about sex, necessarily, although our high school was a pretty promiscuous place. But most of the time it was just getting together to make out. Before we even got to high school, kids in my 'hood played games like "Hide and Go Get It." That's like "Hide and Go Seek," except when you find someone of the opposite sex, instead of tagging them and saying "You're it," you're supposed to make out with them, right then and there. And whether it was games like that or full-on boy-girl encounters, the girls were the instigators as often as the guys. It was just casually accepted that if you liked somebody and they liked you, at some point you'd get together and make out. And if you wanted to make out during school hours, or right after school, or before or after practice, the place to go was the Spot.

You'd hear students talking all the time, like "Guess who I just took to the Spot?" or "You'll never believe who I was just at the Spot with." We all knew exactly what that meant. I'd been to the Spot with a few different girls during my three years at Poly, and it had always worked out fine. It was fun. It was cool. And we never got caught. It was flirty and we'd both walk away smiling. Sometimes it turned into something more. Maybe we'd date a little while, or have a relationship. But more times than not it was just a fun and kind of crazy thing to do, and that was the end of it.

So Tiana went into the bathroom, and I stayed out in the hallway and tried the guy's number a couple more times. If he picked up, I told myself, I would run outside before I even said hello, just so I wouldn't get caught in that building. But he never picked up.

When Tiana came out, I was standing with my back against the wall at the far end of the hall, near the elevator. Instead of heading out of the building, she walked toward me, to the water fountain just across from the elevator. She took a drink, and she turned her head and looked at me while she drank that water, and she smiled all flirty like, and suddenly it hit me: "Oh. This girl's *into* me."

I have to admit, I didn't find Tiana all that attractive. She wasn't someone I normally would've been into, but when she looked at me all flirty from that water fountain so close to the Spot, my teenage hormones kicked into overdrive. I immediately thought, *I wonder if this girl wants to make out with me?*

We talked and laughed real quiet for a minute right there, hoping nobody would hear us while I tried the producer one more time. She was definitely flirting, so I flat-out asked her, "Hey, want to go to the Spot?"

"All right," she said without any hesitation. "Let's go!"

We stepped into the elevator to the second floor. It was clear she knew the routine: when the doors opened, we stayed dead silent. There were five or six open classrooms on each side of the hallway in front of us, and we had to make it all the way to the other end of that hall without anyone seeing us. We had to be ninja quiet as we moved, and we *were*. We walked past all those open doors to classes full of students and teachers. Everyone on that campus knew who I was because of football, so anyone who spotted me for even one second would have known I wasn't supposed to be there. It was nerve-racking. We tiptoed all the way, but we made it to the stairway.

We were both smiling and kind of giggling that we'd make it that far. Tiana then led the way down the two flights to the Spot itself: the landing tucked down under the stairs, right next to a double door with no handles on the outside. *That* was the magic. Those doors were the only exit. They were locked from the outside. So no one could come in through those doors. And if anyone came out into the stairwell above and started coming down the stairs, you'd have plenty of time to hear them and get yourself together and maybe even sneak out before you'd get caught. Because the Spot was under the stairs, no one could see you from above. There were no windows. It was completely hidden from view, this place where a couple of teenagers could fool around in privacy and safety.

Tiana was carrying a hall pass with her, which had come from her classroom. It was this big, clear-plastic, pyramid-shaped puzzle toy with a ball inside of it that the user was supposed to tip and manipulate through obstacles and holes on the inside. It was the kind of thing you'd buy from a gift store at a science museum or something. It was big enough that you almost needed two hands to hold it. She set the pass down on the bottom step and we just pulled each other back into the privacy of the Spot and went at it. We were kissing and touching, and she reached up under my shirt, and I reached up under hers. She was feeling on me and I was feeling on her. And it started to get real heated. So I reached down and started to undo her pants, and she didn't stop me. She got even more into it, like she wanted more, and so I undid *my* pants and she reached right in and grabbed ahold of me.

That's when we heard a door upstairs. A teacher stepped onto the landing above us and started speaking Spanish into her cell phone. We froze, still as could be, and tried not to breathe. A minute or so must have gone by before she ended her call and stepped back into the hallway. We heard a door close again, then laughed in a whisper and started at it again. I pushed my pants down around my knees, and she kept rubbing me, and I pushed her pants down around her knees, too. She still had her underwear on, and so did I, and we were both still standing up, but she seemed so into it and it got so hot and heavy that I thought for a second this might be turning into a whole lot more than a make-out.

And that's when I got spooked. It was way too risky. I didn't want to do this.

"Hey," I whispered. "I gotta stop."

She looked at me like I was speaking another language or something.

"Wait, what?" she said, her voice rising up. I'm sure no one had ever stopped her in the middle of making out before.

"I'm sorry. I gotta get back to class," I said.

She looked at me like she just couldn't believe it.

"It's not you," I said. I didn't want to hurt her feelings. "It's just, like, we'll get back to this another time, okay? We're not through here. Uh-uh." I lied.

I didn't want her to feel bad, but I could tell she did.

I pulled my pants up and she pulled hers up, too, and she kind of gave me some attitude as we got ourselves together. She seemed mad.

"Really!" I said. "I've been out of class for a minute, and I got this girl's cell phone. I've still gotta make this call . . ."

She kept looking at me with her brow all furrowed and this fire in her eyes, like I'd insulted her or something.

"Don't trip, Tiana. We'll finish this, we're gonna get together, we just gonna stop for now," I repeated.

"Whatever," she said.

"All right, I gotta go!" I said to her. "You going back the way we came?"

She shrugged.

"Okay, bye," I said, and I turned and stepped out the double doors into the shining bright light of that burning hot July day.

Thankfully there was no one outside those doors. I looked back and Tiana didn't follow me, so I assumed she went back upstairs, down the hallway, and back down the elevator on the other side of the 700 building.

I went back to class. I gave the girl her phone back, and not too long after that, school ended. I met up with a bunch of other football players and we walked over to Tommy's, the burger joint right next to campus. We had a couple of hours to kill before practice started, and Tommy's was great. That little brick takeout joint had a couple of tables outside with built-in plastic umbrellas for some shade, and a big bag of fries only cost like a dollar. So we all got some food and talked and filled up on burgers and sodas and then headed back to campus.

A group of about six of us were sitting in the middle of the quad, still killing time, when we noticed a couple of police officers on campus. There were cops around all the time in that neighborhood, so we didn't think anything of it—until two more cops showed up and walked into the entrance toward the main office. Then two *more* officers walked onto campus and we were like, "What the?" So me, never being the shy one, I got up and walked over to one of the cops and said, "Hey, what's going on?" The cop looked at me and said, "Nothing. We're just here picking up our diplomas."

"All right, man," I said, shaking my head at his lame attempt at humor. "Whatever."

When I got back my friends were all like, "What did he say? What did he say?" and I said, "Man, he didn't say shit. I don't know what's going on."

We kept talking and chilling for a while, until one of the football players' dads walked over and said, "Banks, let me talk to you real quick." I got up and walked away from the table with him and he said, "Did you get into some trouble today or something?"

He was sort of whispering, like he didn't want anyone else to hear us.

"No," I said to him. "I'm good."

"Okay, well, you know, when I was coming in I overheard the police out there on Jackrabbit Lane. I overheard some police over there saying that they were looking for a kid by the last name of Banks."

"What?!"

"Yeah, that's what I heard."

"Okay. Well, you know, I didn't do anything, so . . ."

"All right," he said, "well, you know, I just want to make sure, because I'm pretty sure I heard him say 'Banks.' You may want to check with your little brother and make sure he didn't do nothing."

That scared me. Was my brother in trouble with the cops?

"All right," I said. "I'll go check on my brother." I knew my little brother was in basketball practice behind the gym, on the outside courts, with the rest of the freshman basketball team. So I ran back there and the coach let me pull him aside.

"Did you do something today?" I asked him.

"No. What's going on?" he said.

"Well, supposedly the police are looking for a kid by the last name of Banks, but if you didn't do nothing, don't trip."

"I didn't do nothing," he said again.

"All right," I said. "Go back to practice."

I watched my little brother run back out onto the court, and I turned and walked back around the gym to where my friends were still hanging out.

I didn't think there were any other kids named Banks in our school, and I started to get nervous. Tiana had a reputation for being a bit of a problem child. She was known for bullying other girls. *What if something happened after I left her?* I wondered. *What if she got caught on her way out of the 700 building and ratted me out?*

I wasn't sure why the cops would care about us being in the building, unless she got into a fight with somebody and they needed me as a witness or something. I hoped that kid's dad had overheard something incorrectly. Maybe it wasn't a "Banks" those cops were looking for at all.

Then my mind started running. *Damn, if this girl did something on campus and somebody saw us walking together and thought I was involved, that could be bad.* And then the rational side of me thought, *Nah, I don't think she could've done anything that would warrant the number of police I just saw.*

It never occurred to me that it could be anything else, and certainly not anything I did.

In my mind, in those fleeting few minutes, I concluded that

the cops must not be looking for me or my brother at all. *It must be someone else*. But I couldn't stop wondering, *Who are they looking for? What's going on?* My curiosity led me to go sit on the steps just off-campus, right outside the black fence on Jackrabbit Lane where all the cops were milling around, just in case I might overhear something.

I sat down in the shade with my backpack and pulled my hoodie up around my face as I leaned back, and right then, from the left side of me I spotted Tiana, her mom, her older sister, and three or four police officers walking out in the opening between those black bars. Tiana saw me. She saw me. I was sure of it. We made eye contact. It only lasted a half a second, but she *saw* me. But then she turned her head back and kept walking with those cops. The whole group of them walked right by not more than three feet in front of me.

I didn't know what to think except, *Oh, shit. It is Tiana. She* did *something!*

If she wanted the cops to find me, why wouldn't she have said, "There he is!" She didn't do that, which made me think that maybe the cops were looking for me to ask me about something she'd done, and maybe she had my back and wanted me to get away or something.

Oh my God, I thought. *They really are looking for me!*

So as soon as they turned left and started walking, I stood up real casual and calm. I kept my hoodie on and started walking really slow in the opposite direction down Jackrabbit Lane, toward the back parking lot and the baseball fields. I walked slow, and then a little bit faster, a little bit faster, a little bit faster, and as soon as I turned the corner by the baseball diamond, I shot like the fastest I could ever run. I ran all the way down that parking lot and hopped over the gate and ran across a little piece of the baseball field and over another gate onto Martin Luther King Jr. Avenue. I ran onto Sixteenth Street and straight to one of my friends' houses—a house where I knew a bunch of my homeboys were at. A bunch of my homeboys who were also on the football team.

Sure enough, they were in there playing video games waiting for the practice to start when I burst through the door like I'd just been shot at or something.

"Whoa! What the fuck's going on, bro?" "What you tripping for?" "What's going on?" they yelled.

"Man, I think the police are looking for me," I said, peeking through the curtains on the front window to see if I'd been followed.

My homeboys all looked at each other and started laughing.

"Man, the police ain't looking for you," they said. "Why would the police be looking for you? Like, what would they want?"

My homeboys found it downright laughable that the cops would ever be after me.

"I don't know, man, I don't know, but I think they really looking for me, bro. I think they're really looking for me. Let me use the phone. I'm gonna call my mom."

I picked up the house phone and called my mom's cell phone.

"Mom, I think the police are looking for me," I said.

"Boy, what?" she said.

"I think the police is looking for me."

"For what?"

"I don't know. I don't know," I said.

"Well, what did you do?"

"I didn't do nothing, I didn't do nothing," I said.

"Well, if you didn't do anything, then you don't have anything to worry about," she said.

I wasn't convinced.

"I don't know, Mom. I don't know."

My mom took a deep breath. "Well, look," she said, "if the police really want you, they'll come get you from home. So you come home."

"Okay, Mom. Okay," I said. "I'll see you at home."

I hung up the phone and decided to bolt.

"Watch my backpack for me," I said, and I gave all my homeboys the five.

"Cuz, you're tripping. You're tripping!" they all kept saying.

"I don't know, man. I'm just gonna go home just in case."

I left my backpack in that house as I ran right out the front door. I ran to the nearest bus stop. It felt like divine intervention when the bus pulled up the moment I got there. I boarded and walked all the way to the back and pulled my hoodie around my face and leaned against the window, and my mind kept spinning over and over about what Tiana could have done. *What the fuck is going on? What the fuck is going on?* I was sweating like crazy, and I swear you could see my heart beating through my sweatshirt.

What did she tell the cops? Or what did somebody else *tell the cops? What could she have done? What?!* But I just couldn't think of *anything* that girl could have done in the last few minutes of school that could have warranted all those cops showing up.

Plus, they weren't walking her out in handcuffs. And her

mom and her sister were there. Maybe it wasn't something she did. Maybe something happened at Tiana's house or something.

Slowly but surely, I started to calm down.

Maybe my homeboys were right. Maybe I was tripping.

Maybe Mom is right. Maybe there's nothing to worry about.

THREE

Accused

As I got off the bus, I looked to the left and looked to the right, and there weren't any cops to be found. As I walked the ten minutes from my stop to our front door on the cul-de-sac, I kept looking left and right and glancing over my shoulders the whole way, and I never saw any police anywhere.

Everything must be fine, I thought. *I'm making a big deal out of nothing.*

My mom had made it home from work before I got there, and she asked me to tell her everything the moment I walked in. "Mom, I don't know," I said. "Somebody told me the police were looking for me, but I didn't do anything."

"Did you do anything out of the ordinary today?" she asked me.

I looked at her and I was like, "No, everything was normal today."

I meant it. It wasn't unusual to go make out with someone at the Spot, and nothing else that could even be described as "unusual" had taken place the entire day. Everything was regular.

"Boy, you ain't got nothing to worry about, then," she said. "Somebody overheard the wrong thing is all. You're fine."

25

She gave me a hug, and I truly thought everything was all right.

"You're right. I'll let it go," I said. "I'm gonna get in the shower. I'm sweaty. I've been running," I told her.

"Okay," she said.

I went up to my bedroom. I got undressed. I threw my sweaty clothes into my clothes hamper and took a long, cool shower. It was still hot when I got out, so I put some boxers on and lay down on top of my bed.

And I fell asleep.

◆ ◆ ◆

The pressure on my back woke me up. Something painfully pressing into my spine.

"Wake up!" a man's voice yelled.

I had no idea how long I'd been out. I was still in the fog of sound sleep, flat on my stomach with my head up near the wall, when I realized it was someone's knee in my back. I panicked. I opened my eyes and saw a gun.

"Don't move, don't move!" another voice yelled. "Stay still, stay still, don't move. Put your hands on your back, put your hands on your back!"

"What's going on? What's going on?" I yelled.

My face was facing the wall so I didn't even know for sure if it was the cops or someone else for a second, until I put my hands behind my back and they handcuffed me and yanked me up off the bed. Besides the cop who was holding me there were three other police officers with their guns drawn. The guns were down, pointed toward the ground, but they were drawn. In my bedroom. Even though I had no clothes on. Even though I had no weapon.

They stood me up and started barking at me, "Find something to wear!" "What do you want to wear?" "Pick some clothes right now!"

I started pointing at clothes with my foot because my hands were behind my back. I was half falling over, extending my leg out like, "All right, those pants right there, and then this and that," while I kept asking, "What's going on?" and calling for my mom. "Mom. Mom!"

"I'm right here," I heard her yell from another room. "They won't let me in. They won't let me in! Let me see my boy!"

They held me and forced my clothes onto my body and one of them asked, "Where are the clothes you wore today? Today?!"

"They're in the dirty clothes. Right there in the dirty clothes," I said. One of them pushed over the whole dirty clothes hamper, which was full to the top, and all my clothes spilled out. "Which ones did you wear today?" he yelled again, and I said, "They're under everything now."

They shifted everything out of the way until I pointed, "That right there, right there," and they gathered my school clothes into a big clear bag.

"Mom!" I screamed again.

They led me out of my room, and I saw my mom across the hall in her bedroom, on her knees, screaming and crying at the top of her lungs with two cops bracing her, holding her back. The look on her face. It was as if she had just seen me lying on the street. Dead.

"Mom!" I yelled, as they rushed me down the stairs and out

of the house and shoved me in the backseat of a police car. I could barely fit. There was nothing but inches between the back seat and the front seats. I had to turn sort of sideward with my knees were all pressed up against the back of the front seat, and it felt like it was a thousand degrees in there. They slammed the door and left me alone with all the windows up and my hands cuffed behind my back and they went back inside the house.

I felt like I was going crazy in there. I don't even know how long it was. It felt like an oven. I was sweating so much. They finally came back out and two of the cops got into the car and we started driving.

I didn't want to yell. I didn't want to provoke anything. But I couldn't stay quiet.

"What the hell is this?" I said. "What's going on? Why is this happening?"

That's the first time they told me why I was in handcuffs.

The police officer in the passenger seat looked back over his shoulder and said, "Yeah, man, there's a girl on your campus accusing you of raping her."

"Raping her?" I said. "I didn't rape nobody."

"Well, that's what she's saying you did," he said.

I couldn't believe it. I just couldn't believe it.

I'd seen enough cop shows on TV to know I shouldn't go running my mouth off, so I just sat back in silence. I stayed quiet the rest of the ride. But my mind wasn't quiet. My mind went crazy. The whole time we were in that car for the long ride back from my mom's house to Long Beach, I just kept thinking, *Why would Tiana accuse me of rape? Why? Why?! I don't get it. This is crazy.* And then I'd start talking to myself in my head, like, *Just stay calm. Just stay cool, man. You didn't do anything. You didn't do anything wrong. It'll be okay. Just be honest. When you get the chance, tell them exactly what happened and it'll all be okay.*

I thought they'd be taking me back to a precinct in Long Beach, but instead they drove me to St. Mary Medical Center. They put me in a room and told me they needed to do a rape kit. We waited and waited, just me sitting on a paper-covered exam table and a detective in the corner, until a woman in scrubs came in and told me they needed to undress me. A woman. They pulled my clothes off. No johnny, no robe, no privacy of any kind. As a sixteen-year-old, it was the most embarrassing thing I'd ever experienced.

They started taking pictures of my naked body. She lifted up my scrotum and looked all around and took pictures of that. She got this brush out, this really hard brush, and brushed through my pubic hair so she could take samples of that. Then they got me back into my clothes and sat me in a little room right next to that exam room, and the detective started talking to me. He came at me all heartfelt, like, "All right, man, I know this is a lot. You know, just listen here, if you just tell me what happened, we're gonna figure this out and you're gonna be okay, all right? Just tell me what happened and everything will be figured out."

I didn't know shit about the law. I didn't know that I shouldn't talk without a lawyer. I didn't know that it's a mistake to talk if you're a minor and your parents aren't present. I felt like this guy was trying to help me, like he was trying to figure out what happened.

"First, I've got to tell you," he said, "you have a right to remain silent. Anything you say can and will be used against you in a court of law. . . ."

He recited those Miranda rights just like we've all heard in movies and on TV a thousand times, and they went in one ear and out the other because I wanted to tell him what happened. I wanted to clear this whole thing up and go home.

All I kept thinking was, *Finally, I get to tell somebody I didn't do this!*

And that's what I told him: "I didn't do it."

"Okay, well, I know you didn't do it," he said. "Just tell me what happened so I can figure this out." So I told him exactly what happened. I told him everything I've laid out in this book right here, every detail.

I told him we were together in that stairwell, at the Spot, and that we'd been messing around, and right after I explained all that, he said, "Okay. All right. Give me some time, we'll figure this out," and he got up and left the room.

I wound up sitting in that room for a solid two hours and my mind kept running over everything again and again. I wanted to make sure I told that detective everything that had happened. And I had. Every bit of it. I don't think I left anything out. I was sure that Tiana would corroborate that story. Why wouldn't she? This whole thing was crazy. It had to be some kind of misunderstanding. I remembered seeing her mom with her and thinking maybe her mom just got mad at her or something and this whole story got mixed up. No matter what happened, I hadn't raped her! They *had* to let me go.

At the end of those two hours of waiting, two officers came in and calmly said, "All right, come with us and we'll take you to the precinct. We have some more investigating to do, but you should be all right."

They took me to the Long Beach precinct downtown, a

gray concrete building with a modern glass front. They took off my handcuffs and put me in a holding cell, which was like a glassed-in room in an office building or something. And I sat there. And sat there. I kept rubbing my wrists. I couldn't believe how tight those cuffs had been. They hurt! And why'd I need 'em, anyway? Didn't anybody know who I was? I'd never committed a crime. I'd never been arrested or put in the back of a police car. I'd never even gotten a jaywalking ticket. I'll admit I was kind of a class clown sometimes. I wasn't the most serious student. But even that was a while ago, before I got serious about football and got my first draft letter from USC at the end of my sophomore football season. And no matter how anyone looked at it, I wasn't a criminal.

The whole time I was at that precinct, no one spoke to me. No one told me anything. Through the windows of that cell I could see all these officers on their computers at their desks, and it made me crazy that no one would come talk to me. I didn't see a lawyer. I didn't see my mom. *Where's my mom? Why hasn't she come to get me?* I wondered.

Four or five hours went by with no word, no explanation of what was happening. But the way those cops acted when they brought me over left me feeling positive that this would all be over soon. So I kept that mind-set. I kept telling myself, *This is gonna be figured out, it's just taking a while. They'll figure it out it. They'll figure it out. It's all gonna be okay.*

Finally two officers came over and unlocked the door. "All right, Banks, come on," one of them said. *Yes,* I thought.

But as I stepped to the doorway they put the handcuffs back on me.

"Is everything cool?" I asked.

"Well, it looks like you've got to see a judge," one of them said. I was dejected. But I still thought everything was going to be okay. So I shrugged my shoulders and said, "Okay."

I didn't fight it. I tried not to let myself get upset. I was innocent. I hadn't done anything. The judge would know that instantly. *This will all get sorted out*, I told myself again.

"Well, you ain't gonna be able to see him tonight," the other cop told me, "but you've got to see a judge within seventy-two hours, so you may see him tomorrow, but in the meantime, we gotta take you to Juvenile Hall for holding, and you got to stay at the Juvenile Hall."

My whole body got stiff.

"Oh my God," I said. "I don't want to go to jail."

"You don't have a choice," they told me. "We can't keep you here."

I started to freak out. I could feel myself shaking. My stomach got all twisted up in a knot. I could feel my heart beating fast in my chest.

They took me out and put me into the back of a police car again, only this time there was someone else in there. A girl. Handcuffed, just like me. We didn't say anything to each other. We just sort of nodded and then looked away as they started the car and took off. It was a twenty-five-minute drive to Los Padrinos Juvenile Hall in Downey. Twenty-five minutes of wondering what in the hell I was going to face on the inside. I had no idea. No concept of what Juvenile Hall would look like. I'd never talked to anyone who'd been there. I'd never imagined I would go to jail, ever.

The cops got out when we pulled into the parking lot, and the girl and I were alone for a minute.

She looked out the window and said, "Yeah, I've been here before."

She was around my age, but the way she said it, it was like she was a veteran criminal or something.

"You've been here?"

"Yeah, man. I've been to this place. This ain't shit," she said. "You been locked up before?"

"No," I said.

"Oh. It's crazy as fuck in there, man," she said. "It's crazy."

Before I could ask her what she meant by that, the cops were back, opening our doors and pulling us out.

I was scared.

They walked me into a room and handed me off to another set of officers, or prison guards, or whatever they were. I didn't know. I just stayed quiet. I didn't want to cause trouble. I didn't want to do anything that might make things worse.

They took the handcuffs off. They took me into a room. They told me to take my clothes off. All of them. "Right in front of you?" I asked.

"Right now," they said.

I closed my eyes. *This ain't happening right now,* I told myself. *This ain't happening.*

"Now!" they yelled.

I stripped down naked, completely naked, and a guard said, "Hands on," and ran his hands over my body. They made me put my arms up in the air and checked my armpits, and open my mouth and stick out my tongue while they looked inside. They told me to bend my head down while they ran a hand in my hair and over my ears, then spread my legs and lift up my scrotum to make sure I didn't have anything hiding under my sac. I felt so violated. So helpless.

"Turn around," they said, and they asked me to lift up one foot at a time and wiggle my toes. Then spread my butt cheeks, squat, and "cough two times."

"That's it," they said. "Remember that routine. You'll be doing it again."

From there they marched me into a shower stall and made me shower while they stood there watching. Then the handed me some inmate clothing, blue and gray, like a cheap sweat suit.

"Get dressed," they said.

They marched me to the medical ward, where a doctor or nurse or somebody poked and prodded me and took my temperature and stuff, and by the time all that was through, it must have been two or three o'clock in the morning.

I was wired. On edge. Exhausted. Scared. I kept telling myself, *This is not my life. This is not happening. This is not real right now.*

They took me to this place that they said would be my module, but someone said the module was full, so they put me into a "day room" instead, and told me that's where I'd sleep for the night, "Until we put you in a cell tomorrow." There was a little plastic cot, like a tiny boat almost, down on the floor with a thin mattress on it. It was about the thickness of an exercise mat.

I was shaking. I was so scared. I couldn't believe any of this was happening. I was alone in that room with one window, and I was glad. I didn't want to be in some cell with some criminal. Who knows what some of the kids in there had done? Who knows what they would do to a new kid like me?

My body finally gave out. The exhaustion of it all took over. I fell asleep. It felt like I'd just closed my eyes when a loud bang woke me up. "Fuck!" I said, popping my eyes open. Somebody had banged on the window, and I couldn't believe it but light was streaming in through the glass. It was morning already. I was so far down on the ground that I couldn't see anything, so I lifted myself up onto my knees, and I stood up. Outside that window I saw a line of about thirty inmates, all dressed in orange, each of them standing with a small towel in his hand, getting ready to go brush his teeth and wash up.

These were kids. Like me. A couple of them noticed me looking and elbowed each other, and pointed, and started joking around about something. The guys behind them looked my way, too. I felt like an animal in a cage. In a zoo.

I wasn't dressed in orange yet. I didn't know what that meant. I didn't know what was gonna happen. I couldn't understand why I was there, why no one had fixed this, why I hadn't seen my mom.

And it all just hit me: *I'm in jail. God. Help me, please. God help me. I'm in* jail.

FOUR

Caged

I heard the key turn. A guard I hadn't seen the night before opened my door. He couldn't have been more than five foot six. He took one quick up-and-down look at my six-foot-one, football-ready body and his eyes went wide.

"God damn," he said. "You are not a juvenile. There's no *way* you're a juvenile."

I didn't respond.

"All right, come with me, son," he said, and I stepped with him into the hallway. As we passed another guard he said right out loud again, "There's no way this kid is a fucking juvenile!"

He brought me into an office, where they made me sit in the corner on the floor. They started calling all of these places, trying to verifying my birth certificate. A bunch of guards stopped in one by one to take a look at me, and I realized I was bigger than every guard there. There was not a guard my size in Juvenile Hall.

In between phone calls, that first guard took a look at my charges, which were printed on a piece of paper he had on a clipboard, and he asked me what happened. And I told him. I explained the whole thing, just like I'd explained to the detective the day before. I said a little bit about who I was, and what high school I went to, and how I'd already committed to USC, and he said, "Oh, yeah! I think I've heard of you. I've heard of you, man."

Finally. I was glad someone seemed to recognize something about me, to recognize that I wasn't their typical inmate. "Well, look, I can tell you're real scared, but if what you're telling me happened the way you say it happened, you'll get out of here just fine. They'll figure it out. I'm sure once you're in front of the judge and everything, it'll be fine."

His words put me at ease for a minute. This was a guy on the inside. A part of the system. A guy who saw stuff, and knew stuff. And if he thought I'd be fine, that I just had to be patient, then I was definitely going to take his words to heart.

They eventually confirmed that I was sixteen and they got ready to house me, but because I had a "sex offense," they said they had to house me by myself. I was kind of glad about that. I was scared of getting put in a cell with some hardened-criminal kid. But once they brought me down to this tiny concrete cell, I realized what "by myself" really meant.

They were putting me in HRO—the High Risk Offender unit. They dressed me in orange, so everyone would recognize just how "high-risk" I was.

When the guard opened the door to that concrete hole, it chilled me. It was a cell for two, with two beds against the walls, across from each other. They were like old military-style bunks, all metal and bolted to the floor. The metal was old and rusted, almost crusty, with graffiti carved all over it. One bed didn't have a mattress. The other, the one with a mattress so thin it looked more like an old worn exercise mat, was for me. There was one window at the back of the cell with chicken wire in it. A mesh of metal so you couldn't bust out. There was graffiti carved into the walls, the ceiling, the door, everywhere.

"Leave your shoes," the guard said. "Your shoes stay outside the door."

I took them off and stepped inside.

"If you want to use the bathroom, knock on the door. When I can get to you, I will come take you to the bathroom," he said. "If not, you hold it and you wait."

He started to close the door.

"Oh, and when it's lights-out, your pants go outside this door, too," he added.

"How come?" I asked.

"'Cause we don't want none of you kids hanging yourselves in the dark."

He shut the door with a tremendous *thud* as I stood there staring at it from the other side. The door was solid except for a small window in the top half, which allowed the guards to peek in and see me. There was a fluorescent light way up in the ceiling, protected by a foggy thick plate of Plexiglas. That was it. Once the echo of the thud stopped, that room fell heavy with silence. I sat on the bunk. It wasn't even as wide as a twin-size bed. I lay down. My feet stretched out past the end of the mat. I had to go on my side and curl my legs up in order to fit. I did that. I faced the wall. And I cried.

How was I supposed to make sense of this? I'd been running around, going to parties, going to practice, going to school, living my *life*! Now I was behind a steel door? Incarcerated?

I didn't see another person the rest of that day except for the guard. But I heard them. At one point some other inmates started talking, then arguing, then screaming from cell to cell.

Then a bunch of them started kicking their doors and shouting and banging, until the guard came down the hallway and yelled, "Quit your hoot banging!"

When it quieted down, I got up to look out the window on the door. All I could see was another cell door across the way, and another cell door on each side of that.

At one point the guard came by and opened my door and told me it was time to eat. I was supposed to go down to the day room. I couldn't. I couldn't think about eating. My stomach was in a knot too tight to accept any sort of food at all.

"Fine. Stay here, then," he said, and he slammed the door again.

As the hours ticked by, it became clearer and clearer that I wasn't going to see a judge that day. Somewhere along the line, someone said something about courts closing at four thirty or something. Maybe someone said that the night before. I couldn't remember who said it. But after the lunch I failed to eat, as I felt the hours tick by in that silence, with the buzz of the fluorescent light getting louder all the time, and nothing but the occasional slam of a door or the shout of some fool down the hall getting through to my ears, I figured it had to be three or three thirty in the afternoon already. Given how much time it had taken to process me into that cell, and the slow-motion way in which everything in that Juvenile Hall seemed to move, I knew there was no way they were preparing to pull me out and drive me all the way back to some courtroom in Long Beach before closing time.

Oh my God, I thought. *I should be at football practice right now.*

I worried what everybody must be thinking about me, and

saying about me. It burned me that I couldn't tell them what really happened. I couldn't defend myself. All that gossip and storytelling would keep spinning till I got home.

I still hadn't seen my mom, or an attorney, or anybody. They said I'd see a judge within seventy-two hours. I'm not sure when that clock started ticking, but even if it had started the moment they pulled me from my bed, only twenty-four hours had gone by.

It had been only one day.

One day, I thought. *What if I'm in here three whole days before I see that judge? Before they figure this out?*

I started to tear up again. I didn't want to cry. I didn't want to show any weakness. I didn't want the guards to see that. But I couldn't help it. I couldn't stop it. That's when I folded the blanket for the first time and set it on the floor right next to that bed, and I got down on my knees, wiped those tears away, and prayed.

"Our Father, who art in Heaven, hallowed be thy name. . . ."

The Lord's Prayer was the only real prayer I had committed to memory. In a way, I'd been praying to God ever since this thing started. But those prayers were more like begging. *Please God. Help me, please. Make this stop! This is crazy!*

The Lord's Prayer? I said that one out loud. I whispered it. I didn't want anyone to hear me. But I felt the need to speak it.

We were the kind of family that went to church every Sunday. My godfather was a preacher who'd built his church with his own two hands, a Baptist church up in Compton. God was in my blood. In my heart. In my history. My mother was raised in Clarksdale, Mississippi, one of twelve kids, and her mother, my grandma, was deeply religious. She's the kind of woman who rises at four o'clock in the morning and prays until seven, every day. And her love of God and trust in God's strength trickled down in one way or another to pretty much everyone in our family. And our family was close. Not just close like we cared about each other, but physically close, too. We were a family who shared when it mattered. When we had an apartment, it always seemed that one of my aunties or cousins would be down on their luck and needing a place to stay, and we always took them in. Sometimes a year or two at a time. And then when we were between apartments or houses, we'd move in with one of them.

Someone always said grace at the dinner table. Someone was always saying a prayer for somebody. Someone was always giving thanks to Jesus when some bad thing turned out okay. And most of the time, no matter how bad things got, things turned out okay in our family. They really did. Other than the passing of my stepdad, I could hardly think of something truly awful that had ever happened to me. For the most part, our lives seemed blessed.

Except for this. Except till now. So with no one and nothing else to lean on, I leaned on God.

Before lights-out, a guard came to collect my pants. He told me to roll them up real neat and place them on top of my shoes outside the door. I stepped back inside. He shut the door. *Thud*. The lights went out. It was pitch black except for a tiny light that gave just enough glow to let the guards look through that four-inch window and see me.

I thought about my mom. The image of her on her knees screaming as they rushed me out my room and down the stairs was burned into my head. I thought about her crying and it made me cry. I hated it. I could hardly imagine what she must be feeling about all of this.

I thought about my little brother, and how the last time I'd seen him he was running back onto the basketball court. How my mom must've told him what happened. I wondered if he went to school the next day. *Today. Was he in school today? It's Tuesday. What if he saw Tiana? They're in the same grade. What if he saw her? Oh shit. I hope he didn't lose it on her. Was she in school, even? Did she go back to school after accusing me of this?*

When there's no one to talk to, a mind tends to spin. And my mind spun hard. Over and over. Reliving the minutes of that Monday, July 8. Retracing every moment of what happened between Tiana and me in that stairwell. Questioning my actions. Wishing the teacher had refused to let me make that call. Wishing the producer had shown up early and taken me out of class. Wishing I'd made that call from right outside the classroom and just gone back in when he didn't pick up, which is exactly what I'd have done if the teacher didn't ask me to take the attendance sheets down to the main office. Wishing I'd said hi to Tiana and then kept on going. Wishing that producer had just picked up the phone, causing me to exit the 700 building while she was in the bathroom. Wishing I'd never asked her if she wanted to go to the Spot.

There must have been a million ways things could've gone down differently. That teacher who'd walked out onto the landing speaking Spanish could've heard us and yelled at us. Hell, if someone had caught us when we tiptoed past all those open classrooms and I'd gotten an automatic suspension, that would have been a whole lot better than this!

I thought about my backpack, sitting on the floor at my friends' house. Was somebody gonna pick that up? Or bring it back to school?

I started to worry about what this was going to do to my football career. I'd now missed two days of practice. *Nobody in a position like mine misses two whole days of practice.* I was a starter now. A leader. This was my big year! I was first on the field. Last off most of the time. I was dedicated. How could I just not show up? *What are my coaches thinking? What if everybody's talking about me? What if people believe I did it?*

God, please don't let anyone believe I could do something like this. I could never rape a girl. Ever. I couldn't even think about it. How could anyone believe I could do something like that?

I worried about missing homework. I wondered if my learner's permit had arrived in the mail. I worried that the documentary crew would finish their film without me.

Oh God. Please, please don't let any of this get back to any of the schools that are trying to recruit me. Don't let it get back to Coach Carroll. Please don't let this stop me from going to USC. Please. Please!

● ◆ ●

The next morning, I still couldn't eat.

I didn't want to socialize. I stayed in my cell even when they said I could go out to the yard.

At one point a guard came and got me and said there was a lawyer there to see me.

Thank God.

They took me into a room and this attorney introduced himself. He said he was a friend of my mom's, and that he was a family attorney, not a criminal attorney, but he was there to help me in whatever way he could.

"Well, thank you," I said. "I'm just glad somebody's finally talking to me. I don't even know what I'm really accused of."

"Brian," he said, "you're accused of raping a girl at your school. Juanita or, um, Wan—"

"Tiana Miller. Yeah. I gathered that. But I don't know what she said, I mean. What did she say I did to her?"

"I don't have those details. The fact is, we won't know until and unless we get a preliminary hearing and start to get some discovery in this case. But the arraignment happens before that, and with any luck, you'll be released on your own recognizance, and we can get this all sorted out then. You have no priors, so I'll be asking for OR for sure. So, why don't you tell me what happened, in your own words, just so I know where we stand and what we might be up against."

I told him the whole story. And he started asking all these weird questions, pressing for details about whether or not it could have "seemed" like I raped her, like if I'd pushed her to the ground or rolled onto her when our pants were pulled down (*No!*), and what the curvature of my penis was like.

"What does that have to do with anything?" I said. "We didn't have sex. We didn't have intercourse. We were touching. We were standing the whole time and we, like, bumped up against each other and touched with our hands and that's it. There was no sex. There was no rape. We were both into it, just making out, until I stopped."

"Okay, okay," he said.

He didn't really explain what was going to happen when I saw the judge, and I left that meeting still not knowing when that "arraignment" was going to happen.

"If we don't get in today, then we'll get in tomorrow for sure," he said. "So hang tight."

"And my mom? When can I see my mom? Where is she? How's she doing?"

"She's real upset, as you can imagine. But you'll see her at the hearing. She'll be there. And then hopefully you'll go home with her from there. Okay? Hang tight, Brian."

"Okay," I said.

Hang tight. Like I was sitting on the bench waiting to get into the game or something. Did this guy have any idea what it was like to sit in a concrete cell twenty-two hours a day? I felt like I was going to lose my mind.

Over the course of the rest of that second day behind bars, a couple of other guards asked me what I was in for, and whether I'd done it. They all seemed to pick up on the fact that I didn't look like some kind of criminal. More than one of them said they could tell I looked real scared and upset, like I didn't belong there. And when I told each of those guards my story, each one of them said, "Oh, I'm sure you'll get out of here after you get in front of a judge."

So I kept on thinking, *I'll be okay. I'll be out of here soon. Once I see the judge they're gonna throw this thing out.*

I kept thinking of what would happen in a day or two when I was back on the football field and everything was okay. The documentary crew had been out there filming us that Friday after the Fourth of July, and our team was on fire. We were gearing up for the most exciting game of our lives. We were getting ready to fly to Hawaii! De La Salle High School had beat us in the national championships the previous season, so they were number one, and we were number two. And the number one and number two teams in Hawaii had gone and called both of our teams out. They wanted to challenge us. They believed they could beat the mainland teams! So they set up a preseason exhibition game in Hawaii that we'd been prepping for all year. Our whole team was flying to Hawaii in just a few weeks, all expenses paid. I'd never been to Hawaii. I'd never been much of anywhere outside of California in my life. I was so excited. Our whole *team* was excited. We were ready to play.

My personality on the football field was pure leadership, and I tried to stay focused on that instead of focusing on where I was. I was the leader of the defense, one of the leaders of the team. I'm the guy who's gonna run us out of the tunnel! I'm the guy in the locker room saying, *Let's go. Let's do this!* The one who hypes everybody up.

I tried to think like that in that concrete cell. I tried to psych myself up for winning my release in front of the judge.

I'll be okay. I'll be out of here soon. Once I see a judge and the judge sees me *this will all be over. They're gonna throw this thing out. No problem.*

I thought those thoughts when I skipped dinner that night. I thought those thoughts as I took off my pants and rolled them neatly and set them outside my door. I thought them as I prayed to God on that concrete bunk, under that thin blanket, as I tried to sleep. I thought them as they took me from my cell the next morning, and took me back to the same place where they'd brought me in, and they told me to strip off my clothes, and I held my hands up over my head as a strange man ran his hands over my body and made me bend over and squat and the whole routine before they put me back in my prison garb and loaded me into a van for the twenty-five-minute ride back to Long Beach. I convinced myself that I would never be going back to that place. Juvenile Hall was now behind me forever.

I thought those thoughts as they put me in a holding cell at the courthouse, a concrete building right next to the downtown precinct where the cops had brought me after my rape kit was finished, and they kept me locked up there for three or four hours before someone finally took me out and put me in a little private room for a few minutes with my attorney. I thought those thoughts as the attorney fumbled over some paperwork and looked real nervous, giving me a vibe like he'd never done anything like this.

But when the bailiff came and took me to the courtroom, walking me into a jury box area off to one side of that beige room, and I looked across the dark wooden tables to the guest box on the other side of that room and I saw my mom, I lost it. I started bawling.

"Mom!" I called. "I want to go home. I want to go home!"

"Calm down, baby," my mom called, making a calm-down gesture with both hands, up and down. "I know," she said. "I know. Shhhh. Shhhh!"

My attorney rushed over and told me to calm down, too. I couldn't act like that in the courtroom, he said. That wouldn't go over well with the judge. But I couldn't stop.

I was shaking as I took a seat. I started rocking back and forth. It all came rushing over me. My mom was there with my dad. My *dad*. He hadn't been like a father to me since he left my mom, when I was three years old. He'd moved away. He was my father with another family. We'd stay with him from time to time, and help him out with his handyman business some summers, and he'd show up on holidays with some cheap gifts for us even though he made good money. But he wasn't my "dad." And now I had to see him like *this*? It was confusing to me. And my sister was with them. My older sister. She'd apparently flown all the way back from Howard University in Washington, D.C., and I hadn't seen her in what felt like ages. I couldn't stand her seeing me like this. What if some part of her believed I did this? What if some part of my father believed I did this? It broke my heart. My mom would never believe it. Never. But what about the rest of my family? *Oh God, please, please let this end!*

I was a mess.

"All rise," the bailiff said.

I tried to suck it up and pull myself together. I stood up, and I felt weak. The judge said, "Be seated," and I nearly fell back into my chair.

The judge was a black man in his late sixties, heavyset under his black robe, with big rimmed glasses and large visible moles on his face. His unkempt Afro was more salt than pepper, and he didn't even look me in the eye. He never looked me in the eye. He glanced over and saw me, but he never looked at me as he spoke. He started talking, and this man who I assumed was the district attorney started talking about the "kidnapping" and "aggravated sexual assault of a minor."

Kidnapping?

And then the judge asked for my plea. I said, "Not guilty,

your honor," just like my attorney had instructed me to do. Then the DA and the attorney and the judge went back and forth about releasing me on my own recognizance, and the DA said something again about the seriousness of "aggravated sexual assault" and the standards for this type of crime, and something about trying this defendant as an adult—which I think meant *me*—and my attorney made some kind of argument about my lack of priors, and my reputation in football, and it seemed like the judge wasn't even paying attention.

"Denied," he said.

Was he talking about my release? My *release* was denied?

I started to panic. I started rocking back and forth again.

"Let's schedule a fitness hearing," the judge said, looking at a computer screen and pointing to it like he was scanning a calendar. "For August . . ."

He stated a specific date, and I didn't catch it, and the DA said it was good for him.

"Okay, bail is set at $1.15 million," the judge said, and next thing I knew he tapped his gavel and got up and left.

My mom started bawling. My sister hugged her. My dad just hung his head down like he was at a funeral.

"What just happened?" I said, looking around for someone to tell me something.

My attorney walked over to me as the bailiff came and put his hand on my upper arm and asked me to stand up. "What happened?" I asked again. "Am I going home?"

"No, Brian. He denied our request for OR," meaning release on my own recognizance. "He decided to set bail."

"A million dollars? Was that the bail amount?"

"One point one-five million, yes."

Oh my God.

"I'm sorry, Brian. Hang in there. You'll get through this."

"Oh my God!" I yelled as the bailiff tugged on my arm to pull me out the side door.

"Mom!" I shouted. "Mom!"

She was bawling as hard as I'd ever seen her as I left the room.

• ◆ •

My attorney came back and they gave us a few minutes to re-group in that little room where we'd met before we walked in. He explained to me that unless we could post bail, I would be held in Juvenile Hall until I had a fitness hearing.

"A fitness hearing? What is that?" I asked.

I didn't know if it was something about physical fitness, or what. But he explained they needed to evaluate whether or not I was fit to stand trial as a juvenile, or as an adult.

"An adult? I'm sixteen years old!"

"Almost seventeen," he said. "And these charges are serious."

"What did that girl say I did? What was that thing about 'kidnapping'?"

"In the state of California, kidnapping is the act of physically taking someone more than ten feet from where they are. So this idea that you dragged her down a hallway—"

"Dragged her down a hallway? I didn't do that!" I said. "She walked with me. Walked. Willingly. She led the way down the stairs to the Spot, just like I told you. Honest to God, I didn't *do* anything."

"I know, Brian. Look, I'll work with your family to see what we can do to get you out of here."

"Are you telling me I'm going to be in jail for a month? More than a month? What about school? What about football? My Hawaii game! My—"

"There's tutoring. You won't fall behind in school. Look, this is really beyond the scope of the work I do, so I'll talk to your family and we'll get you some help. Okay? Just hang in there."

Just hang in there?

FIVE

Tormented

It made no sense. I was innocent. I didn't do it. How could they not release me?

My attorney left. The bailiff put me back in the holding cell. Again. Where I waited for hours until the court closed and the guards put me back in the van. Again. Then they drove me back to Los Padrinos. Again. Where they stripped me naked. Made me squat and cough. Put me back in my cell. Again. Where it all sank in—maybe for the first time since this whole thing started.

I didn't commit a crime. But I'm in jail. In solitary confinement.

I was *sixteen*. Didn't have a driver's license. Didn't have a passport. Where was I gonna go? I was enrolled in summer school. Practiced football every day. How was I a "flight risk"? No priors. No history of violence. Why the hell would they lock me in jail on more than a million dollars bail?

I couldn't even conceive of a million dollars. If everybody in my whole family sold everything they owned, we couldn't come up with a million dollars. I didn't fully understand the way bail worked, either, and nobody explained it to me. There was something about only a portion of it having to be paid in cash or held in cash or something like that, and the whole amount wouldn't be due unless the defendant fled. I wasn't gonna flee. I didn't do anything! But even so, what would that mean? Even 10 percent of $1.15 million was more than a hundred thousand dollars. There's no way my mom could come up with that.

Without bail money, I wasn't getting out. I would stay right here for another month and a half. A month and a *half*. In jail. In *jail*. When I was innocent!

I'd miss six weeks of football practice. Miss the start of school. Miss my whole *life* if I was in there for another month and a half. And then what? Would I even get out that day? No one said for sure. Nobody made that clear. Nobody said anything that made any sense.

A month and a half.

The weight of it hit me like a three-hundred-pound barbell dropped on my chest in the dark, with somebody I couldn't even see pushing down on it, trying to crush me.

I wasn't getting out.

For at least another month and a half, *I wasn't going home.*

● ◆ ●

I couldn't eat.

I barely slept. I lay down and barely moved. But I couldn't sleep.

All I did was cry. And pray.

The guards kept trying to talk to me, some of them in a caring manner, some of them yelling. I "had to eat something." I was "gonna get sick." If I got sick, they said, they'd have "no choice but to force-feed me."

54

In my mind, I think eating that food might have felt like an admission that I was really *there*. In that cell. And I *wasn't* really there. I *couldn't* be there. Things like this just don't *happen*. Innocent people don't go to jail like this. Something had to change. Somebody would speak up. Everybody knew me. They knew I wasn't capable of something like this. They knew I didn't belong here. I just had to hang on a little longer, until somebody figured this mess out and let me go home.

I was innocent. *Innocent*. Why was I here?

I could feel my body wasting away. I could feel my muscles shrinking.

It felt as if my body were starting to eat itself alive.

I didn't care.

I didn't want to leave my cell and learn to get along with the other kids in that place. I didn't want to play games. I didn't want to "program," as the guards kept referring to it. All I wanted to do was go home.

My mom came on the Sunday after my arraignment. We had talked a couple of times on the phone before that, but when she came into Juvenile Hall that first time, it was hard. We hugged, and she kept crying, and I kept crying. It was the first time I'd touched someone in days. You don't even realize how much you miss just a pat on the shoulder or a hug from your mom until it's taken from you. You don't. I had no idea. I don't think she did, either. So we hugged and cried for the longest time.

When we finally stopped and sat down in the visiting room, she asked me all about what really happened with the girl at school, and I told her. Straight up. Just like I'd told everyone else. I told her the truth.

That was painful. My mom didn't know that I was active with girls. She didn't know I'd ever made out with random girls like that. I'd had a couple of girlfriends in my freshman and sophomore years, but we were young. It seemed harmless to her. She still thought of me as her little boy, and I would have been happy to keep it that way for as long as possible. I never, ever imagined talking to my mother about stuff like that. She seemed disappointed in me at first. The look in her eyes almost destroyed me. But when I got to the part about stopping, about telling Tiana I needed to get back to class, and how I walked away, she wiped the tears from her eyes.

She let out a great big sigh and kind of sat up straight in her chair.

"Okay," she said.

She believed me.

"We're going to get a new lawyer," she said. She apologized that the lawyer she brought in didn't get me out the first time we went to court.

"It's not your fault, Mom," I said.

"But it wasn't enough, Brian. It wasn't," she said. "A friend of mine, she knows a lawyer, a black woman who went to school with Johnnie Cochran. She's putting me in touch with her. We're going to talk tomorrow," she told me.

"Mom," I said, "how you going to pay for a lawyer?"

"Don't you worry about that. That's not your problem. All that matters is we get you out of here."

I would learn later on that my mom put our town house up for sale that very week. She sold her car, too. The nicest car she'd ever owned. It wasn't enough quick cash to make bail, but it got her enough money to put down a retainer to buy me the kind of legal representation she fully believed I needed.

I couldn't imagine what all of this was doing to her. She tried her best to stay strong and positive with me, but I knew this must have been eating her up inside. The embarrassment that I felt must have paled in comparison to the embarrassment she felt. She was on the outside, having to live with it all. I wasn't even aware that my story had been in the news until one of the guards mentioned he'd seen me on TV. My mom tried to keep that from me, but when I asked her about it on the phone, she finally broke down and told me. I was all *over* TV. It was a big story. My name was in the newspaper, too.

"So everybody knows about this," I said.

She was silent on the other end of the phone.

I felt so bad that I had caused this for her. For my whole family. And the guilt I felt, even though I didn't do what I was accused of doing, *stung*.

If I hadn't gone with that girl, if I hadn't let my stupidity and excitement get in the way of making the right decision, none of this would have happened! I beat myself up for it, again and again and again.

The next weekend, I beat myself up even worse. My mom brought my little brother in to see me, and he just couldn't take it. The crazy thing is, they don't normally allow other juveniles into Juvenile Hall for visits. It's against the rules. But because the guards in that facility believed me, because they saw through what was going on and thought for sure I was gonna get out of there, they bent the rules for me. They brought my mom and little brother in through a back door where no one would see him and they allowed us to visit in a vacant room.

My brother and I didn't hug a whole lot normally. But we hugged there. He was crying, and I cried, too, though I tried to stop myself and to be strong for him like a big brother should.

We sat down and talked as a family for almost thirty minutes. He was having a real hard time with everything, he told me. He said he saw that girl at school every day. Every day! And it drove him nuts. Every day people kept asking him, "What's up with your bro? Did he do it? Is he going to prison?" It was all too much. He said he didn't want to go to school anymore. And seeing me in that place was too much for him to take.

We hugged tightly before he left, and all I wanted to do was leave with them.

What happened to me was ruining *his* life. And that just about killed me.

With each new day in that solitary concrete cell, something new ate me up, too: *anger*. The anger I felt was something I'd never experienced in my life. It was seething. Burning. I couldn't understand how that girl could be so evil. That word kept rolling round in my mind. *Evil*. The thought of touching her, of kissing her, of smelling her made me sick. I felt like I'd touched the devil. What else could this be? What else could cause someone to hurt me and my whole family like this, but evil? What did I do to deserve something like this? *She ought to pay for what she's done!*

I wanted to punch the walls, but I knew I couldn't. If I hurt myself or threatened to hurt anyone else, I would never get out. The guards made that clear. They weren't fooling around. The other kids I talked to in the yard or in the day room, even though I hardly spoke to more than a handful of them at all, made it clear, too. "They will spray your ass, bruh," they said.

Meaning they'd hit you with the pepper spray. And even if they didn't spray me, it wouldn't matter if I was truly innocent if I got into trouble while I was in juvie, they said. If I got in trouble on the inside, I'd *stay* inside. So I needed to stay cool. But whenever I filled up with anger toward that girl, "cool" was the furthest thing from what I was.

So I turned my thoughts to prayer. I asked God to take care of my mom, and my brother, and my sister, and my dad. I asked God to get *them* through this, and then I asked God to help me, too. I asked God to bring an end to this nightmare. And I'm pretty sure those prayers are all that kept me from bloodying my fists on the white concrete walls around me.

My mother and I talked on the phone every day. Well, every day when there wasn't some kind of lockdown that caused me to lose phone privileges, even though I wasn't out there with the rest of the population and couldn't have been a part of any fights or anything else that went on. That didn't seem fair. It didn't seem fair that I had to call her collect, either, and that she had to rack up big phone bills on top of everything else just to talk to her son. But it quickly became clear to me that things like fairness didn't really exist once you were behind those walls.

Why was this all so drawn out and technical? Why couldn't some grown adults put me and that girl in a room and talk to us and get to the bottom of it and realize that she was lying, and that I had clearly not *raped* her? Nothing made sense. None of where I *was* made sense. I still didn't even know what exactly she had accused me of doing. Nobody showed me a police report. Nobody told me anything.

I just kept trying to remind myself that none of that mattered. *None* of it mattered. Because this wasn't my world.

This wasn't who I was. I was going into my *senior year*. The biggest year of my life! This cell was not where I belonged. And one day soon, this was all going to be over.

After nearly two weeks of not eating, the guards took me into the infirmary. The doctor there put me on a scale. I'd lost fourteen pounds. I was wasting away. I said I felt sick and he gave me some Tylenol and some cold medicine. If I didn't eat, he said, he'd put me on an IV. He said they'd tube-feed me if they had to. "Starving is not a way out of here," he insisted, as if maybe I was choosing not to eat or something.

I went back to my cell and they brought me a tray and I still couldn't eat. I just couldn't.

My twelfth day after going in front of the judge was my birthday. I turned seventeen years old behind bars in Juvenile Hall. There was no cake. No songs being sung. No barbecue at my mom's house. That all seemed like some kind of a distant memory. Before I talked to my mom that afternoon, the only "happy birthday" I heard was from one of the guards. Coincidentally, his name was Angel.

Angel opened my cell door and whispered, "Happy birthday, man," as he tossed two Powerades onto my bunk and told me he'd be back to collect the bottles before he left so I wouldn't get in trouble.

"Thank you," I said. And I drank 'em. But after tasting two brightly colored bottles of flavored water in that colorless place, all I could do was daydream about my real life.

I spent my birthday the same way I'd spent all the days before that. I slept. I cried. I prayed. I raged. I cried. I prayed. I slept again.

Then, two days later, something strange happened.

My cell door opened and a man dressed in street clothes walked in. He didn't look like a prison official. He was a brown-skinned black man, an older guy in glasses, maybe in his fifties, mostly bald, wearing dress pants and nice shoes and an untucked long-sleeved shirt with a button-down collar.

I didn't know who he was. I didn't know why he was here. No one else had ever walked straight into my cell like that.

I looked at him just long enough to take him in, but I didn't make eye contact.

I didn't dare to.

He walked over to my bed and sat down next to me. He didn't seem intimidated by my size, like so many others in that place did. He wasn't fronting all tough like the guards. He had a sort of confidence that seemed out of place in that concrete cell.

He sat there for a few seconds. Silent. And then he spoke to me, slowly.

"I hear you're having a rough time," he said. "I heard you're not eating or interacting with anybody."

I didn't respond. I wasn't even really listening.

Then he said, "Why would you allow yourself to get eaten alive? Not for their sake, I hope."

That's when I started paying attention. I didn't know what he meant by "for their sake." Was he talking about the guards? The people who ran Juvenile Hall? The judge? My accuser? *Who?*

"If you're trying to prove a point—to yourself, or to anybody else—I can tell you it's not going to work," he said.

He looked over at me at that point, and I swear I could feel his eyes on me. He spoke deliberately, in a deep, calm voice.

"I don't know what you're going through," he said. "But you've got to let it go."

His words shook me.

How could someone say something like that? At first I was angry, like, *What the hell do you mean let it go? I'm right in the middle of it all!* But there was a little part of me that understood it—a part of me that understood what he meant by it. This whole experience was killing me. My heart, my spirit, my mind, my body. I was in so much pain and so twisted up, and I knew I couldn't go on like this. I *needed* to let it go, or at least let some of it go, or let *something* go. But I had no idea how to do that.

I started to cry. I wasn't sure why. I couldn't control it.

The stranger in street clothes put his arm around my shoulders—and I let him. I cried right out loud for a good long time.

It wasn't until I started wiping my tears away that he spoke again.

"My name's Mr. Johnson," he said. "I'm one of the teachers here at the Juvenile Hall, and I want you to start coming to my class. I want to start working with you on some ways that you can deal with some of the feelings that you're experiencing right now."

"Okay," I said, nodding a bit and wiping my eyes again. *"Okay."*

The next morning, I did two new things that I hadn't done since the day I'd been dragged out of my bed. I tried to eat some breakfast. Two boiled eggs, dry toast, slippery oatmeal, and half a grapefruit. I hated grapefruit. But I ate some of it anyway. I was starving.

And instead of spending all day in my cell, I went to a classroom inside Juvenile Hall.

Mr. Johnson's class, which I think was supposed to be a history class, wasn't like any other class I'd ever gone to in my life. He spent his time in front of that the classroom speaking to us kids about life, about choices, about what it means to live as good men. He talked about "spiritual enlightenment" and our journey toward "understanding who we are." It almost felt like going to church and seeing a preacher with a sermon about exactly what was going on in my life. Like he'd tailored his sermon just for me. The majority of the kids in class were black or Hispanic. Many of them were poor. Many of them were gang members who'd dropped out of school with little to no education. But he didn't talk down to any of them—or, I guess I should say, any of *us*.

On the first day, he went around to the students one by one and asked the same question: "Who are you?"

And one by one, they would give their names, or they would be rude and say, "Who are *you*!" and some of the kids would laugh. When he got to me and asked, "Who are you?" I told him the same as most kids did. "I'm Brian Banks."

"Well, that's your name. That's how people address you," he said. "But it's not who you are. So who are you?"

I wasn't exactly thrilled that he was suddenly calling me out in front of the whole class like that, but I thought about it for a second and said, "I'm a young black man in prison for something he didn't do." That drew some oohs and laughter, but he shut that commotion up quick with just a look around the room.

"Well, no, that's your current state on this earth. And that body you're in, that's not 'you.' That's simply your earth suit, the thing you wear to survive on this earth, the way you'd wear a spacesuit to survive in outer space. So let me ask you again, if you're not your earth suit and you're not your current state, *who are you?*"

I was silent for a few seconds. I thought about it, and I couldn't come up with anything. So I said, "I don't know."

Mr. Johnson smiled.

"Let's start there," he said.

He started talking to all of us about rediscovering "ourselves." And by "ourselves," he said, he was referring to who we were before we came to this earth in physical form. Our "spiritual selves." It was deep! But instead of laughing like some of the other kids, I found myself wanting to know more.

Just a few days after starting class with Mr. Johnson, I wrote this letter:

> July 31 2002
>
> Dear God,
>
> Hello dear Lord. Lord I come to you now in writing. I know you already know my thoughts but I need some way of explaining myself and getting this off my mind and chest. Lord, why me? I know I shouldn't question your doing Lord but what have I done so bad that this has to happen to me? Lord you and I both know that I didn't do what they said I did. Lord, in my heart Lord, I'm not afraid, but you know people, your children, sometimes think of the worst that can happen. It's just that if they do sentence me for nothing, I don't know what my next step would be. What would I do? What would I do to myself? Now I know that I shouldn't

be thinking like that God, but I really don't think I
would be able to survive mentally in jail or prison.
Lord, I just ask that you come into my heart now
right now and help me. Lord, you know that this is
not a place for me. You and I also know I am not
what they say I am. So please dear God, forgive
me for what I've done wrong in the past to deserve this and give me my freedom and innocence
back. Lord I need you. I need you always. Walk me
through this. Guide me in the right path. Come
into my heart. I need you Lord. Thank you!

Love, your son,
Brian Banks

When Mr. Johnson saw how interested I was in his lessons
after a few classes, he started treating me differently from the
other kids. He sat me off to the side and gave me some headphones. He gave me music to listen to. He handed me a copy
of the book *As a Man Thinketh,* by James Allen, a book about
the power of thought that was written way back in 1903. He
gave me books of poetry and philosophy to read. Sometimes the
musicians and philosophers were one and the same. I read and
listened to the words of black ideologist Marcus Garvey, and Eli-
jah Muhammad, a mentor to Malcolm X, and other black men
steeped in African philosophy and heritage, filled with messages
that resonated so strongly with everything I was going through.
I wasn't the first black man to be falsely imprisoned, and I
wouldn't be the last, and I sort of knew that before all this—but
hearing it all at once in the richness of music and books forced

me to realize I wasn't alone. This path had been walked by many others before me. That gave me some courage, and calm.

The tapes I was listening to stayed with me as I went back to my cell each day. They were teaching me new ways of thinking, including the idea that there was value in listening to myself and my own wants and needs and desires. The idea was that knowing *you*, understanding *you*, mattered.

Mr. Johnson wasn't teaching me history. He was teaching me about love, and hatred, and spirituality—not through religion, but as a whole, in this world and beyond it. It was inspiring, and it motivated me to want to study and learn more all on my own.

I was in some other classes, too. Going to school, continuing to get an education, that's mandatory when you're in the juvenile system. But none of the other classes were like Mr. Johnson's. They were just regular old boring school stuff.

When Mr. Johnson mentioned certain writers or certain books, I'd call my mom and ask her to buy those books for me and bring them the next time she came to visit.

"Where is all this coming from?" she'd ask me.

I told her: "It's this teacher, Mr. Johnson. Because of him I'm going to try to use my time in this place in a positive way, maybe learn something about myself along the way."

So she invested what little money she had left and bought me those study materials. One book, *The Biggest Secret,* by David Icke, looked at conspiracy theories about society and how we can break out of our mental and emotional prisons. Another was *The Impersonal Life,* by Joseph Benner, which supposedly was Elvis Presley's favorite book (right after the Bible).

I had no idea why Mr. Johnson recommended a book that Elvis liked, but as I read it, I found something much deeper than I ever imagined. In those pages, it told me to "be still," and to recognize that God is in control in your life. God is within you, and you are a product of God, no matter what, it said. Don't allow yourself to get so worked up and bent out of shape that you forget that you're not alone in this world. I wasn't sure how to do that, especially given the situation, but I liked the sound of it. I was already leaning on God. I was praying all the time for God's help.

My mom encouraged me to go to church while I was in Juvenile Hall, and I did. I went to the chapel on Sundays. I went to Bible study. I took a Bible back into my cell, and I read it. I started reading it all the time.

My mom was real happy about that, and she sent me notes suggesting verses to read.

"I try to read Psalms 91 every morning and every night," she told me.

So I read Psalms 91:

> *He who dwells in the shelter of the Most High will*
> *rest in the shadow of the Almighty. I will say of the*
> *LORD, "He is my refuge and my fortress, my God,*
> *in whom I trust." Surely he will save you from the*
> *fowler's snare and from the deadly pestilence. (NIV)*

She also forwarded suggestions from my grandma, telling me to read Psalms 27—a section of the Bible that gave me little phrases and thoughts to lean on, again and again, such as:

> *Deliver me not over unto the will of mine enemies:*
> *for false witnesses are risen up against me. (12)*

And this powerful line about patience:

Wait on the LORD: *be of good courage, and he shall strengthen thine heart: wait, I say, on the* LORD. *(14)*

I read, and I prayed, and I waited—as patiently as I could—for results. For the Lord to set things right again. For the Lord to bring an end to this nightmare.

All of that helped to fill and refocus my mind a little bit.

I was taking in so much at once, I couldn't possibly understand it all right away. But that didn't matter. Focusing on faith helped me survive that month and a half. It really did. The simple act of consuming it kept me alive.

On some days Mr. Johnson kept me after class and asked me questions. He asked me things, not just about that day, not just about what happened, but about my life. My family. Who I wanted to be. Who I dreamed of becoming.

Those discussions helped me feel human again. They brought my thoughts back to high school football, on who I was well on my way to becoming, and on coming home. It helped put me in a place of thinking, *It's taking forever to get this figured out, but eventually I will be going home!*

And that was not an easy thing to do. Because what I was about to learn is that "home" as I knew it, the "home" I assumed would always be there for me to return to, the "home" I was living and breathing on a daily basis before I entered Juvenile Hall, was gone.

SIX

No Empathy, No Remorse

I tried to ignore it. I tried to rise above it. I tried not to react to my mom's voice on the phone as she told me what was going on. While I was stuck inside Juvenile Hall, the world outside had already gone and made up its mind. Newspapers and news stations that had sung my praises as a football player, proclaiming to the world that I was the next great football star to emerge from Long Beach Poly—they turned on me. Without proof, without an investigation, without a trial, without anyone listening to what I had to say, they passed judgment.

Despite the fact that I was a minor, they put my name in the paper from the start. And then they used my size against me. My height, my weight, my strength, which had always been talked about as a gift, an asset, something to appreciate, suddenly got used against me. The story the media told the public was like some kind of made-up urban myth, with me as the villain. And it was always some version of this: "Brian Banks, the monstrous 6-foot 4-inch, 225-pound linebacker, dragged a helpless girl down a hallway in the middle of the school day and raped her in a stairwell."

It was fiction. It was made up. But the media made it sound true. They passed judgment—and so did my school.

Based on nothing but an accusation, the school district expelled me. Permanently. They said that I would never be allowed to return to Long Beach City School District, no matter what. That revelation showed up in the newspaper, where my mom had to read it for herself after hearing about it from her friends and our family—before the administration did so much as call her to discuss it, or showed her the courtesy of sending a letter or something, let alone have a hearing to plead our case.

"How can they expel me for something I haven't done? How can they judge me like that?" I asked Mr. Johnson.

He pointed to history. He pointed to the tapes I was listening to. He pointed out the color of my skin. But he also reminded me to stay focused on the truth, and especially to keep reaching for the person I knew I was deep down.

The hits kept coming, though. They were relentless.

First off, my mom got an offer on her house, and she took it. She was packing up and getting ready to move into a rented apartment again with my little brother. Their whole life had been upended because of me. And I realized that my house, the very bedroom I daydreamed about every day in my cell, wasn't going to be there anymore by the time I got out. Which meant I had nothing to envision going home to anymore.

Then it got worse. I was sitting in my white concrete cell one day when I received a letter from someone I expected would've supported me through thick and thin. I saw the name on the return address and I was excited to open it, not just because it was from someone I looked to as a mentor back in school, but because this man was a man of God, a minister, who was always quoting the Bible and preaching the Word. A man whom

I'd trusted and worked hard to please for the last three years: my head football coach at Long Beach Poly.

It didn't take long before I wished I'd never opened that letter at all.

His words burned into my brain like a branding iron.

"Look what you did to your family, your teammates, your team. Look what position you put everybody in," he wrote. "I'm not praying that you get out," he said. "I'm praying that God comes into your life and helps you deal with whatever you're dealing with."

That letter crushed me.

My own coach, a *minister*, judged me in the harshest terms possible based on nothing but accusations and rumors and gossip.

My God, I thought. *If my own coach could judge me like that, how will a jury judge me if this case ever goes all the way to trial? Even if it doesn't, even if the judge tosses this out, will the whole world be judging me like that when I get out of here?*

Thankfully Mr. Johnson didn't judge me. He kept telling me, through every twist and turn, to stay positive. But sometimes I barely even knew what that word meant anymore. What was there to be "positive" about?

"You," he said. "Be positive about you, who you are, and this journey you're on to discover more about your true, deep-down self."

In between the dullness and darkness of the daily routines—wake up, eat, back in the cell, go to school, go back to cell, eat, go to day room to play cards or dominoes or watch some TV if they let you, then shower, then back to cell for the night—he kept hammering that message home.

"Because we are made in the likeness of our creator," he

said, "in order for us to truly have an understanding of our cre-ator, we must first get to know and understand *ourselves*. You need to dig deep, Brian. To find yourself. That's where you'll get closer to God."

He said that the effort to get to know myself was a journey, a journey I was just beginning. He called it the path to enlight-enment.

Like I said, it was deep stuff. It was a lot for a seventeen-year-old kid to take in, for sure. But there was something about Mr. Johnson that made me want to pay attention. It felt like there was a reason he was telling me all of this. Like there was a reason I needed to know it. Like there was a reason it mattered.

Whenever I came to him with bad news, which seemed like just about all the time, Mr. Johnson kept on reiterating: "Don't destroy yourself for *them*. Don't eat yourself alive for the judg-ments and actions of others, which you cannot control."

And through his own words, and through the words of the poets and songwriters and philosophers he shared with me, including the work of revolutionary jazz poet Gil Scott-Heron and the hip-hop group Dead Prez, he kept on hammering one lesson over and over that I just did not want to hear.

"In life, you cannot control what happens," he told me. "The only thing you can control is how you react."

"Well, who's controlling what happens then?" I asked him in anger. "Am I just supposed to roll over and let these people judge me? Am I just supposed to roll over and let these lies dictate the rest of my life?"

"Of course not! But that still doesn't mean you can control it. That's your ego talking. And what does 'ego' stand for?"

He talked about this in class all the time, how the ego is a man-made construct that ignores our true spiritual selves. He even came up with an acronym for it.

"Exit God Out," I said.

"Correct. Look, I know this isn't easy to hear, Brian," Mr. Johnson said. "But ask *yourself* that question: 'Who's in control?' Ask it. Research it. Dig down into it, deep as you can. I'm telling you, the more you dig down deep into who you are, the more you'll see that you have all the answers you need."

Sometimes that philosophical, spiritual-like talk of his made me madder than I already was—even though, or maybe *because*, I knew instinctively that he was right. There was nothing I could do to stop the press from writing their damning words about me. There was nothing I could do to stop members of the Long Beach Poly community or anyone else from judging me, either. There was nothing I could do about any of this but pray that somebody would finally shine a light on the truth and make this whole thing go away.

I hoped the answer to my prayers would show up in the form of the new high-priced lawyer my mom was sacrificing so much to hire. The lawyer that "went to school with Johnnie Cochran." But I didn't get a great feeling about her from the moment I met her.

She was an older lady, maybe in her fifties, with dark skin and a strong jawline. Her hair was real short, like a half-inch Afro type of style, with little gray pieces throughout. The first time we met was maybe a week before we were set to go into that "fitness hearing," and all she really did was ask me to tell my story again. I asked her if she'd read my file, because I'd told the story over and over again already. She said she had, but she "needed to hear it for herself." So I told her what happened between me and that girl at school.

She didn't react. She stayed kind of stone-faced. But I got the sense that she didn't believe me. She gave me no assurances at all that we would be able to beat this charge, or that the case would get thrown out, or that she'd be able to get me out on my own recognizance in the meantime, which was something me and my mom were still hoping for once a new attorney was on board. She did say that the upcoming hearing could "help" me, and mentioned something about getting an evaluator to help see the big picture, but she didn't explain it in a way I could understand. She said she would see me at that hearing, and then left.

A week later the guards woke me up before dawn, put me through the strip search routine, and loaded me up to transport me to the courthouse, where I waited my turn once again in a holding cell.

When I entered the courtroom, once again I looked across and saw my mom, and my dad. My sister wasn't there this time, but I was glad my dad was there again to support me. I was glad, but I was still upset that this was the circumstance that finally got him to come around and see me. This wasn't how I wanted my dad to think of me, and this isn't the setting where I wanted to remember seeing him.

Once again, the same black judge walked in, and the dialogue was all between the DA, the judge, and my attorney. No one talked to me. No one really looked at me. I felt like I wasn't even there.

The judge reaffirmed that he wasn't going to change my bail, which I sort of half-expected, I guess, but then they went back and forth over the details of the charges, and my age, and whether this was a clear case of a charge that should automatically see me tried as an adult. In the end, they decided that an outside evaluation needed to be done to determine my mental state and whether I was, in fact, "fit" to be charged as a minor. That meant I was going back to Juvenile Hall, to wait to be evaluated, and to wait for yet another hearing that was set yet another month out, in late September.

Right about the time I should be flying off to Hawaii with my football team, I thought. *You have got to be kidding me. This can't be for real!*

Once again my mom started bawling. Once again it was back to the holding cell, then back to Los Padrinos, then stripping down for another embarrassing strip search. Clothes off. Hands on. Hands up. Mouth open. Tongue out. Head down. Hair and ears. Lift sac with one hand, sweep under with the other hand. Turn around, one foot up at a time, wiggle toes. Spread your cheeks, squat, cough two times. Get dressed. Then back to the concrete cell.

Amazingly, a few days later, my attorney gave me some news that made me think that maybe, just maybe, this whole thing could actually get dismissed. Some news that gave me hope.

During one of our pretrial meetings, she told me and my mom that they had performed a DNA test on Tiana Miller. Apparently she had a rape kit done after school that day, not unlike the one they police had forced on me, and during that test they'd taken a DNA sample. If any of my DNA was on her, then that would confirm without a doubt that sexual contact occurred.

My lawyer told us all of this in what could only be interpreted as a damning tone—as if it was going to serve as proof that I'd raped that girl.

"I didn't have sex with her, so they can't find my DNA on her," I told her.

"Well, let's just hope and pray it comes back negative, okay?"

"Why hope or pray? I didn't do it. I didn't have sex with her. It can't be mine," I told her again. "It's impossible."

And once again she said, "We'll see."

That lawyer didn't make anything seem like it was going to be easy, and I had no idea how long it would take before that DNA test result came back. Given the way everything had gone for me so far, even knowing that there was no way anyone could have found my DNA on that girl, it was hard to have hope.

Back in Mr. Johnson's class, I tried to make sense of how to deal with all of this without driving myself crazy. How to deal with the insanity of it all while not going insane myself. How to make myself a better person when everything seemed to be working against me. It became a discussion point in class one day, and some of the other kids started asking about it, too.

We had read about the biblical concept of being "*in* this world, but not *of* this world." And the class was having a real hard time understanding how to make sense of it. And suddenly it hit me. So I raised my hand.

"Yes, Brian."

"I think what you're saying is this: in order to evolve one must not be *in*volved."

Mr. Johnson put his hand on his chin and put his head back a little and looked up toward the ceiling.

"Yeah, yeah, yeah, that makes sense," another kid said.

"Like, sometimes you gotta step outside of something to really see what's going on," said another.

"He means don't get caught up in all the petty shit that's going down," another kid said. The class laughed at that. "Be your own man. Be bigger than that shit."

Mr. Johnson smiled and gave me a little nod.

I lost track of how many days went by before the evaluation lady showed up. But she came. She introduced herself and told me she was a clinical psychologist. She said she had a PhD, and she seemed nice enough, and I told her I was ready to tell her whatever she wanted to know.

Man, she put me through hours and *hours* of questioning and filling out forms, including detailed questions about my sexual history. Like, whether or not I used condoms (I did) and all kinds of stuff I was embarrassed to talk to this strange woman about. But I did it. She asked questions about my family history. She wanted to know if my parents were alcoholics or drug addicts. She wanted to know if I'd ever been abused, or whether anyone in my family had been abused. And of course she asked me all about the events between me and Tiana Miller. She asked me specifically if I had forcibly touched that girl or forced her to have sex with me, and I said, "No."

When she pressed me about it, I said there was no reason for me to exhibit that kind of behavior. As a football player, I said, girls were generally attracted to me. "So I don't have to force anybody to have sex with me. I could have sex if I wanted to. But I wouldn't force sex on anybody, ever," I told her.

She kept trying to get me to say more about whether what I'd done with Tiana Miller that day was wrong. And at some point I said something like, "Sure, I messed up some." Meaning I shouldn't have been there. I shouldn't have gone to the Spot with her. I'd had a lot of time to think about this stuff, and of course I had regrets. I tried to express those regrets to her.

She asked me how I felt about Tiana having endured something like this, and I reminded her, very clearly, "I didn't do it." *I didn't assault her!* So I'm not sure what she was referring to when she said Tiana was "enduring" something. I still didn't know what exactly that girl had said I'd done!

Over the course of the interview I talked about how much this whole thing had affected my future. I told her about Pete Carroll and USC, and how my whole life had been put on hold and basically taken away from me because of these charges. I expressed myself as openly as I could. When she asked me about my future goals, I even mentioned some of the new things I'd been learning from Mr. Johnson. In addition to saying that I wanted to be a football player, and make a lot of money, and play for the NFL, and have a good family, I said that my ultimate goal was to "find myself."

I meant it! As awful as this whole thing was, I was inspired by Mr. Johnson and all of those books I was reading. I wanted to evolve, to move forward from this, to put this all behind me, to create an even better life for myself and my family than I'd envisioned before this all of this happened. I was ready to dig down deep and get closer to God.

When it was all over, I went back to my cell and prayed that it was enough. I prayed that this would be what was needed to keep me from being tried as an adult. The evaluator stayed pretty stone-faced during our meeting, just like the new attorney. But I prayed to God that this would be enough for us to clear things up, enough for this case to get dismissed, so I'd be able to start rebuilding the life that had been taken from me.

I'd been imprisoned long enough, though, that alongside all of that hope, I felt fear. Fear that what I said wouldn't be enough. Fear that something I said might work against me. Fear that this system was working against me instead of for me right from the start—because I was a black man. Fear that this evaluator lady had judged me by size, just like the newspaper stories did, let alone by the color of my skin. Fear of the reality of my situation.

Over the course of that second month behind bars, Mr. Johnson asked me to write poems like the ones I'd read and listened to in his classroom. And I did. I wrote. I wrote things like this, just days before my next hearing at the end of September. A poem that I've kept in a notebook all these years:

I am a stranger to this world
Am I really here?
Do I possess strength and longevity?
Has there ever been a need to fear?
I am a stranger in this world
And this world most strange to me
Can I be invincible like time?
Will I only suffer in defeat?
Pages flipped in my book by wind unannounced
Pages unread . . . pages unnoticed,
Only I know they exist

But they insist that I persist for persistence is my
    test;
Persistence is our gift
Or my demise?
My spiritual nemesis in disguise
I am a stranger to this world
By choice or by fate?
Hands spiral segments of time
I'm afraid my time has run far too late
I am a stranger to this world
I am not safe
Unforgiven experiences, my love no more
My love replaced with hate
Where has my innocence eloped?
I am a stranger to this world
I am controlled by remote.
No hope . . .

On the morning before I went back in front of the judge, I debated not praying. I worried that my prayers were jinxed or something. A part of me felt like the more I'd kept praying, the more things kept getting worse. In church, growing up, we always heard encouraging phrases, like "God might not be there when you want him, but he's always on time." And I had always hung on to that, like "Amen! That's true!" But it's hard to keep hanging on when you're in a desperate situation, when all you can think is, *God, please, I need you here* right now! *Please show up!*

Still, after thinking about my mother, and my grandmother, and everything I'd read in scripture, I went ahead and prayed anyway.

Before we walked into the hearing, my lawyer told me I should make a plea offer. "My recommendation is that you plead guilty," she said, "and take life in the California Youth Authority."

"Guilty?" I said. "I'm not!"

"Yes, but—"

"And what do you mean take 'life'?!" I asked.

"In the California Youth Authority. It's not a bad place," she said.

I'd heard stories about life at CYA from other kids at Los Padrinos, and either those kids were full of it, or she was just plain lying. There were other places in the juvenile system called "camps," where kids were rehabilitated through sports- and outdoors-type programs. The judge had already ruled that he wouldn't agree to any settlement for me to go to a place like that. I knew from what I'd heard that the California Youth Authority was more like a prison. A *real* prison. Designed for really bad kids. There were fights there, and race riots, and occasionally some kid got killed behind those walls. The way she was speaking to me, it's like she was trying to convince me that going to CYA would be like going off to summer camp.

"And 'life' in juvenile just means you go until you're twenty-five," she said. "I truly believe it's your best chance for avoiding trial as an adult at this point."

As if going to jail until I'm twenty-five is no big deal?

I was shocked.

"Why would I plead guilty to something I didn't do?" I asked her.

She sighed.

"Because the results of your evaluation were not good, Brian."

"What do you mean, 'not good'?" I asked.

"The report makes it sound as if you premeditated the attack," she said. "It says that you showed no remorse, no empathy toward the victim."

"The victim? What attack? What *victim*? What about *me*? How can I be remorseful for an attack I didn't commit?" I asked her.

"Calm down. There's no arguing with the specifics of the psychologist's findings, regardless of what you think is correct. The judge will have already read the report, and her finding is that you're not suited for the juvenile system."

"What?! Can I see it? Can I see what she wrote?"

"No. The reports are 'sensitive' and aren't to be shared with clients. The specifics when taken out of context can be troubling—"

"Damn right they're troubling!" I said. At this point I wasn't yelling as much as I was almost *laughing*. It felt like some kind of a sick joke. *How could that woman interpret anything I said as me "premeditating" an "attack"? Like, this can't really be happening right now.*

"Brian, if you go into the adult system, you could get life in prison for these charges," my lawyer said. "*Life.*"

I froze. I could barely breathe when she said those words.

"Life. For something I didn't do," I said.

"That's the maximum sentence, yes, for these charges."

"I need to talk to my mom," I said.

"All right. Let me go see if I can find her. I can't stress enough how much I recommend we offer that plea, and I've told your mother the same thing."

"Wait. You already told my mom I should take a plea? You told my mother I should go to jail till I'm twenty-five?"

"I think it's the best option, yes," she said. And she left the room.

I couldn't sit down. I started pacing around. I couldn't even imagine how upset my mom must be. So I was completely shocked when my mother walked in two minutes later looking like she was all pulled together.

"Mom," I said. "She wants me to take a plea deal. For—"

"I know," she said. "Brian, I just have one question. Did you do it?"

"No! Mom, you know I didn't do it!"

"Then you don't take that plea. You fight this. You tell them the truth."

"But they might try me as an adult if I say no."

"Then we'll take it to trial," she said.

"I could get li—"

"Brian. You didn't do it, and you're not going to say you did. There is no way you're putting a felony on your record and giving up your whole life and going to some *youth prison* till you're twenty-five years old for something you did not do!"

My mom hugged me and I shook off the tears before we asked our lawyer to come back in. We told her I absolutely would not make any kind of deal that forced me to admit to a crime I hadn't committed.

She did not look happy.

"Okay," she said.

We walked into the courtroom. A few minutes later, the judge walked in. After talking about some legal stuff I didn't understand, he confirmed that he'd read the psychologist's report, and he said that he agreed with her recommendations, as well as the recommendations of the district attorney.

Before I had a chance to catch my breath, and without so much as a chance to speak the truth to anyone in that courtroom, the gavel came down.

The judge ordered me to be tried as an adult.

I closed my eyes, and I heard my mother start to cry, and I pictured Mr. Johnson's steady face, and I did everything I could not to get lost in the storm that washed over me.

I felt the bailiff grab my arm, but I kept my eyes closed. I tried to focus. I tried to go inside. I tried to believe.

None of this matters. This is noise. This is noise. This is all a distraction from my path of enlightenment. This . . . this is not who I am.

I pictured one of the letters I'd received from my mom. The one with the Bible verses on it. The verses that my grandmother suggested I read and hold dear. In my mind, I could see my mom's handwriting, written in blue ink on a page of lined paper, pulled from a binder that she used in her classes with her students, and suddenly I remembered: Psalm 27. *Psalm 27!*

> *The Lord is my light and my salvation—*
> *whom shall I fear?*
> *The Lord is the stronghold of my life—*
> *of whom shall I be afraid?*
>
> *When the wicked advance against me*
> *to devour me,*
> *it is my enemies and my foes*

who will stumble and fall.
Though an army besiege me,
my heart will not fear;
though war break out against me,
even then I will be confident.

Even then I will be confident, I thought. *Even then I will be confident.*

◆ ◆ ●

Los Padrinos Juvenile Hall handles only juvenile inmates, not juveniles being tried as adults. And as soon as I got back to Los Padrinos, right after they stripped me down, an officer informed me that because I was now to be tried as an "adult," I couldn't stay at Los Padrinos anymore. In the morning, they said, I'd be transferred up to Barry J. Nidorf Juvenile Hall in Sylmar, California—way up in the San Fernando Valley, north of Los Angeles—a facility that specifically houses juveniles whose crimes are serious enough to warrant adult charges.

I was about to be locked up in a juvie facility full of kids who were actual rapists, murderers, and God knows what else.

Not only would I have to move, but now the whole process would start over for me. *Everything* would start all over again in the adult judicial system. That meant a new arraignment. New hearings. New *everything*.

I'd learned the hard way that it wasn't unusual for a month or more to go by between hearings. It was almost October. I'd been brought here at the beginning of July. Assuming it took as long as this process had already taken me, I figured it would be sometime in December if not the new year before we got a chance to present anything of substance in front of a judge. We could renew our request for me to be released on OR. We could even ask again for an outright dismissal of this case. But would any of that happen?

This had all gone on for too long. I was starting to feel numb inside. And now I was looking at more *months* of my life? Not days, but *months*? I didn't want to think about the possibility that it could get worse. I didn't want to think of any possibility other than at some point this would all get cleared up and I'd be freed. *I can't be sent to a prison for a crime I didn't commit. I just can't!* And yet, here I was. Locked up. And about to leave this facility that I'd grown accustomed to, which meant even more uncertainty and change.

As awful as Los Padrinos was, as bland a place, as bleak, at least I knew where I stood there. And at least I had Mr. Johnson.

I wasn't even sure I was going to see Mr. Johnson by the time I got back and got through the strip search. But as fate would have it, he was there.

We were allowed a few minutes of family time after we returned from court, and my mom had driven out to see me. She and Mr. Johnson were together in the family visiting room when they brought me in.

"Oh, man. I'm so glad to see you," I said.

"And I'm glad to see you, Brian," he said. He'd stayed late for a meeting and had just gone back to his classroom to pick up his things. He saw the court bus pulling up, he said, and then he spotted my mom. He had picked her right out of the whole crowd of parents and relatives and asked if she minded if he went in to see me.

"Well, maybe it was meant to be," I said.

"Maybe so," Mr. Johnson said. "Take a seat. Tell me how things went."

I can't even explain how hard it was to tell him what had happened—and to tell him that I was leaving in the morning.

"I don't want to leave," I said. "I mean, I do, but not like this."

"I know what you mean, Brian," he said. "I'll be sorry to see you go."

"Your classroom is the only place in this whole facility where I can go to forget about everything, where I can go and not worry about my case and not get all stressed out about what's going to happen to me," I said. "It's the only place where I focus on where I need to be in my mind, and in my heart."

"Well, I'm glad you've found that here, but now you need to find that wherever you go."

"How do I do that?" I asked him.

"Just keep listening," he said. "Keep reading. Keep doing what you're doing. It'll come."

I only had a couple of minutes before I had to be back in my cell. So I didn't waste any time. I just came out and said what I wanted to say.

"I just want to thank you right now," I said. "Thank you for helping me get busy learning about the world, and searching for answers about myself and everything. I just don't understand, though. I even told that lady!" I said to him. "I told that evaluator lady that one of my greatest ambitions was to 'find myself,' Mr. Johnson. I told her that. And I meant it. You've taught me so much."

Mr. Johnson bowed his head a bit and shook it slowly back and forth. Almost like he was resigned that this was gonna happen. Maybe because of his years of experience working in the system, he knew that I didn't stand a chance of *not* getting moved into the adult system.

But Mr. Johnson didn't keep his head down for long. He didn't get all sad or emotional on me. Instead he raised his head, and he looked at me with those knowing eyes of his, and he said, "Brian, no matter what the situation is, no matter what the outcome is, no matter in which direction you're headed, up or down, I hope you'll continue down the path you've started here. The path of enlightenment. Of understanding *you*. Of getting to know yourself," he said. "Because you're something special."

I can't even explain how good that felt. Especially for him to say something like that in front of my mom.

"Man," I said. "I don't know. All I've been told in so many words, all day long, and all last month, and for the whole two and a half months I've been in here is that I'm some sort of monster who needs to be caged up!"

"Don't listen to all that outside noise, Brian," he said. "Be still. Stay focused. Keep getting closer."

"I will, Mr. Johnson. I will. I promise," I said.

I still wasn't sure what he meant by all that. I was just barely beginning to grasp the concepts he was teaching. He and I had known each other for only eight weeks. But those eight weeks felt like a lifetime to me, in both good ways and bad. And he'd changed me in those eight weeks. He really had.

In the middle of all the blistering static of worry, fear, and pain, Mr. Johnson was able to turn my mind to a different channel. He showed me how to escape what was happening and try to find a deeper meaning in the mess I was in. He allowed me to recognize myself as separate, and worthy, and to move my mind beyond the lies, and beyond a justice system that made no sense.

He gave me that, and I was grateful for it. I knew I wouldn't let that go.

I gave Mr. Johnson a big hug good-bye.

"Thank you, again," I said.

"Brian, thank you," he said. "You take care now."

He left and I gave my mom a big hug, and she told me to stay strong. I promised her that I would. There really wasn't anything more to say after that. We both felt defeated. But having her there that night meant the world to me, and I knew she believed in me and would continue to support me as much as ever. Seeing her stay strong made me feel strong, too.

I tried to keep my mind on that, and on what I'd learned from Mr. Johnson, as the guards woke me up before dawn, stripped me down, packed me into a van, and took me on an hour's drive north to Sylmar—to a facility I had never seen, even farther from my mom, and even farther from what felt like a sputtering memory of my city, my school, my family, my *life*.

My home.

SEVEN

In the Cave

The first thing I noticed walking into my second Juvenile Hall was how much cleaner it was than the first—and how much more it felt like a prison. Los Padrinos was like a comfortable old run-down barn compared to the cold, hard walls I was walking into in Sylmar.

I looked for it on a map before I got there, and noticed it was right off Interstate 5 on the way to Six Flags Magic Mountain. That's the big roller-coaster theme park that kids all over Southern California beg their parents to take them to. It seemed almost cruel that this juvie facility was so close to it.

I went through the strip search and some orientation with a new set of guards. These guards seemed harder. I didn't see anyone who looked like an Angel. I couldn't imagine any one of them tossing me a Powerade.

When they walked me back to the module that would become my home for the foreseeable future, the kids' faces seemed harder, too. Every one of them was facing murder and gun charges, or rape charges, and major time in prison. And I knew I would have to interact with these kids right from the start because we were all in mandatory school classes together.

I thanked God that I was as big as I was, because walking

into that place not looking like I did, I think I would have been terrified.

They housed me in a solitary cell again because of the sex offense charges, and this cell wasn't even meant for two people. It had one small window on the wall in the back, up sort of high, with horizontal metal bars going across it. And below that window was the bed, a concrete slab sticking out of the wall and with one of those superthin mattresses on it. This mattress was green. There was a thin blanket folded on top of it. No pillow. The concrete walls were painted white all the way around the tiny room.

The door was solid except for a four-inch-wide window that stretched diagonally across the middle from the top left corner to the bottom right corner. But just like before, all I could see was a hallway, and more cells.

A few weeks went by before I heard from my attorney. My mom came to visit every week, even though it was a longer drive. My dad even came to visit me, which was helpful. I loved my dad. I loved seeing him. I was pretty sure I'd now spent more time sitting across the room from him in a courtroom and across the table from him in Juvenile Hall than I'd spent with him in the last few years. I was glad he was there. I was glad he'd promised to help my mom with some of the lawyer fees. And it felt good to know that they could come together like this, for me, as my parents.

Sometimes, though, seeing my mom and dad was more just a reminder of how bad my situation was. When they talked to me about my brother, and what was going on in their lives back home, I realized again and again just how much this was affecting them—and how much I wished all of us could just put this all behind us. But the possibility of that seemed to get further and further away—especially when I realized just what kind of sentences the courts were handing down to other kids in that facility.

One kid I met and got along with, a black kid who was seventeen, just like me, only tiny—he couldn't have been more than five two—missed class one day to go to court, and when he came back, he looked shell-shocked. He looked like he'd just seen a ghost.

"What'd you get? What'd the judge say?" all of the other kids asked him.

"I got seventy-two years," he said. "They're transferring me to Chino tomorrow morning."

This kid was a gang member. A Blood. And as part of his initiation he'd tagged along while some other guys shot someone. He didn't hold the gun. He didn't pull the trigger. But he followed the gang code and wouldn't rat on his fellow gang members, so the system made an example of him. He took the punishment for those gangbangers who probably don't even remember this kid's name. All he got for his loyalty was the rest of his life behind bars.

Seventy-two years. He was just a kid. It was insane.

In those first few weeks, I watched a couple of fifteen-year-olds get forty years and thirty years each, and my jaw hit the floor with every one of those sentences. *If these kids are gettin' those kinds of sentences, what's the judge and jury gonna lay on me?*

Multiple times over the next two months I went back and forth to court, getting up before dawn, then being strip-searched and transferred to a solitary cell in Central Juvenile

Hall in downtown Los Angeles for a minimum of twenty-four hours before and after every hearing. They put me in true locked-down solitary confinement in that facility every time because they didn't have any other holding facilities for an "unfit juvenile" like me. And even after all that, nothing changed for me. I wasn't released on my own recognizance. None of the charges were dropped. Half the time we showed up in court only to face a continuance, because one of the lawyers or the judge had a vacation coming up, or wanted to take time off for the holidays—all while I sat in Sylmar with my life hijacked, waiting in limbo. The whole first half of my senior year of high school ticked away with no movement whatsoever on my case.

In those first few months, the only kids I saw who got out of Sylmar without a heavy sentence were the white kids. No joke. That's not an exaggeration. They were the only ones. The difference in sentencing was like day and night. Every white kid who came through was released.

I could hardly believe it. I mean, I knew that white privilege existed. I saw it here and there with my white friends. But I never saw it like I did in the juvenile system. One of my best friends in the world was white. I had no animosity toward anyone because of the color of their skin. But in here? It wasn't personal. It was automatic. It was a given. Blacks and Hispanics were treated one way, whites were treated another way. No one denied it. No one tried to hide it. It was just the way it was—the way it always was, and still is.

There was one white kid in there for molesting his little sister, and he didn't even deny that he'd done it. He just kept saying, "My dad's gonna get me out of here. He's gonna figure this out." And sure enough, within a couple of weeks, he was walking out with a smile on his face.

On those days, when someone got out, I watched their eyes light up. I watched their whole demeanor change. And at night I'd dream it was me. But every morning I'd wake up to the same nightmare.

It's like I was living three different lives in that jail. One life was just a daydream, a memory, some part of me that was holding on to what I thought was real, the life I'd always known. A life where I could get along with everybody, and play football, and walk over to Tommy's for a burger and fries without anybody asking where I was going. Another life was just surviving jail, continuing to read, continuing to try to stay on the path of enlightenment that Mr. Johnson had set me on, trying to keep to myself and mind my own business and not get caught up in all the noise of the fights and the lockdowns and the tension that happens when you lock a bunch of angry young guys in on top of one another. The third life was the emotional roller coaster of going back and forth to court, not knowing what was going to happen, the waiting, and the waiting, and the waking up thinking this could be a really good day, or that it could be a really bad day, or that it could be a nothing day that led to nothing but another continuance and more weeks of waiting despite all the trouble and expense it took just to get there.

Nobody cared what those continuances meant for me. There was certainly no consideration of my constitutional right to a "speedy trial." (In addition to my spiritual readings, I had started reading up on the law.) There was zero consideration of the fact that I was still a minor and that I'd been ripped away from my family for so long. I missed my family. I needed my family. No one cared about what this was doing to my brother, who my mom insisted was all but ready to quit school entirely, and whom I hadn't even seen since July. No one cared that I wasn't doing what I was supposed to be doing with my life, even though I hadn't been found guilty of a single thing.

There was no weight room in juvie. So there was no chance of keeping up my old physical routines. No chance I could stay in the shape I needed to be in when I got out and got back on the football field.

I wound up reading about my old classmates from Poly in the newspaper, reading about how they played in the big games that I should have been playing in that season. It crushed me.

I won't get into how depressing it was to have Thanksgiving behind bars. Those special days and holidays that people cherish or dread or just plain take for granted on the outside, they're just days like any other on the inside. Filled with tension, and fighting, and noise. Slamming doors and angry voices.

By the end of November, I was depressed. It felt like I'd been in there forever. I felt myself getting angry again. Angry more often. I was afraid something in me might pop.

And just like that, like a sign from above, I got a letter from Mr. Johnson:

11-27-02

To: My Spiritual Son

Out of the 20 plus years, I've seen many young men cross my path and me theirs, but I've never experienced someone with the spirit of Moses. These words are not expressed to feed or pump up your ego (Exit God Out) but they are to share my observation.

Since you have been physically away I placed on the wall: "In order to evolve one must not be involved." Be in the world but not of the world.

Your words to your fellow peers were very inspirational. What comes from the heart goes to the heart. Remember to lean on His understanding and not the understanding that is false according to how it (understandably) is filtered through the ego.

If it is possible, I would like to send you a book titled "The impersonal Life" or would it be better to send it to your mother and she can give it to you. Let me know ASAP.

Do you have access to the internet?

Words of inspiration and encouragement are important to share. When one sows good seed they will reap good. If one throws out lies they will reap lies so be it with anything we do or say.

Keep in mind when you speak to others about the real, speak to them as if you are talking to yourself.

Do you want people to attack you?

Do you want people to judge you?

Do you want to be forgiven?

Do you want to experience Divine Love?

Whatever you want you must give it away!

THIS WORLD IS NOT FOR COWARDS
Do not fly. Look not for success or failure. Join
yourself to the perfectly unselfish will and work on.
Know that the mind which is born to succeed joins
itself to a determined will and perseveres. . . . Live
in the midst of the battle of life. Anyone can keep
calm in the cave or when asleep. Stand in the whirl
and the madness of action and reach the Centre.
    If you have found the Centre, you cannot be
moved. VIVEKANANDA.

That last part was a quote from Swami Vivekananda, an Indian Hindu monk who's credited with introducing all sorts of Indian philosophies and spirituality in the Western world, including yoga.

That letter reminded me in every way that I wasn't alone. That I needed to look inward. That I needed to be in this world but not of it.

It helped to remind me, even after everything that had happened, that it was okay to keep my mind on the future. Because deep in my heart I still felt like, *At some point this is going to get figured out. They'll realize I'm innocent and send me home!*

Sports had taught me perseverance and keeping a positive mind-set. My mother and going to church had taught me to have faith. And Mr. Johnson taught me how to combine those things on a deeper level while I focused on my path of enlightenment. So I held on to all of that. I held on to it hard.

I held on to it through Christmas. I held on to it through New Year's Eve.

As I turned the corner into 2003, I was preparing to finally face the false charges in adult court, and on January 13, it happened: the Los Angeles County district attorney filed a felony complaint charging me with two counts of forcible rape and one count of sodomy, each count involving a "special circumstance" of kidnapping. Worst-case scenario, those charges could yield life in prison if I was convicted. How could that be real when I didn't do any of it?

It was time to prepare for the preliminary hearing on my case. It would be the first real chance the prosecution would have to submit evidence in front of a judge at Long Beach Superior Court. It would be the first out of all the hearings I'd had in which my accuser, Tiana Miller, would be expected to be present in the courtroom.

Over the next few weeks, I wound up sitting down with my attorney for a whole bunch of meetings to prepare for that day. She assured me I wouldn't have to testify. She grilled me about every detail of the incident with Tiana. She wanted to be able to blow holes in her story, she said, and she made reference to the fact that Tiana had already changed her story several times about exactly what happened that day.

"Well, did anyone investigate that? Someone changing their story a whole bunch probably means they're not telling the truth, right?"

"That's not what this hearing is for. That's what a *trial* is for," my lawyer said.

Really? I thought to myself. *'Cause I thought investigators were supposed to gather evidence before these things went into the court system. Was everything I was reading about how the law was supposed to work just not true in the city of Long Beach or something?*

I rode to the courthouse thinking about how much time had gone by.

Nine months. Nine *months*.

Maybe that's enough time to push Tiana to tell the truth. She must feel guilty. She has to feel guilty. Maybe she'll just let it go. Maybe this whole thing will end today.

I kept on thinking positive right up until the moment I set foot into that courtroom and saw my mom, and my dad—and laid eyes on Tiana Miller for the very first time since that day at school.

EIGHT

Time

"All rise . . ."

Tiana sat down with her mom and her sister, and her mom kept glaring at me. While the DA and my attorney and the judge started talking about some paperwork and legal files, Tiana didn't look at me *at all*. She kept staring at the ground, or looking the other way.

Just the sight of her brought all of the anger I'd ever felt rushing up to the surface in one big tsunami. Any sympathy I had for that girl went away.

As far as I could tell from the legal talk that was happening, her story was the only "evidence" the DA was presenting in the case, except for the report of the medical examiner who'd done her rape kit.

No one talked to me. No one asked me anything. But then, all of a sudden, the DA asked Tiana to take the stand.

Tiana walked up to the witness stand full of attitude, and the moment she opened her mouth she started lying. As the DA questioned her, the story Tiana told sounded more like the fictional incident described in the newspapers than what really happened. I sat there staring at her, just hoping she'd make eye contact with me and put a stop to this whole thing. I kept on wishing she could hear me thinking, *How can you do this? Stop. Look at me. Look at what you've done. Just stop this, please, right now! Look at me!*

She said I followed her into the 700 building and stalked her outside the bathroom.

Wrong.

That never happened.

She told the judge that I'd grabbed her wrist and pulled her into the elevator.

No.

She said that once we were in the elevator I lifted up her shirt and started sucking on her breasts.

Not even close.

She said I pulled her into the stairwell and pulled her pants down and forced myself on her. Then I turned her around and tried to force myself into her behind, and then I turned her around and forced myself into her again.

My God.

When my attorney got the chance to cross-examine that girl, she definitely found a few holes in her story. For example, Tiana said the water fountain was just a "foot" from the elevator, but when she pressed her on it, she admitted it was more like *eight* feet. And she pointed out discrepancies between what Tiana told police when she first reported the incident and what she was saying in the courtroom, about whether I pushed or pulled her into the elevator, and whether she stepped out of the elevator on her own or whether I pulled her by the wrist.

To me, all of those little things mattered. They showed Tiana wasn't truthful or accurate in her recollection, and that she was changing her story as she went along.

My attorney asked Tiana how long the hallway was on the second floor of that building, and she responded that she wasn't sure. She asked her how many classroom doors were open on the second floor of the building, and she said "one," which conflicted with the answer she supposedly gave in a police report: "Two." And both of those answers were untrue. There were multiple classrooms up there, and *all* the doors were open. I know because I was there! It's an easily verifiable fact that any investigator could have proven. But my attorney didn't press her about it.

She did ask Tiana why she didn't call for help, and Tiana said, "I wasn't thinking at the time."

"Because you didn't feel any fear at the time, did you?" my attorney asked.

I thought that was a great follow-up, but when Tiana answered "Yes, I did," she didn't follow up on that, either. She moved on to what happened in the stairwell. And instead of pressing her about why she didn't say anything to the woman speaking Spanish on the cell phone, she basically answered her own question and said that Tiana didn't say anything because she didn't think the woman would understand her. "Is that correct?" my attorney asked, to which Tiana responded, "Yes."

It felt like she wasn't driving any of these points home.

She got Tiana to admit that her story seemed off, but she never nailed her the way I thought a lawyer was supposed to do. She never made a big, crystal-clear point to the judge that screamed, "Hey, this story doesn't make sense!"

Why wouldn't she follow up on the fact that there could be no way Tiana was trying to get away from me in that hallway or someone would have noticed? Even if only one door was open—let alone all of them, as they were—any kid in a classroom who heard the squeak of a sneaker on a tile floor or anything else would have looked our way. That's just how kids are. Even if they didn't hear us, any one of those dozens of students, or teachers for that matter, certainly would have noticed a girl struggling to get away from a guy my size in that hallway, even if they only spotted it out of the corner of their eye. But they didn't. There were no witnesses. Why? Because we were both quiet. Because we had both chosen to be there.

Which means I didn't kidnap her!

But my attorney didn't mention anything about that.

She did manage to ask Tiana about the hall pass she was carrying, pointing out that she was carrying it the whole time I was supposedly pulling her by her wrist down the hall and down the stairs. She even got Tiana to mention how she stopped and placed that large hall pass on the last step when we were at the bottom of the stairs.

"Did you place it there in order to be able to touch Brian's penis?" my attorney asked.

Tiana said, "Yes."

She set it down so we could make out! I thought. *It was her choice as much as mine!*

That seemed like a huge point to make, but my attorney didn't follow up about that, either. She didn't make it clear to the judge. She just moved on and started asking about something else. Again.

It wasn't until the district attorney brought up the hall pass on a second short round of rebuttal questioning that Tiana admitted that both of her hands were *free* before she put the hall pass on the ground. She had previously claimed I'd been holding her by the wrist throughout everything that happened that day. Another major discrepancy in her story.

But my attorney didn't hammer that home, either.

I knew this wasn't a trial, but this was the one hearing that could have stopped the trial from moving forward. It was the one shot we had of getting the judge to drop some of the charges. I couldn't understand why she didn't press harder. I couldn't understand why she didn't say, "That makes no sense at all."

It made no sense. At all.

Even so, when the hearing was all over, I still thought that what she got Tiana to admit on the witness stand would be plenty for a judge to say, "There was no way this girl was kidnapped," and maybe even to think, *This girl was likely not raped, either.*

The judge didn't make a decision that day, though. Everyone went home, and I went back to Sylmar, and we waited until his decision came in the mail.

When it did, I opened the letter in my cell.

The case wasn't dropped.

None of the charges were dropped.

The judge set a trial date.

For July. Almost four months from that day. An entire *year* since I'd been home.

A year of my life. Hijacked. Kidnapped. Destroyed.

I dropped my head between my knees and tried to breathe.

My entire senior year. Gone.

I wasn't going to graduate from Long Beach Poly.

I was going to graduate from high school in Juvenile Hall.

My name, my reputation, my family's peace, my friends,

and possibly my future—college, all of it—had been taken from me.

Would I ever be able to get my football career back?

An entire year of my life.

Gone.

"God," I prayed, "I don't know if I can do this. I don't know if I can take any more of this."

• • •

I had a couple of pretrial meetings with my attorney, at which she continued to mention that she would do her best to get me a plea deal. I reminded her that I didn't want to admit guilt for something I hadn't done. I know my mom reminded her of that, too.

Then at one of those meetings, my lawyer walked in carrying a manila envelope in her hand.

"What's that?" I asked her.

"Oh, it's your DNA test results," she said.

"Oh, okay, cool," I said.

I wasn't overly excited or anything. I knew what the result of that test would be.

"All right, well, let's see what it is," she said, and she opened the envelope right in front of me. As she started to read the report, she damn near jumped out of her seat with excitement.

"Oh my God," she said. "It's negative. It's *negative*!"

"Yeah," I said. "I've been telling you that. It's impossible for it *not* to be negative."

Her reaction just confirmed to me one last time that she hadn't believed me the whole time she'd been representing me. This woman, like everybody else in the system, had prejudged me.

"This is good. This is *good*. We'll spring this on 'em when the time is right," she said.

I didn't understand one bit of her strategizing like that with my life. How could the right time to show my innocence not be *right now*?

If a judge saw that none of my DNA was on that girl right after I supposedly raped her, wouldn't that raise enough reasonable doubt to throw this case right out? I wasn't a legal expert, but that DNA evidence seemed like all the proof anyone would ever need to see that Tiana made the whole thing up. A smoking gun if there ever was one.

But it wasn't up to me.

Nothing was up to me.

It seemed I had no choice but to keep on waiting.

● ◆ ●

Jury selection began on July 8—the one-year anniversary of my arrest, to the day.

We were minutes away from stepping into the courtroom when a guard brought me into a claustrophobic conference room and closed the door behind me. There were no windows. I could stretch my arms out and touch the walls. I sat on the tiny metal stool that was bolted to the floor, folded my hands together on the cold, hard ledge, and looked through the bulletproof window in the middle of that room, waiting for my lawyer to step in on the free side.

About a minute later, she walked in—with a great big smile on her face.

"I've been talking with the DA, Brian, and we've got a deal."

"A deal?"

"Yup. A *great* deal. Let me walk you through it," she said. "This deal, if you plead no contest to one count of rape, you're to undergo what is called a ninety-day diagnostic. This ninety-day diagnostic will be at Chino State Prison. And what that means is you will be sent to Chino State Prison for ninety days. You'll be placed in general population. You will live as an inmate for ninety days. During that ninety-day period, you will be interviewed by a psychologist and a counselor, and they will determine on a ladder system at that point whether you will receive one of three choices: felony probation, three years in prison, or six years in prison. And that's it."

"So, *prison*. For something I didn't do."

"Take this deal, Brian," she said, "because I am confident"— she looked me square in the eyes—"I am confident, Brian, you will get the favorable report. You're a gentleman. They'll see that. You will get the probation. I am sure that, at the most, even if something was to go wrong, you'll get the three-year sentence. *At most*. You've already been locked up close to a year. So the most you'll serve is about eighteen months more. You get on out of here. You'll still be young, you can play football, you can go to school and move on with your life. Get this out of the way."

What?

No, I kept thinking. *Why are we even talking about this. No!*

I think she saw that I wasn't chomping at the bit to take the deal.

"Look, Brian, if you don't accept this deal, you've got to walk into that courtroom. We're going to start selecting this jury. And you're likely going to get an all-white jury. And an all-white jury will take one look at you and they will *auto-matically* think that you're guilty—because you're a big, black teenager. They're going to assume that you're guilty as soon as they see you."

This cannot be happening.

"And, Brian, they're not just going to think it, but they're going to *find* you guilty."

No.

"You're facing forty-one years to life in prison," she said. "So it's up to you: ninety days, or forty-one years to life."

No!

I started crying. I couldn't hold back.

"There must be some other way," I begged her. "I didn't do this. Please. Can't you do something else?"

"This is it, Brian. I worked hard for this deal and it is the best thing for you."

She looked at the clock on her cell phone.

"We got ten minutes."

"Ten minutes?"

"That's it. If we step into that courtroom and start jury selection, this deal is off the table. So what do you want to do, Brian? What do you want to do?"

"I want to talk to my mom," I said.

"No," she said.

I was shocked. I'd talked to my mom before every decision we'd made.

"What do you mean?" I asked.

"I mean, no. You can't talk to your mom," she said. "You're in an adult court now. You have to make adult decisions on your own."

I have always wondered how true this was. I've gone over it a million times in my mind: Couldn't I speak to anyone I wanted? If I needed more time, couldn't she have pressed the district attorney or gone to the judge for a ten-minute recess or even ask for a continuance? I'll never know who was playing hardball here. I do know that my lawyer made me feel that I had no options. And I do know that her fears for what would happen if I went to trial were real.

"I'm going to step out for a few minutes and let you think about it, but when I come back, I need to know," she said.

She stood up. She turned to go.

"And Brian?"

"Yeah?"

"Take the deal."

My attorney walked out the door on the free side of the glass, and that door started to close itself slowly behind her.

I put my elbows on the table and put my head in my hands. I felt like I was going to pass out. How in the hell was I supposed to make a decision like that? To not fight the charges? To admit to something I never did? To agree to put a felony on my record? For life? To agree to another ninety days? In jail? In a prison full of grown-ass men?

The door kept closing. I could hear it through the glass, creaking on its hinge.

My head felt like it was going to spin off the top of my neck. I felt sick to my stomach. How was I supposed to make this decision all by myself at seventeen years old? My heart started beating as fast as it beat when the cops woke me up with a gun in my face.

I couldn't breathe.

All of a sudden the door snapped shut with a *thud*.

This was it. The clock was ticking.

I thought about my mom and how much my going to prison would kill her. I thought about my brother and sister and how they'd never be able to cope with me going to prison for forty-something years, let alone for *life*. And I thought about the stories we all hear about state prisons, about the violence, the stabbings, the rapes in the shower, and all the other awful things that go on behind those walls.

I was sure I couldn't take another year in prison, let alone spend the rest of my life behind bars. I couldn't do it.

An all-white jury. Automatically guilty.

I closed my eyes and pictured a gavel coming down. I saw myself being dragged off in chains and shackles in an orange jumpsuit with my mom crying her eyes out, screaming, "No, no, Brian! My baby!" with the same face full of agony and shame that she showed me on the day I was arrested in our home.

I opened my eyes and stared at the empty space through the glass in front of me.

Our home was no longer there. Because of this. Because of *me*.

My city. My school. My team. My dreams. My family. My life! I can't let them keep taking it. They've taken it all! I need it back!

I'd made it a year. I could make it ninety days.

Ninety days or the possibility of life. How can that be my choice right now? How? Would they really lock me up for my entire life for something I didn't do?

I knew they would. I knew it. I'd seen it firsthand. *Thirty years, fifty years, seventy-two years—for a young black kid who was just a bystander. Seventy-two years!*

Ninety days started to sound pretty good.

I looked like a grown-ass man now, and this system was treating me like I was fully grown already. Surely that meant that I could make it in prison for a short stint. What more was ninety days? I could *do* that. I could *survive* that.

No! I'm innocent. I didn't do it. I can't admit to a crime I didn't commit.

There has to be justice. Someone has to see this is wrong. Someone has to see the truth!

Wake *up,* man! No one's gonna see it's wrong! You're a big black teenager. If they were going to see the error of their ways they would've seen it long before now. You're nothing but a number to them. You're not even human. They're going to make an example of you. Make a *decision*!

I could feel my pulse beating, beating, beating in the temples of my forehead.

"God, I need you," I prayed. "Right now. Please. Right *now*! I need you to tell me what to do, God. Please!"

The handle turned and my lawyer stepped in. I could see the door closing behind her as I once again closed my eyes.

"So, are you gonna take it? Will you take the plea deal?" she asked.

I closed my eyes as tight as I could and pressed the palms of my hands into the sides of my head, trying to keep it from exploding as my mind spun round and round and round.

Ninety days, or the possibility of life? Ninety days, or the possibility of life?! How could it come down to this? How can this be the only choice?

"Brian, I need to know. Right now. Will you take it? Will you take the dea—"

"Yes!" I said, throwing my hands out and opening my eyes as wide as I could—staring at her, staring into her soul with anger and fear. I looked that woman in the face and said, "Yes, I'll take the deal. I'll take it."

NINE

Step by Step

I 'll never forget the first time I set foot on the USC campus.

I was nine years old, and my stepdad took us on a tour of Los Angeles. My grandmother came to visit, along with two of my cousins who flew in from Chicago, and he thought it would be cool for all of us—all of them, plus me, my brother, my sister, and my mom—to experience that great city on foot. So we started out early in the middle of downtown and then toured all over by foot, by bus, and by train. And at some point in the afternoon we toured the campus of USC. I thought it was beautiful. All those cobblestone sidewalks and brick buildings and perfectly green lawns. I didn't understand how a place like that could exist right in the middle of a great big, busy city. And to think that place was a *school*. A *college*. I hadn't thought a whole lot about college at that age, other than to acknowledge the fact that my mom had gone back to school to get her teaching degree. As far as I knew, the school that she went to wasn't a place like USC. This seemed like a million light-years away from what my public school looked like back home. And it amazed me when my stepdad pointed over to the Los Angeles Memorial Coliseum and reminded me that this was the home of the very same USC football team that I'd seen on TV: the Trojans.

Growing up in Long Beach, which is only about thirty miles south of Los Angeles, it seemed as if everyone was a fan of either USC or the University of California, Los Angeles (UCLA), and for some reason I just naturally gravitated toward USC. After that campus visit, I was all in. I was a Trojan fan. USC football was everything.

I was into watching the NFL on TV, too. Football got really big in the 1990s. And by big, I mean it seemed larger than life, with all of that symphonic music and the slow-motion replays, and watching these giant men with steam coming out of their mouths go slamming into each other. To me it didn't seem all that different from watching WCW and Nitro wrestling matches on TV. My brother and I would try to mimic all the moves we saw on those shows, along with all kinds of karate moves we picked up from old Bruce Lee and Chuck Norris movies.

We were a sports family going back as far as I can remember. My brother, my sister, and I were all involved in sports. I ran track and played football and basketball and took karate lessons, and I already mentioned that my stepdad taught us tai chi once he was around. My sister was into all kinds of sports, too. And my mother was always getting us up super early in the morning on Saturdays or Sundays to take us on a road trip to some match or meet for one sport or another in Palm Springs, or Temecula, or even all the way in Las Vegas one time. We had trophies and ribbons all over our house.

Football wasn't my natural sport early on, though. I was nine when I first tried out for a Pop Warner team that practiced at Long Beach Poly. There were four or five teams practicing at the same time on three fields. I was so big and tall for my age that they put me on a team with a bunch of experienced *twelve- and thirteen-year-old kids*! The first time I got hit, I thought, *I don't like this. I don't like football at all!* I didn't quit, though. I stuck with it. My mom always told us, "Don't quit. If you join, you commit." But I didn't go back the next year. Instead I played some flag football, and then followed where my height and speed naturally led me: to the basketball court.

Basketball seemed to be my thing. It was just where I belonged. Everyone thought I was on my way to be six foot ten when I was fully grown, and because I was the tallest kid on the team, my coaches always played me at center.

At age twelve I could dunk on a regulation rim—hop up, sink the ball, and hang from the rim ten feet in the air. I was athletic, too. I could block. I could steal the ball. Everything.

By the time I finished middle school, I was basically a star player. The summer before my freshman year I started working out and practicing with the high school team.

But right around the end of that summer, fate stepped in.

I was walking into my house when this black guy who was visiting his mother in the house next door walked over to me and said, "Hey, man. What school you go to?"

"Poly," I said.

"Oh, I'm a coach at Poly. Are you on our football team?"

"Nah, I didn't sign up," I said.

"Wow. As big as you are, you should be playing with us. Like, come on!"

"I don't know. I'm really concentrating on basketball," I said.

"Man, just come try it out. I'm telling you, we could use somebody like you on the team. Just looking at you I can tell you'd most definitely be a starter. You're a big guy. We *need* you."

By the time I showed up and the assistant coach took me in to meet the head coach, I had already missed all of the summer workouts with the team. I figured they wouldn't want someone who'd missed so much time, and this meeting was just going to be a waste of my time. But the head coach looked up at me and the first thing out of his mouth was "Goddamn, boy. Where the hell have *you* been?"

They gave me some gear and suited me up and tried me at three or four different positions, including *quarterback*, before they determined that my size and speed would serve them best on defense. They liked the way I could come off the edge and rush the quarterback, so they gave me a starting spot as a defensive end on the team.

Sophomore year, they bumped me up to varsity. That almost never happened at Long Beach Poly, just because our school was so full of good players.

I did okay, but I didn't think I was playing my best— I honestly thought I was still a much better basketball player, and I proved that during basketball season—until the end of that sophomore season, when the coach decided to try me out as a linebacker. That's when everything fell into place. It just clicked. Linebacker was *my* position. It was like I'd been meant for that spot my whole life.

My junior year started with an injury to my ribs that kept me out for five games. Even so, by the end of that season, I was ranked eleventh in the nation and just about every Division 1 football school in the country was clamoring to have me on their team.

None of those other schools really had a shot, though, because for me, it was always USC. That's where I wanted to go. And as fate would have it, that's the school that wanted me first.

At the end of my sophomore season, my coach came up and handed me my first recruitment letter. When I went to grab it, he held it tight and he gave me a little speech, something along the lines of "Hey, I'm gonna give you this and I want you to understand how important this is. This letter is why it's important to continue to work hard at school."

"Okay," I said.

"And remember," he said, "this school isn't the only one watching you. So don't go throwing all your eggs in one basket, and get those grades up!"

"Got it."

He let go of the envelope and I turned it over and saw the USC logo in the top left corner. My eyes got all wide. A couple of my friends looked over my shoulders and I got this great big smile on my face. I opened it up right there and read it, and I'm sure it was just a standard-issue prospect letter. But to me it felt like I'd just won the lottery.

It was just a preliminary thing, like "Congratulations, we're looking at you! We just want you to know you're on our prospect list. We noticed you as a player, and we hope you keep up your good work and good grades, and we'll see you again soon."

I was practically jumping out of my skin when I ran home after practice to show that letter to my mom. I was a sophomore and I already had a college prospect—and it was my dream school!

My mom was funny about it. If she wanted to be a poker player she'd be great at it, because she was never one to show too much emotion about things like this. My sister was already going to California State University, Northridge, and my dad was a college grad who taught for a while, and my mom had her own teaching degree by then from CSU Dominguez Hills, so it's not like I was breaking new ground on the college front for my family.

"Wow, okay. All right, that's nice," she said. "That's nice. So, now, you gotta keep your grades up." *Boom*, she went right back to being the diligent mother.

"Mom! Just be excited!" I said. I was jumping-up-and-down excited.

"I'm excited," she said, "but this letter won't mean *anything* if you don't get to go to that school because of your bad grades."

"Okay," I said. "I'll do better. I promise."

I meant it. I really did. I made up my mind right then and there to dedicate myself to football and improving my grades, full-time.

I quit basketball and gave all of my attention to football (maybe too much attention, which might be why my grades slipped a little bit over the course of that year).

And next thing I knew, I was talking to USC head coach Pete Carroll. He came to watch me from the sidelines during practice. That may seem unusual, for a head coach of that caliber to be hanging out at a high school practice. But Long Beach Poly is just one of those schools. I remember even as a freshman seeing Pete Carroll standing on the sidelines one day. "Oh my God! That's Pete Carroll!" He was there looking at some of our seniors who would eventually go on to play for the NFL, and I just remember thinking, *Someday. Someday I hope he's here looking at me.*

I hoped and prayed he would come to watch me someday. And he did.

Pete Carroll wasn't just a coach to me. He was the coolest coach in the world. You could see that his players always had fun. You could see how well he got along with them. And the very next summer between my sophomore and junior years, I was off to USC to participate in one of his training camps.

I was so fired up, I played better than I'd ever played in my life. I went to a Nike camp and couple of other camps, too, and the sports sections of magazines and newspapers ran articles about my performance. I ran a 4.49 in the 40-yard dash. Just blew people away.

Lots of recruitment letters from other schools came in after that, and every one of them felt like the possibility of a dream coming true. I had *options* about what college I wanted to go to, and any one of them was ready to give me a full scholarship to go, not only to play football, but to get an education. It felt like the whole world was opening up to me.

There really is nothing like the excitement of receiving those recruitment letters. Seeing the school logo on the envelope. The anticipation of what it's going to say. Opening that letter and reading "Congratulations!" or "We are pleased to inform you . . ." There's nothing like the power of those words from some prestigious school telling you that you're *wanted*.

Then my mom surprised me in my junior year: she took my brother and me up to see a game, in person, at USC. That's when it went from feeling like a dream to feeling real.

Sitting in those stands, surrounded by more than ninety thousand fans in USC gear with their faces and bodies painted in Trojan colors at the Coliseum, I looked down at the field and spotted their linebacker and I thought, *I've practiced with those same coaches. I've played with some of those same players. If I keep playing well and working hard, pretty soon that's going to be me!*

• ◆ •

One by one over the course of that year—one by one while I sat in two different Juvenile Halls on false charges—every one of those scholarship offers was rescinded.

They notified me by letter. One by one. And opening those letters came with just as much dread as the recruitment letters had come with excitement.

"We regret to inform you . . ." Again and again. From all those prestigious schools.

There was a part of me that still held out hope. Whenever a new letter came for me, I'd say, "Well, at least it's not USC."

Until it was.

One of the very last letters of all to arrive that year was from USC. And when I read that phrase, "We regret to inform you . . ." I cried.

That was it. The door was closed. My USC dream was over.

So when I took that plea deal, one year from the day it all started to unravel for me, the idea of going to prison for ninety days just seemed like lousy icing on the cake of a defeat I'd already swallowed.

I'd already been punished beyond imagination.

I could hear my mom weeping behind me in the courtroom when I entered that plea. She was shocked.

I wouldn't get to explain it to her until I called her that evening on the phone, from juvie.

She was mad. We had vowed that we would make our decisions together. She was angry that the attorney she hired had let her child make such a big decision without talking to her first.

But it didn't matter how angry she was. It was too late now.

My whole life had been ruined.

So now what? I was off to prison?

So what? I told myself.

Not juvie. Not some special place where they'd keep me safe because I was so young. I was off to Chino State Prison—the "California Institute for Men" in Chino, California—way out east of Los Angeles in the middle of a bunch of uninhabited farmland. More than an hour's drive from Long Beach. One of the largest prisons in the state. Home to 2,500 inmates. We're talking *prison,* prison. Hard-core.

You'll adjust, I told myself. *It's only ninety days. You've done a year. Ninety days will fly by. Then you'll be home. You'll be done with this. You'll be free.*

Was I scared to walk into a prison full of grown men? Life-long criminals? Murderers? Of course I was. I had no idea how bad this might get. I heard from other kids in juvie that Chino was one of the "scary" prisons. I remember one kid telling me, "Don't be no punk. Don't be scared. Don't be scared of *shit.* Regardless, you may not know what's going on, but don't be scared. But don't try to come in there and be hard like you the tough guy or something, like you're gonna come and defend everything or win every fight. That'd be worse. But don't get pushed over."

Another kid told me that I'd get "banged on" by a Crip and a Blood as soon as I walked in. I would have to either declare who I was with or let them know that I wasn't down with being in a gang. "Just don't make anybody hot, and put some respect on it."

So I simultaneously had to be smart enough to not act tough, but to act tough *enough*, to tell gang members that I didn't want to roll with them, and somehow do it without offending them?

"Man, you piss off the wrong guy up in there and you'll get packed. They be shankin' fools in there," they said.

When I asked them how they knew all this, they always seemed to have an older brother or a cousin or some uncle who'd been through Chino. They knew the ropes. They'd been prepared for it.

I kept holding on to my faith. I kept holding on to Mr. Johnson's words. I kept thinking about everything I'd learned on my journey so far. And I reminded myself of who I was, deep down, and I tried to convince myself it would all be okay.

And I prayed.

I knew I wouldn't leave until sometime after I turned eighteen, which was sixteen days away. I didn't know when or what day they'd come get me, for security purposes. So I just prayed day and night. I begged God to stand by me and to help me get through this final part of my fight.

The one thing I couldn't shake, though, the one thing that truly deep-down terrified me more than anything about my transfer, was that someone at Chino might find out what

I was in for. In prison, rape, child abuse, molestation, and even some spousal abuse cases are all considered terminable offenses. There's a revolt against crimes against children and women, governed by men who are no saints themselves. In prison, people will kill you. Everybody knows that. You see it in movies. You see it on the news. That's just the law behind those walls. And it was all I could do to keep myself from believing that maybe the judge and the DA and maybe even my lawyer wanted it that way. Maybe they all believed deep down that I did it. Because they didn't investigate the ridiculousness of Tiana's story. Because they didn't consider what the results of the negative DNA match really meant before they cornered me with a plea deal at the outset of my trial. Because no one in the whole judicial system did their job.

All I knew is that if anyone in that prison found out what I'd been labeled, *anyone*, it wouldn't matter that I was innocent. It wouldn't matter that I took a plea.

It would mean that I'd get seriously hurt or killed.

When the night of my eighteenth birthday came, the night before they transferred me out, I couldn't sleep. Not a wink.

I couldn't shake it.

I was afraid.

TEN

Ninety Days

From the outside, Chino looked like some kind of military installation.

On the inside, it felt like some sort of prison camp.

The guards put me through the usual strip search, issued me the bright orange uniform of a convicted felon, then walked me into my dorm. They called it a "dorm," like I was going off to college or something.

I wasn't.

To say the California Institute for Men was overcrowded would be an understatement. My unit was set up in a former gymnasium that had been converted to hold hundreds of prisoners all together. It looked just like a high school gymnasium, only the light-colored, all-wood basketball floor was covered with bunks stacked three high, just a foot or two apart from one another, as far as the eye could see.

This was my new temporary home. And that home was segregated by race. There was a white section, a Hispanic section, and a black and "other" section. Everything in prison was divided that way. Everything. Why? Because eventually, as other prisoners moved out, inmates in that gymnasium would get rotated into cell blocks. The segregation was designed by the inmates themselves. Why? Because if there was a race war out in the yard one day and the guards were forced to put everyone back in their cells, different races that were housed in the same cells would keep fighting and wind up killing each other. So rather than let that happen, they segregated everything from the start, including this packed-full gymnasium.

Someone pointed me to my bunk in the black area. It was way off in the far corner. I was the new guy, so the top bunk was mine. I climbed up just to take a look around, and all I saw was a sea of some the scariest people I'd ever laid eyes on in my life. There were a bunch of white supremacists walking around the perimeter with their shirts off, brandishing giant tattooed swastikas on their chests and stomachs. We're talking giant, six-foot-five, 260-pound neo-Nazis. A couple of them had swastikas tattooed on their *faces*. I'd never seen anyone like that in the real world. It was disgusting. It made me angry. Where did these people live? How could they walk around like that? There were tatted-up black and Hispanic gang members gathered together in groups, too, looking at us newbies like prey. Imagine the deadliest, angriest gang members from every gang in the world being plucked out and dropped together in one room. That's pretty much the room I was in.

I climbed down so I wouldn't get noticed, and I spotted a big black guy walking right toward me. I don't think I had been in that dorm more than three minutes and already I thought, *Here we go.*

I stiffened my body as this guy walked straight up to me and said, "You Banks, right?"

"Yeah," I said.

"Brian Banks?"

"Yeah," I said.

"Oh, okay, you were just up at Sylmar, right?"

"Yeah, just left there. Why, what's good?"

"You know my cousin!"

He said the name, and sure enough, I knew the kid.

"Oh shit, for real? That's the homey."

"Yep, we are crimmies. Us and my two other cousins. I got word from him you may be coming up this way," he said.

He kept talking and talking, and it quickly became clear that this guy wasn't my enemy.

"Yeah, he told about your situation. Well, I already kinda know about it. Shit, the whole city do. Shit is fucked up what you're going through, cuz."

He leaned in real close and whispered, "I work reception up in the front. So when your paperwork came through, I took care of it."

This guy was dressed in orange. He was an inmate.

"You took care of my paperwork?" I whispered back. "What do you mean?"

"Yeah. Us inmates here have jobs. Mine's in the front office. So I watched for your paperwork and, like"—he leaned in further and whispered again—"I already processed it. I took care of it. It's all good, man."

I didn't quite get it. I said, "You mean . . . ?"

"I filed it already so no one else will see it."

"Yeah," I said. "I get it. Wow." I leaned back a bit and looked him in the eye and said, "Thank you."

"No problem, man. No problem," he said.

Remember all that praying I'd been doing for the sixteen days before I transferred?

Some of my prayers worked.

I mean truly, how was that not some kind of divine intervention? This guy happened to be related to a guy I was in Juvenile Hall with, who happened to go to the same high school as me, and he happened to know me as a football player, and so, he looked out for me, *big-time*. If it wasn't for this one random guy who just happened to work in inmate processing for this dorm having stepped in to make sure the nature of my charges got swept under the rug, my very first night in prison could've been a whole different story. I could have got rushed. I could have got stabbed. Jumped. Anything. And I never would have seen it coming.

"All good, cuz. Let me get back to work. I'll come get at you later."

I closed my eyes as he walked away and thought, *Thank you, Lord*.

No sooner did he leave than I got approached by members from both Crip and Blood 'hoods, "banging on" me just like I'd been warned.

"Aye, where you from, Blood—"

"What up, cuz—"

"You bang, my nigga?"

"Who you roll with?"

They were right in my face, looking me up and down, scanning for fear. It was hyperaggressive.

"I'm from Long Beach," I said.

"Oh, you from Long Beach? All right then, Blood," the guy from the Bloods said, and he proceeded to throw up his hood with his fingers, like sign language, to let me know where he was from. He walked away and the Crip representative stuck around.

"What you in here for?" he asked me.

"Home invasion," I said. I'd come up with a whole story on the bus ride in, to provide me with a little cover. "Took the rap for the homey," I said. I went on to explain that a close friend of mine robbed a guy we all knew. "The guy suspected it was either him or me. So instead of snitching on the homey, I took the rap for him.

"They picked me up, and because I didn't snitch on him I ended up getting time."

I noticed my bunk mate was listening in on us a little bit while we talked. He was an old dude with the nappiest braids and all kinds of prison tattoos. Looked like he'd been in prison forever.

"Oh, man. So you in here taking a rap for somebody? Damn, cuz. I hope he's looking out for you," the Crip rep said.

So far so good. That whole conversation left a knot in my stomach. I wasn't used to lying, and here I was lying to this man's face about my charges and conviction. I was scared to death that somebody would see a hole in my story and start asking questions, or somebody would see my paperwork and rat me out.

Turns out this Crip rep was also my MAC rep. He was the black inmate who represented us on the Men's Advisory Council, a sort of liaison between the warden and prison administrators and the inmates. Those representatives were chosen by race, too, and in reality, he was basically the guy who was the decision maker and peacekeeper for the blacks in our dorm. One thing quickly became clear: the guards and the warden don't run things inside the prison. In prison, the inmates are in charge.

The inmates run the prison and its politics; the guards just enforce the punishment and safety of the facility. And my MAC rep was about to show me the ropes.

"All right, cuz. Follow me," he said. "Check this out. You see them two showers, those are ours. Don't touch those four. Those two sinks, that's ours. That water fountain over there is cool. That's ours. Don't walk down that hallway. Stay out this aisle way. That table over there is for the Mexicans; don't sit there. Those two phones, we cool with those on Mondays and Fridays, but don't touch them the other days. This is the day room. This TV, you can look at them, but on Tuesday, Wednesdays, the Mexicans get to sit in the front row. You gotta sit in the back row, whites sit in the middle. And then it rotates. Don't touch the TV when it ain't our day."

It was implied that messing up on any of these rules would get you DPs, which I figured out meant "Disciplined."

"When you hit the yard, make sure you stick with your people," he said. "We share our basketball courts with the 'others'; the Mexicans and whites got theirs."

It was a lot.

"You gon' need to remember all this, homey, feel me? It's politics and rules in here."

I had to pay so much attention absorbing the rules, absorbing the culture inside those walls just to keep myself safe, there was no time to think about what day it was, or what hour it was, or how I would have been buying supplies and getting ready for dorm living at USC right now, and playing football right now with Pete Carroll as my coach. I didn't have time or space in my mind to think about my mom, or even my little brother, who'd decided to drop out of Poly because he couldn't take the pressure and the stress from everything that had happened to me. My mom wasn't allowed to visit me during the ninety-day eval. I wasn't allowed any visitors at all. I wasn't allowed phone calls, either. The only way I could communicate with the outside world was through the mail. So I wrote my mom letters telling her, "I'm fine. I promise you, I'm good in here. Everything's fine." I hated lying to my mom, but I had no choice. If I didn't lie to her, if I told her what I'd seen in my first week alone, she never could have made it. She would have worried herself to death.

The fact is, prison was a minute-by-minute, hour-by-hour existence. The only thoughts I had were about what I should and shouldn't be doing all the time. I had to think about not looking anybody in the eye unless we'd already established a good relationship. To think about how to reconcile the fact that I was seeing all kinds of violence around me, every day, and how to live with the prison mantra of no matter what, "You didn't see shit."

No matter what happened, you looked the other way. If anyone asked you about it, "You didn't see shit." That was the one and only answer, or else.

Just a few days into my sentence I walked into a bathroom to go brush my teeth and saw a guy slumped in the corner of the shower, bleeding out. He'd been beaten. Stabbed. I had to suppress every natural instinct I had—to call for help, to rush to his side, to try to stop the bleeding—and instead just turn around and walk back out of there.

I didn't see it. I didn't see that. I'm just gonna brush my teeth over here instead.

After three days in the gymnasium, they transferred me to

an actual prison yard, with six dorms on each side of a dirt track. Right after I got there, word got around that a guy in the next module killed someone with a broomstick. Broke the broomstick off between the bars of his cell and stabbed the guy right through the chest.

The third time I hit the yard, two Hispanic inmates got into a fight. The guards yelled at them to stop. They wouldn't stop. They yelled, "Everybody down!" and everyone in that yard, including myself, hit the dirt. Flat on our stomachs. Our hands up on the back of our heads. That's when the gun came out. A guard shot one of the two guys who were fighting with a block gun—a rifle that shoots rubber blocks. Those blocks don't kill you, but they take a chunk of meat out of you. The guy was spraying blood everywhere from the hole that that gun caused.

This was my introduction to prison life.

Were there times in those early days at Chino when I was tested and had to defend myself? Yes. Am I proud of it? No. I did everything in my power to avoid getting into fights. And I thanked God that I was as big as I was and could handle myself the couple of times that it happened, because I won. I established to everybody in that prison that I wasn't a punk. And that was important. But you'd better believe I prayed every night that whoever I fought wouldn't come back later seeking revenge, with a knife, or with a few of his homeys.

As for the physical pain, I could take it. I was a football player. I was used to being tough and taking hits. I was aggressive on the field. But nursing bruises and tasting your own blood feels a whole lot different in prison than it does on a football field. This wasn't a game. In prison, they play for keeps.

But the pain I felt on the inside? The emotional toll of deal-ing with all of that? There wasn't any support system to help me or anybody else get through it. There are no coaches in prison. There are no counselors. There's no mom or friend there who will let you cry on her shoulder. There are no hugs in prison. Whatever you're going through, you just deal with it. If you're having a bad day, you're not allowed to show anything except anger and frustration. It's okay to be angry in prison. People expect it. Everybody's angry just about all the time. But you cry? You're labeled weak. And that could get you killed.

For all of the violence I encountered at Chino, I was told that it wasn't the worst prison in the system. I heard stories, lots of stories, about how bad some of the other prisons were. And the worst of them wasn't even a "prison." It was Los An-geles County Jail. The stories some of the inmates shared about that facility were more terrifying than anything I'd ever seen in any horror movie. Stories about guys screaming for their lives while the guards just looked the other way. Stories about white kids getting tortured by gangs of blacks and Hispanics as pay-back for all of the privilege and injustice of the system. That jail had sewer problems. Infestations of rats and mice. There were stories of people screaming all night long. It sounded like the seventh circle of hell.

More than one inmate said to me, "Don't ever go there if you can avoid it, man. You ever get into trouble again, do it in Orange County. Do it up in the Valley. Don't get caught for nothing in LA County, man."

It always struck me that most of the inmates I talked to were always making plans for how to deal with whatever trouble they got into next. This was life for them. There was no rehabilitation. There was no reform. Prison life was *life*. What happened on the inside carried on outside these walls. I started to wonder if the racial divides, the gang wars, the drug smuggling—all the bad things that were happening in cities all over America—were a reflection of what was happening inside the prisons, not the other way around. It's like the prisons were designed to train inmates how to be lifelong criminals full of anger and hatred toward the world around them. It normalized division, caused ongoing rivalries in the gangs, stoked the racial divides, all of it.

A few weeks at Chino and I was more grateful than ever for the teachings of Mr. Johnson. I think he probably knew I might get here. He had seen it a lot. Injustice. Kids being railroaded again and again in a justice system in which black lives really and truly do not matter. Not one bit. Not to anyone who had any power to make a difference. I think that might be why he taught me the things he did so early on.

He told me one time, "When you're in prison, you are forced to make a decision: are you gonna be still, or are you gonna run from yourself?" Sitting in Chino, seeing what I saw, knowing I had to make it through ninety days, I could have easily grabbed on to something to help me deal with it all. Something bad, like drugs. Drugs were everywhere in that place. There was a whole system of smuggling them in, and lots of inmates were using.

Most of the people around me took on prison in really destructive ways. If it wasn't the drugs, it was the constant violence. Like I said, everybody was angry. Really angry. And they'd rather raise hell and let that anger out onto something or someone else instead of facing it themselves. I had my own anger and I had my own set of problems, but I used every cell in my body to try to stay still like Mr. Johnson had taught me and not be my own destructive force. I kept reminding myself, over and over, that I was here by accident, a mistake, a miscarriage of justice, whatever you wanted to call it. But I was *not* here of my own doing. So I was *not* going to further destroy myself. I was *not* going to add to the sentence by getting into trouble and being someone that I'm not. The only thing that mattered to me was getting out. I *needed* to get out.

My biggest fear wasn't that I'd get hurt or killed. Truly. My biggest fear was that I'd get caught in a fight, even if I was just defending myself, and I'd wind up in the hole—therefore jeopardizing my ninety-day plea deal. If I didn't get a favorable report during that ninety-day eval, they would keep me in prison for the next six years. Or worse, if something really bad happened, I could wind up facing new charges for something I got caught up in during my stay, and those charges could keep me in prison much longer. I can't even explain how tense it is, trying to walk that fine line of surviving in prison while trying to not do anything that could jeopardize your future.

I felt so unbelievably lucky to be the size I was, so big that most people didn't try to mess with me. But I learned in my first month or so that there was a lot more than my size to thank for that blessing of being left alone. I had homeys in the street life on the outside. They knew me and knew that I was innocent. They knew me as a rising football player. They knew I had a shot at making it, of getting out of Long Beach on the straight and narrow. They sent word ahead that I was coming. "Oh yeah, he's from the city. He's good."

That combined with my knowledge from hanging out with

homeys, my knowledge of the 'hood, of OGs in the city, that all validated me as a true Long Beach guy.

In prison, even if you're not a gang member, you still roll with your city. It's called a "car," as in "We're all from the same city so we roll in the same 'car' together."

I ran with the Long Beach car.

• ◆ •

I did half my time, a full forty-five days, before I saw the psychologist and the counselor for the first time. They were both scheduled back to back on the same day, two black women, and over the course of their evaluations they both separately came to the very same conclusion. At the end of the day, the two of them shook their heads and said to my face, "This is insane. You should not be here. You should not *be* here!"

Neither one of those women could understand how *anyone* who read my case file, which included the police reports, the testimony from Tiana, and the fitness evaluation, or anything else could possibly think that I belonged in prison. I still hadn't been allowed to look at any of those files myself, but they told me, once again, that my accuser had changed her story multiple times. Her details were so inconsistent, they said, that it seemed obvious to them—as professionals—that the charges were made up. "Especially considering that the DNA from the rape kit wasn't a match!" they said.

They also commented on how well I was handling prison. I'd picked up a job by then and was working with other inmates on R&R—Reception and Release. I worked with whites and Hispanics, and together we were responsible for taking new inmates' clothes at intake, storing them properly so they could receive them again when they got out, and giving them their prison clothes. I did cleaning work, too, like a janitor position. And that allowed me to be out and about in the bathrooms and hallways in the R&R building, which showed my evaluators that the guards and the MAC reps trusted me. They seemed impressed by the way I got along with everybody, from my bunk mate to my white and Hispanic coworkers on R&R. And they were both impressed by the way I talked about trying to stay centered and true to myself, just as Mr. Johnson had taught me. I had been working on that daily.

It turns out that the "ninety-day evaluation" was really just about one visit from the evaluators. That was the only day they "observed" me. And at the end of that day, they pulled me into a private room and told me the best news I'd heard in fifteen straight months: They said they were giving me a favorable report. They said they were recommending to the judge that I be released on "time served" and serve out the rest of my sentence on felony probation.

"Thank God," I said, closing my eyes and squeezing my hands together. "Thank you, Lord!"

I looked them both in the eyes and I said, "Thank you. Thank you so much. Thank you for caring. Thank you for *listening*." I got teary-eyed but sucked it back in before I left the room.

I was so happy I wanted to shout it out loud and jump up and down on the way back to my dorm. But I held it in. I needed to keep my poker face. I still had time left. I couldn't let anyone get jealous and try to jeopardize my release.

"What's up, youngster?" my bunk mate said. I think he'd

seen me enough to recognize that something was different on that day. "How you feeling?"

"I'm feeling pretty good," I told him.

That's as close as I would come to telling anybody on the inside that I was about to be free.

I climbed up on my bunk, pulled out a pencil and a piece of paper, and wrote to my mother: "We've got it, Mom! We got the favorable report. They're recommending felony probation. Which means I've only got a few weeks left. I'll be home in no time, Mom. This is it. It's happening. I'm coming home!"

ELEVEN

Of Mice and Men

For the next couple of weeks, I walked around Chino with a little bit more pep in my step.

Freedom was right around the corner.

I could taste it.

Soon I'd be called for transfer back to Juvenile Hall, back to Long Beach Superior Court to face the judge and receive my sentencing.

With just a few days to go, I stood there in the middle of the hallway, mop in hand, staring at the glare on the floor from the fluorescent lights above, sidetracked by the possibility of going home, replaying the words of the psychologist and counselor in my head intertwined with the repeated sentence: "We got the favorable report!"

It's only a matter of time, I thought, *before—*

"Banks!" a CO—correctional officer—barked out from the front desk of R&R.

Setting the mop back in the bucket, I hustled my way over to the front desk.

"Yes, sir?"

The CO was a muscled six-foot, four-inch middle-aged white man. He was baldheaded with no facial hair, no facial expression for that matter, and he didn't raise his eyes from the *Los Angeles Times* as he plainly asked me, "You enjoying your time here?"

Confused by the random question, I replied, "Uh, I mean, not really."

"That's too bad," he said nonchalantly. "You're on the transfer list. Pack it up."

Transfer list. Pack it up?

Did I really just hear him say, "Pack it up"?

"Now, sir?" I asked.

"Yes, Banks, now," he replied.

Here we go. I'm out. All I got to do is see the judge and I'm done.

All I kept thinking as I went through strip search—spread 'em, squat, cough two times—was *I survived. I survived prison. I'm done.*

I knew I'd be held in another facility for a few days. Maybe more. That's just how court dates from prison work. When you're transferring from prison to court, you're transferred back to a jail facility. And from what I understood, whatever facility you left before going to Chino would be the facility you'd return to, which meant I was going back to Juvenile Hall.

The guards entered the cell and began shackling us for transfer. Arms, waist, ankles. All chained. As they led us out onto an empty bus and drove us out of the last security gate of the prison, I felt myself exhale.

I made it out.

I'd gone to prison for three months and made it out alive. I looked back only once, to remember. To never forget.

I sat back in my seat and closed my eyes, and just for a moment I felt thankful. I had no desire to go back to Juvenile Hall, but between juvie and Chino, juvie was something to look forward to. *And pretty soon all of this will be over,* I thought.

No more than five minutes into the drive, one of the transfer guards up front stood and made his way back to the locked gate, which separated us from them. He carried a clipboard in his hand. It was time for roll. I'd done this enough times now on the inside to know the routine. When my name got called, I had to respond immediately with the last two digits of my prison number, which every one of us had to have memorized or we'd never hear the end of it.

My prison number was V13109.

"Alvarez!" he yelled.

"Yea," Alvarez loudly replied. The bus squeaked, bounced, and cracked.

"Last two?" the guard asked.

"Four three."

"Thank you, Alvarez," the guard replied, inking a check next to the prisoner's name on the clipboard. "You're transferring to LA County Jail."

The guard moved on to the next name: "Banks!"

"Yes, sir," I loudly replied.

"Last two?"

"Zero nine."

The guard glanced over his clipboard, then marked a check. "Thank you, Banks. You're transferring to LA County Jail."

LA County Jail?

My heart dropped.

"Sir, LA County Jail? I'm supposed to be transferring to juvie," I said with confusion.

"Well, it says here you're transferring to County."

My heart began to race. I tried to play it cool. "But sir, I came from Juvenile Hall. I'm supposed to go back to where I came from, right?"

"Well, it says here you're eighteen, right?"

I nodded.

"That means you're too old for juvie, Banks. You're going to County. You can take it up with them there."

God, no, I thought. *Don't let them send me to that place. Please. Don't let them call my name when we get there. Let this be a mistake. Don't put me in that place!*

He finished roll and I knew I had maybe an hour to mentally prepare for where I was headed. I started going over scenarios. *What if somebody pushes up on me? How will I respond? How am I gonna respond when they come up and ask me where I'm from? How am I gonna walk? What's the facial expression I'm gonna use when I'm looking at people or if somebody talks to me? Okay. What's the best countertechnique if someone swings on me?*

The raw emotion hit me all at once. *Don't cry. Don't get emotional. Keep a straight face. Don't let the other guys on the bus think you're scared to go to County. No big deal. All right.*

I already felt like I'd been kidnapped, and now my kidnappers were taking me from one dark dungeon to an even darker one, for more torture. And I was helpless to do anything to change it. I couldn't walk away. I couldn't run away. I'd been so happy thinking it was almost over, and now I didn't know when it was going to be over. I didn't know what I'd find on the other side of that door. No clue what I was about to experience except for the nightmarish stories I'd heard at Chino.

We pulled up to County and a giant door slid open to let the bus through. It closed behind us, then another giant door opened to let the bus into the lot. They filed all of us off and took us into a ten-by-ten room.

"Strip it down!"

A busload of men, all naked, squatting, coughing, and guards with flashlights looking into cracks and crevices.

"Get dressed."

They took us to a big room with rows of benches, where one by one we were called to a glass window to talk to a man or woman on the other side who would start the intake process. There were guys sleeping on benches, and in corners. Who knows how long they'd been there. Gang members started talking to each other. Some people sat quietly. Others were fidgety and pacing around. It felt like one off comment would spark a riot in that room.

"Banks!"

I walked up to a black woman behind the window. "Ma'am, I'm not supposed to be here," I said. I tried my best to put it on thick. "I just turned eighteen a few *days* ago and I left Juvenile Hall, and I was told that I was gonna go back to Juvenile Hall."

"Okay. Let me do a chart check and see what we can do," she said.

It seemed like she really wanted to help.

"Thank you. Thank you!" I said to her.

A few minutes later she called me back up, and I thought, *Okay, God. Here we go.*

"Mr. Banks, you turned eighteen, so we can't send you back. You've gotta stay here until you go to court."

There was a pay phone in that room, and as soon as she

was done handing me my wristband to get all checked in to LA County Jail, the guy using that phone hung up and I rushed right to it.

"Mom!"

Thank God she picked up.

"You've got to call the lawyer and tell her to get on the phone with the county and get me transferred. I can't be here. I gotta get out of here. This is the place I was telling you stories about."

"Well, why do they have you there?" she asked.

"I don't know. It's got to be a mistake. Please call her. I'll call you back. Hopefully you can reach her before they take us in."

It took forever to process everyone. It gave me enough time to get to the phone again and call her back. My mom had reached the lawyer. She said she'd made a call—but there was nothing we could do. I was eighteen years old. Whichever county jail they put me in was where I had to stay until we went to court—which wasn't going to happen for almost two weeks.

"Two weeks?!" I yelled.

"I know, Brian," my mom said. I could hear the sadness in her voice.

"That's longer than ninety days. That's way longer," I said.

"I know," she said. "She says there's nothing we can do. There's nothing anybody can do. There's a backlog of cases, and that's it."

I was speechless.

"I'm sorry, baby. Please stay strong. You can do this. You're almost done."

One last test, I thought.

But why am I being tested? Why, God? Why?

"I love you, Mom," I said.

"I love you, too, Brian. I love you so much. You stay strong now," she said.

"Bye."

"Bye."

I hung up. I closed my eyes. I tried to pull it together. I had to pull it together.

My evaluation was good. I'm going home. I'm getting out. That's what matters.

Remembering that kept me going.

A few minutes later, they took the whole group to another holding cell. They passed out a bunch of trash bags.

"Everybody gets a bag," the guard said. "Take one and pass them down."

Once everybody had a bag, he said, "Now strip down. All your clothes get stored inside a bag. If it's personal property, you'll get it back when you get released. If it's not personal, we're taking it away from you."

All I had were my prisoner clothes from Chino, a small brown pocket Bible, a few letters I'd received, and some loose papers with phone numbers, addresses, and notes I had written while I was there. I put it all in the bag, and stood there with the rest of the naked men. They filed us out and handed each of us a shower roll: a towel and a bar of the cheapest industrial soap imaginable. As we walked across a nasty floor that looked like it had never been washed, we passed posters on the walls that warned us about hepatitis C and staph infection and whatever else was going around in the prison those days. They led us all into a giant shower that—no disrespect—reminded me of the gas chamber in the movie *Schindler's List*. I had watched that film as a kid, and thought it was one of the most powerful films I'd ever seen in my life. The gas chamber scene haunted me. This room looked just like it. The metal door slid open. They put the whole group of us inside and slammed its giant metal door shut. We were locked inside. A riot could have popped off. Anything could have happened. There were no guards inside this locked room.

The sound of pipes filling echoed off the walls, and then jets of cold water came bursting out all over us.

I had put on deodorant that morning. I decided not to wash it off. I had no idea when or if I'd see any kind of deodorant in the days ahead, and I needed to preserve whatever was left there under my arms.

They marched us out of the shower to a room where a bunch of inmates were handing out blue prison garb.

"Size?"

"Three-X," I said. The guys looked around.

"We only have two-X," he said, handing me a 2X scrublike shirt and pants, and a pair of shoes, like slippers with rubber soles. I got dressed in that too-tight shirt and those pants that ended a couple of inches above my ankles, and they took us through medical, and then they put us all into holding cells. Thirty or forty of us per cell. Divided by race.

The guards went away and basically never came back—for the next two days.

In the black cell there were two long benches against the walls, facing each other, and a toilet/sink in one corner. We were all pressed up against each other. The only way to sleep was to lie against somebody else on the floor, which meant sleep was nearly impossible.

There were no windows. No way to tell what time of day or night it might be.

I thought for sure somebody was going to pop from the frustration and start a fight, and who knows what would have happened with all of us right on top of each other like that.

The concrete floor was covered in spit. There was a puddle of old urine in the corner.

They told us they had nowhere else to put us because LA County Jail was overcrowded. They said we wouldn't get moved into cells until other inmates left. And for the whole two days, all anyone talked about was how bad it was going to be once we did leave that holding cell and finally went into the tower.

"Just make sure you don't go to this block or that block," guys said, as if any of us had a choice in the matter. "That's where it really pops off. Riots and fights. It's mainly gang affiliated."

I kept praying that I wouldn't wind up in one of those blocks.

On the third day, the door opened.

"On your feet! When you hear your name, give me your last two and step out."

They took us in lines through long, dark hallways that felt like they were deep underground. It was like a boiler room or basement, with pipes overhead and cement floors beneath our feet. Many of us had no idea where we were going. No idea what was ahead.

"All right. You, you, you." They pointed to me and a couple

of other guys. "You guys are going to 700. Go get in line over here. You guys over here."

It wasn't one of the blocks I was warned about. I felt good about that.

More hallways. A door opened. They led us into an enclosed cage of bars and wire mesh. I could barely see through—but I could hear the rumble of the cells. The noise. The inmates knew some new blood was approaching.

And I could smell it.

The jail smelled like death. It smelled like a port-a-potty that had never been changed. The wretched stench of hundreds of un-showered men, and shit, and blood, and God knows what else.

The guards wouldn't walk us to our cells. They told us which cell to go to and we had to walk alone, past the glaring faces of men behind bars. This was a two-tiered module, cells on the bottom and cells on top, right above them. Without making eye contact, I looked into those cells. They were six-man cells. Six men all packed together in every one of them. Six men in a cell that only looked big enough for three people. There were three-tier bunks on each side of a tiny aisle, only as wide as the combination toilet/sink at the back of the cell. No room to walk around. No room to breathe.

There was barely any light. No windows. When my cell door opened, I looked in and saw four Hispanics and one black guy. I panicked.

I stopped dead and looked back at the guard and said, "I can't go in there."

"What was that?" he yelled.

That's when the black guy ran right up to the bars. "It's cool, cuz. It's cool in here. You straight."

I walked in, and sure enough the guys were okay. The black guy was from Compton. A year older than me, fighting a pretty heavy charge and looking at fourteen or sixteen years. The Mexicans were all gang members, but they weren't looking for any trouble. They wanted to stay cool.

I was lucky.

I noticed there was a pay phone on the wall inside the tiny cell.

"Yeah, it's like a buck sixty or two bucks a minute," one of the guys said. "That's how they make money. They know we gonna use it. They know that's our lifeline. Our only connection to the outside world."

"Yeah, yeah, and they'll shut 'em off just to make everyone crazy. Watch, homey. You watch," one of my other cellies said.

They weren't kidding. Not an hour goes by in that place before it hits you: You want to call your lawyer, you want to call your mom, you want to call anyone you can because you're never coming out of that cell. At LA County Jail, there is no yard. There is no rec room. There is no day room. No music. No TVs. No radios. No clocks. You don't know when the sun is up. You don't know when the sun is down. The only way to tell time is with the phone.

If you want to know what time it is, you listen to see if somebody above you or next to you is on the phone and you yell out, "Can I get a time check, please?" And whoever is on the phone will ask what time it is.

"It's four thirty-five p.m.!" they'll yell out, and then everybody will know.

I realize that sounds sort of civil, but this was happening in a place that was an absolute gutter. It was nasty. It was dirty.

There was no cleaning crew that came to clean these cells. There wasn't even anyone coming around and handing out mops, saying, "Here's some cleaning solution so you can clean the walls and floors and toilets yourselves."

Nothing got cleaned.

I know people who are scared to use a public bathroom at a busy McDonald's, but that is like a palace commode compared to this place they had put me in. I swore I would never complain about having to use a public bathroom for the rest of my life once I got out of that place.

I swore I'd never complain about having to wait for my brother to get out of the shower again, either. In this place, they only allowed us to shower every four days. When it happened, it happened at 5 a.m., with no warning.

From a sound sleep, I was jarred awake by a voice yelling, "Shower, shower, shower!" The cell doors opened and closed within thirty seconds. If I didn't gather my soap and towel and make it out before that door closed, I'd have to wait another four days. And the shower I got was the same one I took after intake. The gas-chamber-like shower with cold water.

After a few days, I got the routines down. I was lucky not to see any violence in 700 block. So, overall, everything was pretty chill—until they moved me.

"Banks! Pack it up!"

They took me to a different module, one door over. They put me in a four-person cell, way down in the corner. It was two Hispanics and a black guy—and God stepped in once again.

We did the "What you in for?" and "Where you from?" and it turned out the black guy was from Long Beach. He went to a different school than me, but we realized that I had been in juvie with his cousin. "Wait! You're that football player," he said. "Man, bro, you're going through some fucked-up stuff right now. We were talking about you before we got locked up. The whole city heard about what happened to you. And man, I just want you to know, I'm sorry you're going through what you're going through."

The Hispanics in my cell were chill. They didn't want any trouble. They were just waiting it out like I was. But the three Hispanics in the next cell over? They were a different story. They were all gangsters, and they were angry. They were looking for trouble.

The very next day, the guards sent a white guy into their cell. He was young guy, maybe in his twenties, with long hair. Kind of a hippie-looking kid who I'm guessing was in on a minor drug charge or something. In fact, he looked like he was just coming down from whatever high he was on.

No sooner did he step into that cell than the gangsters stripped him naked and beat him. They made him sleep on the concrete floor, under the metal bunk. They stepped on him when they went to use the toilet. And for the next three days, every time he tried to get up, they beat him some more. They tortured him to within an inch of his life.

When he screamed, they yelled "Agua! Agua!!" and all of the other Hispanics in all of the other cells started flushing their toilets, those industrial-type toilets, over and over—*Whoosh! Whoosh! Whoosh! Whoosh!*—making so much noise that nobody could hear the young man scream.

Even when you could hear him scream, no guards came.

No one cared.

On the fourth day, they opened his cell first thing in the

morning, and when his three cellies went to the shower, he crawled out, crying, "Help me. Help me." The guards down the way started laughing. "You fucking punk, bring your ass up here so I can deal with you," they said. They wouldn't even come get him. "You're a fucking mess!" they yelled. "Now we gotta do paperwork, you fucking pussy."

I watched that guy crawl on his hands and knees, naked, beat down and bleeding, to the end of the cell block—where the guards yanked him up off the floor by his arms and dragged him out screaming to who knows where.

Then the toilets backed up. The whole system. Our module flooded with backed-up feces and piss, three inches deep all over the floor. Mice started pouring out of the cracks around the pipes, dozens of them, climbing up all over our bunks trying to escape the flooding. And we all had to climb up on our bunks to escape the flooding, too. They didn't even evacuate us. Two whole days went by before we finally heard some pumps running to drain the place out. But no one came to clean anything up. Once the water was gone, the piles of wet human shit just stayed on the floors.

Finally, after the sewer water receded, I heard the words I'd so desperately wanted to hear.

"Banks! Court! Long Beach Superior, tomorrow morning."

My court date was finally here.

I welcomed the sight of the filthy bus. I welcomed the sight of the familiar holding cell in Long Beach Superior Court, and just tried to stay out of the way and not get hit when a fight broke out between a couple of Crips in the holding cell that morning.

I welcomed the peace and quiet of the familiar interview

room, with the bulletproof window and the metal stool bolted to the floor.

I even welcomed the sight of my lawyer. The lawyer who forced me into this plea deal in the first place. She came in smiling, all happy that we had the positive report. Happy that my parents and a whole bunch of supporters had written a large stack of supportive character letters that she was going to give to the judge.

I'd written a letter to the judge myself, before I left Chino. I wrote that I was sorry that both of our families had been put through this ordeal, and thanked him for allowing me to go back to my family. I planned on reading the letter out loud in the courtroom.

"I don't want you to do that, Brian," my lawyer said.

"Why not?"

"I'm afraid it will come off as unremorseful. It could rub the judge the wrong way," she said.

I was so tired, so tired of all of it, that I just nodded my head and said, "Okay."

"I'll put your letter on top of all the other letters, though," she said. "So he'll read it first."

"That's fine," I said.

"You ready?"

"Are you kidding?" I said. "You have no idea."

I saw my mom sitting at the front. She was always there. She never missed a court date. And this time, I knew she had a bag with her. A bag with some of my street clothes in it, just in case she was allowed to bring me home that very day.

God, please let it happen.

My dad was there too. I looked around for my brother or

sister, but they weren't there. Of course they weren't. My sister was in D.C., going to Howard University, and my brother was still too shook up to want to see me. It was just too much for them. But I missed seeing them. I hadn't seen either one in so long. Seeing them would have meant a lot.

I was surprised to see one of my mentors from my basketball days there. He looked over and made eye contact with me and nodded his head in support. My eyes welled up with tears for a second and I had to wipe them away. I hadn't noticed at first, but my auntie was sitting right next to my mom. She waved her arms at me and smiled her big beautiful smile. My stepfather's best friend, Kurt, was there, too, and some other family friends. Everyone was there to hear the good news. They didn't seem as tense as they had been at past court appearances. I could tell they were all glad to see me, and excited at the thought that they would finally be able to take me home with them that morning.

For this proceeding, I wasn't seated beside my lawyer at the table. They sat me behind my lawyer in a chair up against the wooden half-wall that separates the viewers from the participants in the courtroom. The DA was at the next table. And behind him, in front of the little wooden wall, sat Tiana, her older sister, and her mother.

The judge walked in, and all of my confidence and faith flew out the window.

Fear and doubt are never far from belief, and the fear that grabbed me was the kind that makes you shake uncontrollably. The kind of fear that makes your legs go numb and give out. The kind that makes your heart go from beating fast to aching in agony. It was fear of the unknown; of opening a door and having no clue what's on the other side. The same fear you get when you've been underwater too long and you're now racing back to the top for air just in time, *hopefully*. I was beyond afraid. I was helpless, silenced, spoken for, ignored, humiliated, pushed along. To have gone through all that I did, and then have my freedom dangled over my head in this moment. Nothing else in the entire world mattered to me but the judge's decision.

He started off by addressing the district attorney: "Is there anybody that would like to speak?"

"Tiana's mother would like to speak," she responded.

Tiana's mother got up and she proceeded to give a long speech about how I took advantage of her daughter, how I stole her virginity, and how I didn't give her an opportunity to choose when she wanted to lose her virginity, because I'm a monster.

She went on and on about how I'd stolen her daughter's future and destroyed her life. She said she wished that I was facing more than six years.

"That isn't enough time for what he's done," she said, looking dead at me. Everything in me wanted to yell right in her face: "I didn't do it!" I wanted to plead with her, "Ma'am, I promise you, your daughter is lying." But I couldn't. I knew that if I raised my voice, or stood up, or showed any emotion, it could cost me everything.

The judge asked Tiana's mother, "And how has your daughter been, ma'am?"

"Oh, she's doing better day by day," she said.

"And how are you? How is the family?"

"We've had better days," she responded.

The judge then looked at my lawyer and said, "Do you guys want to say anything?"

My lawyer stood up and reminded the judge that I'd just completed ninety days of hard time at Chino, and that I'd walked away with an evaluation strongly recommending my release on felony probation.

"We also have these character letters," she said. "And Brian wrote a letter."

She brought the letters up to the judge, and he said, "I'm going to go back in my chambers and read these letters, and then I'll make my decision."

I fixed my eyes on the floor. Heart racing, aching. I could feel myself rocking back and forth while we waited.

We gave him at least thirty to forty minutes' worth of reading material.

He came back in less than five minutes. It felt to me like he'd gone in the back, taken a drink of water, and come right back out. There is no way he could have read all of those letters. *No way,* I thought. *He didn't read a damn thing.*

He came back in. He sat back down. And he said, "All right. The defendant is to receive six years in prison. . . ."

What?!

The words hit me like shots from a gun.

My lawyer dropped her expensive pen to the table and jolted back with her eyes all wide.

This can't be happening.

Out of the corner of my eye I could see Tiana and her mom and sister, all happy, pumping their fists like they'd won a big game or something.

This cannot be happening right now.

And behind me, in the front row of the visitors' section, I could hear my mom crying.

I dropped my head. In that moment I could have expressed myself through any variety of emotions. But I just laughed. I knew even then that it seemed like a weird reaction, but I dropped my head and started laughing. I wanted to scream. I couldn't. I wanted to stand up and yell at that judge. I couldn't. I wanted to pick Tiana Miller up and shake her and make her tell the truth! To tell her mother that her girl was a damned liar. To run out of that courtroom and tell the world this system is a joke. It's cruel. It's broken. It makes no sense.

I couldn't. I couldn't do anything.

So I laughed.

"This is a joke," I mumbled. "This is a joke!"

This can't be real.

The judge read off a long list of instructions, droning on and on as I sat there with my head down, unable to grasp a word he said. And then his gavel fell.

I'm done, I thought. *That's it.*

When the bailiff stood me up to lead me out of the courtroom, I still had a weird smile on my face. I was still shaking my head. Maybe I was in shock. I don't know. I just kept thinking, *This cannot be real.* It was truly beyond comprehension.

My heart stopped racing. My fear went away. My anger subsided. My hope was nowhere to be found. I was done. I was depleted. Exhausted. I had no fight left in me.

I looked back at my mom and my family and friends and everyone was crying. My dad was comforting my mom. He had this stoic look, but there were tears streaming down his face, too. I realized it was my dad's birthday that day. His birthday, of all days.

"I love you guys," I called out. "I love y'all."

They called back, "We love you, Brian!"

The last thing I heard as the courtroom door closed behind me was the sound of my mom's voice, crying, "No! This can't be happening. My Brian. *No!*"

TWELVE

Thoughts and Prayers

In the holding cell, back among the other inmates, I started shaking. I bent down and put my hands over my eyes, pressing against my eyelids to keep the tears from coming. I tried to hide it from everyone around me but my arms and hands just wouldn't stop shaking.

My mind kept spinning, trying to make sense of it all. But I couldn't make sense of it. None of it made sense.

How could this happen?

What should I think now?

How should I feel?

What do I do next?

I felt like I had died.

• • •

I did the math in my head, figuring how long I'd served and how much time I had left. Under California law, I'd be forced to serve 85 percent of my sentence. The sentence was six years. So that was . . .

Four years and two months.

After time served, I was looking at four more years and two more months.

In prison.

Longer than I'd spent in high school.

By the time I'd get out, I could have finished college and probably been playing for the NFL.

That life—*my life*—the way life should and could have been, kept flickering like a broken movie projecting in my mind. But there wasn't really time to do much thinking after the judge made his ruling. Not a lot of time for working out my emotions or anything like that. Not a lot of time to work through the anger I felt burning in my chest. I had to get back to surviving. Cold, hard surviving.

Within a couple of days I was transferred from LA County Jail to the county jail known as Wayside or Peter J. Pitchess Detention Center, farther north, up near Magic Mountain again. I would stay there until they transferred me to prison. *For rape.* I was on edge the entire time thinking that for sure somebody was going to see the charges on my paperwork now and I'd suffer a prison-level penalty for the crime I didn't commit. Every time the cell door opened, I thought for sure somebody was coming to beat and stab me to death while everybody looked the other way and "didn't see shit."

I could hardly sleep, but when I did, I'd wake up thinking, *Well, at least I didn't get killed last night. That's a good thing.*

And then I'd wonder, in all seriousness, *Is it?*

I sat there wondering if maybe I'd be better off dead.

I never thought of suicide. That wasn't it. I just wondered what good it was for me to be alive anymore. What was the point. Why did life matter?

I felt like I'd already died.

That's what they'd brought me to. That's what this *system* had brought me to.

What a joke, I thought. *This is all some kind of a sick joke.*

◆ ◆ ◆

I was locked in my cell when I found out that Tiana Miller and her mother had filed a lawsuit against the Long Beach city school system, claiming that the school had fostered an "unsafe environment" that allowed Tiana to get raped.

They sued the school system for millions of dollars in damages.

They filed the lawsuit on July 7, 2003—the day before I plead no contest. One day before my case was set to go to trial. It made no sense. I went over and over and over that detail in my mind. Why would they do that? Did they know something I didn't? Did they know I was going to do time no matter what? Was my sentence a done deal before I ever set foot in the courtroom? What if I'd been found innocent? That lawsuit would have gone down in flames, right? So what did they know that I didn't know?

The anger in my chest burned hard. I wanted that girl to suffer. I wanted her mom to suffer. And now they were looking at getting paid? I clenched my fists so hard at that thought, I nearly drew blood with my fingernails.

I became paranoid, too, wondering if my lawyer, the judge, and the DA had been talking and making deals behind the scenes or something. If there were really millions of dollars to be made suing the school system, who wouldn't want in on that money? Who was *getting* that money? Was it all some kind of a shakedown? A scam at my expense? Was this all rigged against me from the start? Was I just a pawn in some moneymaking scheme? Is that what this was all about?

I'd get all wound up about it, and then talk myself out of it, and then get upset again just thinking about the fact that Tiana and her mother were trying to get rich off of putting me in prison—on a lie! A lie that for some reason the system flat-out believed.

Why was it that no one believed *me*?

What a joke, I thought.

• ◆ •

After a few weeks in county jail, they shackled me and bussed me over to Delano State Prison in Kern County. Delano is "the reception prison," they told me. The one everybody goes to first.

There a group of counselors would interview me to determine where I would serve out my sentence—in a minimum-security or a maximum-security facility.

Great, I thought. *Because all of my evaluations have turned out so well for me!*

When they brought me to my cell, there was no one else there.

It was the size of a small walk-in closet, but there were only two bunks. Which meant only one cell mate. *A step up from where I've been*, I thought.

They told me I would be there for forty-five days. And because of the mixed nature of the population in that prison, we were all on 23/7 lockdown. That meant twenty-three hours a day in the cell. On alternating days, we'd get an hour on the yard, or an hour in a day room to watch TV, play cards, play chess, or just hang out.

Twenty-three hours a day. Every day. In a closet-sized room. With a stranger who, for all I knew, might try to fight or kill me as soon as I turned my back.

I was setting my things on the top bunk when I heard the cell door slide open behind me. I turned around real quick and laid eyes on a man who took up the entire doorway. A black man. Six foot ten. Easily upwards of four hundred pounds, most of it muscle. And I thought, *Oh, shit. Am I gonna have to fight this dude?*

He looked down at me and said, "What's up, man?"

"What's going on?" I said. As if this were some normal conversation.

"So," he said. "You're my cellie?"

"Yeah."

"All right, cool, man. Well, let me tell you some of the rules in here. . . ."

Lucky for me, my giant "cellie" wasn't a fighter at all. He had a heart as big as the muscles on his six-foot-ten frame, and a whole lot softer. He was actually a cool guy. He was in a gang and he'd been caught selling drugs a few too many times, and he'd gotten himself a twelve-year sentence. The last thing he wanted was to cause himself any more trouble, and when you put the two of us big guys side by side, whether out on the yard or sitting playing chess together in the day room, there was just no way anybody was going to mess with us.

Which meant there wasn't as much to worry about while I was at Delano.

They had a commissary there, and my mom put some money into my account for me. Which meant I could get deodorant, and decent soap and shampoo for my every-other-day shower. I could even buy some ramen noodles to eat instead of the standard-issue prison food they delivered to our cells on plastic trays. Compared to LA County Jail, it felt like a major step up.

There were times when my cellie would get mad at me for beating him at chess and he just wouldn't talk to me for three or four days straight.

Which meant it was quiet.

Which meant I had twenty-three hours a day with nothing but my thoughts.

My thoughts—and my anger.

A few days in, I got a letter from my lawyer saying she could no longer represent me. In order to appeal my case, I needed an appellate lawyer, she said. There was an appellate lawyer in her office whom she was now referring my case to. She asked me to sign a document ending our attorney-client relationship. And I did. I signed off on that.

I never heard from her again.

The appellate lawyer never came to see me. Never wrote to me. Nothing.

I wasn't allowed any phone calls from Delano. Only letters. So I wrote to my mom, and she wrote back, and she told me she never heard from the new attorney, either.

My mom said she tried calling, but the attorney never answered. She found out that our former attorney had closed her office. She took down her website.

It made no sense. I couldn't make a call. I couldn't get to the bottom of it. There was no one to talk to about it. All I could do was wrestle with it and try to work things out in my mind.

My thoughts. My anger.

I didn't ask God to help. I stopped praying altogether. What had praying gotten me? Every time I prayed to God my situation just got worse. So I stopped.

All I had were my thoughts.

I started to doubt my mom's letters. Was she lying to me? Was she trying to protect my feelings or something? Had she fired the attorney? Given up on me? Was there really no way of beating this? What had I done to deserve such mental, emotional, and spiritual punishment? My mother had spent everything she had trying to defend me. And look where that got us.

Maybe Mom decided that she can't afford to defend me anymore.

Yeah.

My thoughts.

Nothing but my thoughts.

It's real easy to get paranoid when you're stuck in prison and no one's talking to you.

Twenty-three hours a day in a cell with nothing but your thoughts.

It got dark.

You're not going home.

You're not playing football.

You're not going to college.

You're in prison.

Prison.

This is your life now.

This is YOU now.

Fuck everybody. Fuck EVERYBODY!

I was filled with anger. I was filled with rage.

I could feel my heart pounding in my chest at night. Hear the blood pumping in my ears. I wanted *revenge*. I wanted to *hurt someone*. I wanted the people who put me here to *suffer*!

But then? There was nothing to do with all that anger. I stuffed it down inside because there was no place for that anger to go. There's no therapy in prison. No rehabilitation. Nothing. Want to know why there are so many fights in prison? So many killings? So many rapes? Because there's nowhere else for the rage to go.

For better or worse I was locked in a cage with a cellie who would have been ideal to rage out on, like the system, an opponent much bigger than me. But he wasn't the one I was angry at. I kept reasoning with myself. Working it out. Trying to be still. Reminding myself that nobody in that prison was the one who put me there. All that fighting or lashing out at someone would get me was me was a guaranteed spot in maximum security for the next four years, if not a harsher sentence on top of it all.

But it was *hard*.

My mind just kept spinning.

Four years. Four years of this shit.

I'll never make it.

I just want to disappear.

Please, God, just take me away from here.

And there I was praying again. It kept coming back to God. Even though I'd given up on prayer, I had no other way to express what I was feeling than to put it back in God's hands.

And the best I could do was pray for him to *take me away*?

I didn't want to pray that prayer.

Prayer has gotten me nowhere! I thought.

So I didn't.

I forced myself to stop praying altogether. Again.

I vowed that I wasn't going to ask God for *anything*.

• ◆ •

Toward the end of my forty-five days, I met with the group of counselors to determine where they would send me next. They explained that their determination would be made on a point system. "Anything twenty-seven points or less and you'll qualify for minimum security," the lead counselor woman explained. "Any more than twenty-seven and you'll be placed in one of the two levels of maximum-security facilities."

"Okay," I said. "I understand."

They interviewed me from a long list of questions, ranging from my age and whether or not I was a high school graduate (yes) or a college graduate (no) to talking about my charges— my real charges—and comparing notes against my file and my (nonexistent) prior criminal record.

And by the time they finished adding my points—three points for this, minus one point for that, two points for this other thing—I had 29 points.

I was two points over.

I freaked out.

"What?!" I said. "You've got to be kidding me. Please, please," I said to her. "Can't you just take those two points off. Please!"

They nodded to a guard who stepped in and stood at the door as a signal for me to exit the office.

"There's nothing we can do. Your score is twenty-nine points. We can't make exceptions," they said.

"But I have no priors," I argued. "I just turned eighteen. I—"

"Look," the lead counselor said. "After a few months you can petition for another eval, and with good behavior, chances are you can get moved to a minimum-security facility within six months."

Good behavior. In a maximum-security prison. Do any of you people even know what prison is like?

What a joke, I thought.

On the way back to my cell, I started thinking all kinds of thoughts. Even violent thoughts. The rage inside of me wanted to bust out once and for all.

Man, fuck this shit. These weak-ass guards, those punk-ass counselors and their point system. Fuck ALL of this shit!

I had never felt that kind of anger in my life.

The system had nearly broken me.

But a few days after I got back to my cell, divine intervention stepped in and reminded me that I didn't have to be that way.

"So, where they sending you?" my cellie asked.

I looked at the paper they gave me.

"CMC," I said. "The 'California Men's Colony,' wherever the fuck *that* is."

I was still raging.

I climbed up on my bunk and threw the paper down. My cellie picked it up.

"Oh shit!" he said. "CMC San Luis Obispo. You going to Club Med!"

"What? Where am I going?" I asked.

"Man, this is one of the coolest prisons you can go to," he said.

"Really?"

What about prison could possibly be "cool"?

"Yeah, man. You get a key to your cell. Like, you get to open and close your cell door, you know, when they give you the permission to, and you get a lot of hours on the yard, and it's really not that active there," he said, referring to the violence. "It's a level three, but it's not crazy at all, cuz. You know, you'll be straight there."

"I'll be good there?"

In my mind, I didn't think I was going to be "straight" anywhere.

"Yeah, man," he said. "This here's a blessing."

THIRTEEN

Seeing Stars

The first time the night air hit me, I felt like a whole new man.

My cellie was right. The California Men's Colony *was* a blessing. Compared to the places I'd been, and others I had heard stories of—the places I could have been sent—CMC felt like a consolation prize.

In addition to the cell door privileges, and more hours of free time, and access to a library full of books, and a commissary that allowed me to purchase deodorant and ramen and upgraded sweat pants and socks that were actually comfortable on my skin, CMC allowed us inmates to occasionally have some night hours in the yard. And the first time I stepped outside for night yard in that place was the first time I had been allowed outside in the darkness in nearly two years.

This was still prison. I wasn't supposed to cry. I wasn't supposed to let anyone see me shed one tear. *No weakness.* But when I looked up and saw a sky full of stars, I could not help it. I stepped off to a corner where I could be by myself, and my tears ran in silent streams down my face.

I saw freedom in that sky.

It didn't matter that the moon was low on the horizon, and

that its sliver of white light was cut in half by the razor wire at the top of the fence. I could *see* it.

I could feel that night air on my skin, and I thanked God for giving me that gift.

It didn't matter that I was in a prison yard, on a patch of California dirt with nothing but a pull-up bar and a track that I wasn't allowed to run on: "Only jog, or the guards might think you're trying to escape or hurt somebody or something, and they'll hit you with the block gun, or worse, the M16 rifle."

None of that mattered.

All that mattered was the sky.

On night yard was when I did some of my deepest reflection at CMC. It's hard not to reflect on who you are and how you got where you are when you're penned in under that big, wide-open night sky.

I was still holding on to a lot of anger, though. As days and weeks and months rolled by, I stopped hearing from the people I usually heard from. Friends, teammates—people stopped inquiring about me. Stopped writing letters. Some stopped answering my calls. Once the hope of my release was gone, people just seemed to fade away.

For some, I think, there was an overwhelming sense of helplessness. Not ignoring where I was, but rather knowing there was nothing they could do about it. So they went on with their lives, distracted from the pain of what happened to me, and my absence.

My mom was the only one who came steady, every other weekend, even though it was a three-and-a-half-hour drive in each direction. She was always there. My sister, Minah, came most of those visits, too, once she'd moved back from college in D.C. But my dad? He didn't come anymore. My brother? He was still too shaken by it all to see me. He got old enough to drive and took off in the Honda Civic that was supposed to be mine. He just avoided the whole situation.

I was stuffed in the smallest of all the cells I'd ever been housed in, too. It was only two bunks, and two inmates per cell, but one of the bunks folded up against the wall. And when it was down, there was no walkway left between the bunks. That's how tight it was in there.

My first roommate was this annoying small, husky brotha in his forties who'd been in prison for years. I was nineteen. We had nothing in common and I swear he just intentionally bugged me. I kept getting angry and wishing he'd leave.

When you've got no lawyer, and therefore no hope of getting your sentence reduced or making some kind of appeal, it's real easy to fall back on anger. It's *easy*.

When you're looking at four more years in prison with no hope of changing it, you stop looking forward to things. You can't look forward to things. Especially to getting out.

Before I left Kern County, they gave me my release date: August 29, 2007. I was sentenced to six years, but unless I messed up, I'd only serve 85 percent of that sentence.

August 29, 2007, was way too far in the future for me to wrap my mind around. It was too painful to even think about. And even if I wanted to think about it, what would I think about?

When you first begin a prison sentence of several years, you can't look forward to life. You quickly realize you *have* no life. Your life is gone.

So it just keeps getting dark.

I was pretty much in that exact same state for my whole first year at CMC. Darkness. Confusion. Consumed by all kinds of anger. Without even trying, I'd grown accustomed to the ways of an inmate. I had *become* an inmate. That was my position in life. I found myself holding on to the bitterness of anger and grudges, taking parts in fights and riots, drinking pruno—prison alcohol, made from leftover fruit, and bread, and hot water, secretly fermented in plastic bags. You adapt when choice is no longer possible.

I got prison tattoos, too. I learned how inmates made their own tattoo guns by repurposing the whirring motors from portable CD players, and the tubes from Bic pens, and how the "G" string from an acoustic guitar becomes the needle. They put time and skill and patience into building those tools, as well as the work they do with them. I marked my skin with the permanent remembrances of my prison number, and an intricate design of a ghetto city and pyramid all pointing "To the Top," to the *Truth*. I even tried to give one to myself, "LBC" for Long Beach City, but I had to give up because it hurt too much. So there it stood, incomplete on my skin in the distinct faded color of greenish-black ink of those who've been through the system. Something convicts see and recognize in each other forever.

The system turned me into a "convict."

They replaced my name with a number: "V13109." And in that inhuman state, I lived in constant rage.

The me I knew seemed all but gone. The kid I was, the football player with a future, was a distant memory.

I was a convict now.

Until one day, something extraordinary happened.

The prison had been locked down for yet another violent

altercation out on the yard. I lay there, caged in my cell, raging in my mind like I always did, getting all worked up about the system and how unfair it was, when suddenly the cell began to brighten. The sun came piercing through the small window at the back. I was shocked at how bright the cell became. I wanted to feel that sun on my face, so I climbed off my bunk and stepped over my sleeping cellie to the back of the cell, a small space just barely wide enough for a man to relieve himself. I stood there, facing the window as the sun's rays shined and warmed me to my soul.

I took a deep breath, held it, then exhaled.

And then—an epiphany.

I had stopped praying to God with my requests a long time ago. I had stopped praying altogether. But there was something about the sun in that moment that silenced my mind.

I became fixated.

I was still.

And suddenly, it felt as if someone were standing next to me. And they began to speak.

"You are not in control over the things that are occurring in your life."

I thought of Mr. Johnson's class: "Be in this world, but not of this world."

I recalled his earliest words to me back in juvie. His plea that I not "let them beat me." That I not eat myself alive for them. To "be bigger than this." Bigger than all of this.

I thought of his classroom teachings, and the question, "Who are you?"

Prison isn't me. This sentence isn't me. These made-up charges aren't me, I thought.

I don't want to be here. I shouldn't be here. But I am.

I can't control that.

What can I control?

My reaction.

I won't let this define me. I am who I say I am. I cannot allow any of this to destroy me.

Who am I?

Why am I?

Brian Banks, now what?

I closed my eyes and what felt like hours went by without answers. It was so quiet in my mind that I stopped asking questions. I didn't want to ask any more questions. I wanted to be still. I needed to listen.

Stillness.

And time.

And the sound of my own breathing.

My breathing, and the beat of my heart, were the only sounds I heard.

And that's when I heard the words:

"I'm here."

It wasn't some big, booming voice. It wasn't some lightning bolt from the heavens. It wasn't anything I could see, or touch, or even physically hear. It was consciousness.

"I'm here."

Deep inhale. Exhale.

"I'm here."

God was with me. He'd always been with me. And even though the worst had happened, although I'd held off on praying, I never lost my faith.

God wasn't *out there* somewhere. He was *in here*. He was

with me all along. He was here. I felt Him. I believed in Him. I always had.

So why wasn't He helping? Why wasn't He making things better?

I felt myself tense up when I asked those questions. My mind started racing. I went back to being angry. I hated the way that made me feel.

So I stopped.

"Be still."

I stayed still. I realized I had to stay quiet and listen to my breathing in order to feel better.

And when I did that? Consciousness returned.

"I'm here."

The more I silenced my mind, the more open I was to receiving His words.

And at my quietest, when my mind was most still, only then did I ask, "God, how do I get through this? What do I do now? What do I *do*?"

And the answer given was this:

"Be you."

Be me?

Again I asked, *Who am I?*

"Rediscover."

"Rediscover"? What does that mean?

I had plenty of time to think about it. All I had in that place was time.

The first thoughts that came to me weren't about who I *was*. They were about who I *was not*.

I realized that lashing out and fighting wasn't me.

I am no criminal.

Being angry all the time wasn't me.

I am not an inmate.

I agreed that I was not in control over things that were happening in my life. And that's where the epiphany really kicked in.

But I do have control over me, I thought.

I was surrounded in darkness.

But I am light.

"Rediscover."

Makes sense, I thought. *But how will that set me free?*

I didn't receive all the answers in that moment. Or maybe I did and I just didn't understand them. Clearly this was going to take a while.

All I know is that something changed in me. Right then. Right there.

In my darkest of moments, I discovered my light.

I didn't have to search for it. No one handed it to me.

It was there. In me. The whole time.

I just had to rediscover it.

I wasn't dead, even though sometimes it felt that way. I was very much alive.

My light had been dimmed, but it wasn't out. If I kept going the way I was going, I could've smothered it. I could've caved in the face of darkness. I could've done the job for "them"— those responsible for this. I could've fed the anger.

But I didn't. I wouldn't.

Why?

Because God was with me. *In* me.

While standing at that window and standing at a cross-roads, when I could have continued to turn my mind and body toward the distractions of anger, violence, drugs, or anything else that is self-destructive, I looked inward and listened for Him.

I remembered an old saying: "We have two eyes and two ears, but only one mouth. We should look and see more than we speak."

Stepping away from the window, I climbed back onto my bunk, stayed quiet, and kept listening. A few things immediately became clear. There were things I *did* have control over. I had no choice in where I was, or why, but I did have choices.

I realized that I had spent my time at CMC filling myself up with anger, rage, torment, and stress. Almost every negative emotion you can think of, I had it. I even thought about revenge—of taking revenge upon those who I felt were responsible for what had happened to me. I obsessed over it. I wanted someone to pay. But as I listened, as I quieted my mind, I realized that those people I was spending so much energy on had no idea how I felt. They couldn't feel my rage. More than likely, they didn't care. I was the one who was suffering that rage. Not them.

Until that moment, I'd been so fully consumed in the negative, the evil thoughts, that I'd left no space for God.

As the hours and days and weeks passed by, all intertwined and never-ending, piece by piece, like bloodied armor after battle, I began to shed those demons.

I was still surrounded in darkness. Prison is still prison, and there was still plenty to be pissed off about, to stress about, to send me into a state of rage. Falling into our adolescent ways of reacting to circumstances is easy. It's a habit. In my knee-jerk reaction to news I didn't want to hear or the million rules

I didn't want to follow because I knew I didn't deserve to be in that prison, my anger flooded in again and again.

But after that day, I knew I didn't want to be that way.

I became aware that every time I got angry or felt those negative vibes, it wasn't "me." It was my reaction to my physical condition. And yet, I was allowing those reactions to direct my emotional well-being, and I no longer wanted to allow those experiences to govern the way I felt. *That* was something I had control over. Or at least, I tried to take control over it.

Like anything else, it would take time and practice to master. And I had nothing but time to practice.

I'm not sure I could have done that if it weren't for the angels God placed on this earth for me, and the tools that were given to me by them: passively as a child at first, from my mother and being raised in the Baptist church, and then actively by Mr. Johnson in my first few months of incarceration. Without their early guidance and intervention, I could have easily chosen the route of drugs, violence, or even my own death after facing this prison sentence. Those roads are not uncommon answers for many who wind up behind these walls.

After all, this *wasn't* "Club Med." And for anyone to think that any form of prison was "Club Med" was irrational. What kind of a world was it that threw an innocent child into a prison system so torturous and debilitating that he shed tears at the sight of the moon, the comfort of the night air, or the ability to simply put deodorant on in the morning?

One night in my cell, deep in meditation, quieting my mind and listening, I was reminded that the answer to escaping those atrocities was to not participate in them.

"In order to evolve, one must not be involved."

I had to stop taking part in my own destruction.

"Be you."

I needed to focus on being my best self, not some version of the number the system wanted me to be. I had to find more effective ways of dealing with the unpleasantness and horrors of my circumstances, and instead focus on finding my peace.

The message I kept hearing, the one I kept receiving, is that pursuing this "self-mastery," going within me, making "me" stronger, was the only way I would truly find freedom.

I had begun a journey toward self-mastery with Mr. Johnson. I had walked away from that path when I was convicted. And now I was returning to that same path.

In the hours between prayer and meditation, I started reading. I read constantly. When I had nothing else to read, I would read the dictionary. I'd seen the movie *Malcolm X* when I was a kid, and I remembered vividly a scene in which Malcolm begins reading the entire dictionary. I decided I'd do the same. And I did—cover to cover.

I also read the thesaurus.

I started using all sorts of new words when conversing with other inmates, and I wasn't the only one. Lots of those men were educating themselves behind bars. Some of the smartest men I've ever met were inside, and we discussed and debated all sorts of topics: politics, religion, prison reform, spirituality. We shared poetry, music, and positive affirmations. Iron sharpening iron.

I dug deep in my studies into Pan Africanism and Afrocentricity. I spent hour after hour reading spirituality and self-help books. I read books that discussed spiritual energy and vibrations, our chakras and how they are the energy centers in our body through which energy flows. I studied the importance of self-love, value, and accountability.

I wanted to understand myself. I wanted to better understand people, and the human spirit. I wanted to improve myself, to be better than the accusations that were made against me and the brand of "inmate" that was forced upon me. I wanted to be a better *me*.

And through it all, I wanted to fully believe that God was leading me with some greater purpose—that He knew exactly what was in store for me even if I didn't know what it was myself.

I wondered, *Is it possible to move forward without fear?*

What if I had moved forward with no trepidation at all? From the beginning of this ordeal, and even before then: what if my faith had been stronger than my doubt and worry?"

How many sleepless nights had I spent worrying and wondering if I was about to get killed while I was in prison because of the charges I'd pleaded to? Yet here I was. Very much alive.

Why?

Because God was there with me, working for me, all along.

I kept reminding myself, every day: *I needn't have worried. I needn't worry now.*

I need to listen to what God is trying to tell me.

He saw me through this—not in the way I wanted. He didn't release me from this hell. But he didn't fail me, either. He gave me everything I needed in order to survive. He kept me alive. He kept me safe.

And now I felt God was doing what I had prayed for: he was setting me free. Not from prison, but from my circumstance. He was setting me *mentally* free. *Spiritually* free.

For one that is free in the mind is free no matter their physical condition.

It wasn't easy. As the months went by, there were times when my focus was taken from me: when a riot broke out in the yard, when someone was stabbed, when we were all put on lockdown; or the time it rained so much that our module flooded, and they moved us to another yard with modules so filthy that the MAC reps got together and decided that all races would join in a hunger strike to protest the conditions.

Even in all of that chaos, I found my stillness. I meditated. I listened. And what God kept telling me is that I had to be patient. I needed to be at peace. I needed to keep working on myself, to prepare, to dig deeper, in order to move forward.

I was clearly a work in progress myself, but even so, I used some of what I was learning to help other inmates get through their own ordeals. In a place that felt like some sort of demented amusement park—a dark Magic Mountain, full of emotional roller coasters built on fear, anger, mistrust, and despair—I gained a reputation for being a life coach. I started to become a man to whom other inmates came for help; to work through mental roadblocks, to talk people down from their ledges, to help them set aside their distractions and focus on what matters.

We had talks about "doing the time, and not letting the time do you." Talks about stress. Talks about dealing with family. I did my best to share some of Mr. Johnson's teaching with other young inmates, including one who was the same age as me, whom I met, and who got out, and who returned to prison again within a year. I saw a difference in him once we started talking, as he started to learn more about himself and to think about working on himself instead of constantly reacting to the people and circumstances around him.

I found that it felt good to help other people, and that I always learned more about myself in the process.

It wasn't college. It certainly wasn't USC. But prison was definitely turning out to be an education.

An education that was about to serve me well.

One day, out of the blue, I received a piece of legal mail. Legal mail was the only type of mail that wasn't opened before they gave it to us. Months had passed since I'd received any news from anyone about my case, so I opened it immediately, hoping it was from the long-lost appellate lawyer.

It wasn't.

It was a letter from the Long Beach Civil Court office informing me that attorneys for Tiana Miller and the Long Beach City School District were coming to San Luis Obispo in a couple of weeks to depose me as part of the lawsuit Tiana had filed against the school.

I was basically told to "lawyer up" in order to get ready for that meeting.

At first I let myself get angry. I didn't want to do anything that would help the school district after those teachers and administrators had let me down the way they did. If they had to pay out millions of dollars in damages, so be it. Of course the thought of Tiana and her mother getting rich off the lies made me angry, too. But I quickly remembered that anger never got me anywhere and that stressing over a problem never changed the outcome. So I ignored it altogether. I knew that all I needed to do was to deal with where I was, and *who* I was, and when the time came to be deposed, I'd do what I'd done from the beginning: keep it real, and tell the truth.

"Be you."

Sure enough, a couple of weeks later attorneys for both Tiana and the Long Beach Unified School District arrived at CMC to carry out a deposition. I was escorted out of my cell, out of my module, off the prison yard, down a corridor, and into a small interview room, where two attorneys who'd never met me asked me all sorts of personal, accusatory, and ugly questions. I told them the truth. My version of the story of what happened that day had never changed, and that seemed to frustrate Tiana's attorney. Clearly my story and hers were two very different things.

But when it was all over, when they got up to leave, the school district's attorney asked the guard if he could stay and talk to me by myself for a minute.

"Yeah, that's cool," the guard said.

The attorney walked back into the room and closed the door. He looked me in the eye and said, "I just want you to know that I'm sorry that this happened to you. You shouldn't be in here."

I was shocked. I didn't show it, but I was surprised as anything to hear those words from an attorney. I knew what the truth was.

Does he? I wondered.

I just looked at him. I didn't have anything to say. I looked at him, and he looked at me, and that was that. He got up and left.

About a week later I received some more legal mail. This time it was a big, thick manila envelope from that same school-district attorney. I went back to my cell when my cellie wasn't around and I cracked that envelope open. It took me a moment to realize what I was looking at.

It was my files. *All of them*. Police reports, transcripts, evaluations, DNA results—copies of every bit of paperwork on my case, which I had never been allowed to see going all the way back to the day I was arrested in 2002.

I closed my eyes and thought about something I'd read in one of the dozens of books I'd devoured in all those months. A quote from Buddha:

> Three things cannot be long hidden:
> the sun, the moon, and the truth.

I took a deep breath. I opened my eyes—and I started to read.

FOURTEEN

Truth

The Long Beach Police Department incident reports on my case were full of lies. Full of inconsistencies. Full of things I didn't say. Full of things I didn't do.

One report stated that after the police put me in handcuffs in my bedroom, I told the officers, "I know why you're here and it was consensual."

I never said that.

I don't even think I knew the word *consensual* when I was sixteen.

There was something about them having to search for my clothes in that room, they said, because I tried to hide them. *I didn't hide them. They were right on top of the laundry basket. The officers knocked the basket over.*

The report said I told them I saw Tiana "earlier in the day in the hallway of the 700 building at Poly High School" and then "saw her coming out of the girl's restroom and told her to come over and talk to him and she did." The first part wasn't true, and the second part didn't happen that way at all. We ran into each other outside, on a walkway.

Those details might seem small, but they weren't small to me. They were false. They weren't accurate. They painted a different picture of what happened. Those little details made it seem like I was guilty or trying to hide something.

And Tiana? She painted a different picture every time she was interviewed over the course of the two and a half years since that day at school. In one report she said I followed her into the 700 building and asked if she "needed any help" as she headed into the bathroom. In another she said that we ran into each other in the hallway inside the 700 building. In one report she said that I'd asked her to have sex with me a month or two before that day. In another she said that I'd asked her to have sex with me on multiple occasions. In one report she said that she followed me into the elevator. In another she said that I'd grabbed her by the shoulders and forcibly pulled her into the elevator. In the first report, she didn't respond when the interviewer asked why she didn't call for help or make any noises during the incident. In another, she said she was "trying" to make noise. *"Trying" to make noise?* She mentioned the teacher who was speaking Spanish on the phone on the stairs above us, but never explained why she didn't cry for help except to say I was "telling her" not to say anything. How could the investigators not question her story when there were so many questions raised, and so many inconsistencies? If either my lawyer or the investigators themselves had ever pointed those things out in the courtroom, I wouldn't be sitting in prison.

I had to read the details in the file over a couple of weeks. I couldn't read those files when other people were around. And to be honest, I couldn't stomach it all in one sitting. I couldn't process it. I couldn't believe that all this stuff that I was reading was about *me.*

The investigator who interviewed *me* included all sorts of

things that I never said at all. I was reading words in the police report that were attributed to me, when I never said or did those things.

When I got to the results of the rape kit on Tiana, my heart started racing.

According to the sexual assault nurse's report, Tiana showed "multiple tears/lacerations" to her labia, as well as to her "posterior fourchette" (I didn't even know what that was), and to her "clitoral hood." She also had an "anal tear at 6:00 o'clock." And the nurse found "clumpy white matter inside of Miller's vagina by her cervix."

The report said the incident was "consistent with her account of what happened and also consistent with penetration."

How can that be? I thought. *I didn't rape her! We didn't have sex! My God.*

I felt like I'd been punched. I was staggered. Like the world didn't make any sense.

I thought I heard my cellie coming back, so I stuffed the papers back into the envelope and hid them under my mattress. If anyone saw those papers, I'd be a dead man.

It wasn't him. Two other inmates walked by my cell.

I pulled the paperwork out again and kept reading.

That's when I found the DNA report. I already knew that they didn't find any of my DNA in her rape kit. My attorney made that clear to me when the report first came in. But what I didn't know just about knocked me over: the DNA report said that there was, in fact, male DNA present—but that DNA wasn't mine. It wasn't a match. It belonged to somebody else.

Tiana had another male's DNA on her underwear.

My mind started spinning: *Was she raped by somebody*

else? Did she have sex with somebody else and then try to cover it up by blaming me? Was she being abused by somebody or something?

Wait. Why does it even matter? It wasn't mine. The DNA wasn't mine!

How is that not 100 percent proof that I didn't rape her?

How did that not come out in court?

Why didn't my attorney tell me, or tell my mom, or tell the judge or anybody? Why?

My heart was pounding.

Didn't the district attorney have that report, too? Why would he have moved forward with the case knowing that Tiana had somebody else's DNA on her underwear on the same day I supposedly raped her in that stairwell?

The evidence, the only physical evidence they had, pointed to the fact that they had the wrong guy.

I was fuming.

Who was liable for this? The DA should be. She had this information the entire time and did nothing with it. The judge, too, for overlooking the facts. And my attorney: she should face consequences for how she misrepresented me.

I stuffed the paperwork under my mattress again and did my best to calm down. It took me the rest of that day and night to recenter myself.

The next time I was alone for a long stretch of time, I read the rest of the files and discovered that pretty much everyone, every step of the way, came at my case with a presumption of guilt based on Tiana's initial story and, most important, how her story seemed to be corroborated by the sexual assault nurse's report.

The assumption of guilt played directly into the fitness hearing evaluation I went through when this whole thing started—the evaluation that led to me being tried as an adult.

The psychologist who interviewed me included the details of the sexual assault report on the front page of her evaluation. She put the details of the vaginal and anal tears directly under a paragraph stating that I denied the charges and said, "As a football player, I don't have to force anybody to have sex with me. I can have sex if I want to."

She took those words completely out of context. The way it was presented in the report made me sound inconsiderate and egotistical.

And after our whole conversation about my goals for my future, she wrote that I wanted "'[t]o be wealthy, to have a good family, a family that is problem-free, and to play in the NFL.' When he was asked about his main goal in the future, he answered that his main goal is 'to find myself.'" And then she made me sound as selfish as selfish could be: "With regard to his thoughts and feelings related to the instant incidents, Brian expressed that he is feeling sad because he is afraid that his future plans are damaged. Attempts were made for Brian to express some empathy for the alleged victim, but no empathy was shown toward the alleged victim. Brian believes he 'should be going home.'"

Finally, she put all of her presumption of guilt into play when describing the "degree of criminal sophistication" that I exhibited in this crime. Based on Tiana's telling of the story, combined with the rape kit evidence, she wrote: "it appeared to this examiner that the alleged victim was pre-targeted. There was a high degree of sexual violence involved, inasmuch as the minor sustained several injuries. . . . It also appeared to this examiner that the minor's alleged sexual misconduct stemmed from wanting to be in control and wanting to have a sense of empowerment over the alleged victim."

What?!

The report was written before the DNA test findings were even done.

And she wrote that the "victim" was "pre-targeted"? To state as a fact that there was a "high degree of sexual violence" that stemmed from my "wanting to be in control" over Tiana Miller? How was there any evidence of that unless she believed Tiana's story and presumed that I was guilty?

It is astounding to me that throughout this process, not one person who could have made a difference—not one—showed any empathy to *me*. There were people in the prison system—guards, officials, hard-core criminals—who exhibited more common sense, decency, and empathy toward me than the people whose job it was to investigate these claims ever showed.

The files also contained some transcripts of video interviews of Tiana in which her story changed again, getting a little more violent and a lot less believable every time she told it. All somebody had to do was go to the school and take a look at the hallway full of open classroom doors to realize there was no way I was "forcing her" and "dragging her" from that elevator without somebody noticing. If one person had done that, just one person, I thought, *I might not be sitting in this cage right now.*

But I kept coming back to the DNA. The DNA evidence was rock solid. No room for error. No room for interpretation.

No room for "maybes" or "yeah, but, what-ifs"? No "he said, she said" at all.

Facts. Concrete facts.

It should have been case closed.

◆ ◆ ◆

The attorney for the school district sent his card with the files. Here was one person who had read through all these lies and who was also connected to the case. I decided to call him to see if he could help me.

When I finally reached him, he said he had made numerous attempts at trying to contact my attorney. He said he called her multiple times and sent emails while my case was ongoing.

She had never responded.

He wanted to offer his services, and compare notes, and essentially give me the backup I would have needed to clear myself of the charges. His motives in that were somewhat selfish, I suppose, because it would have pretty much ended Tiana's baseless lawsuit against the school district.

He stated more than once on that phone call, "You shouldn't be in prison."

"So what can I do?" I asked him. "Can you help me?"

"I can't," he said. "It would be a conflict of interest. People would frown on the fact that I sent you your own files as it is. But I wish you luck. I really do. I'm so sorry for what's happened to you."

"Thank you. You have no idea how much I appreciate what you've done here," I said.

"You take care now," he said. And he hung up.

"I'm so sorry for what happened to you."

Those words echoed in my mind.

It was the first time someone professional saw the truth. And cared.

Thank you, God. Thank you.

I'd been patient. I'd been listening. I'd been preparing for something, even though I wasn't quite sure what it was I was going to be.

This was a big step in my journey.

All the reading I'd done, all the studying—it was time to put it to use.

I was able to get the addresses of all the Innocence Project offices in California. I sat down and started to write letters that very night, hoping someone would respond. The Innocence Project was very well known in the prison system. Everybody had heard about their work. They were life savers, helping innocent people clear their names.

I did a little research and found the Innocence Project closest to me was based in San Diego, at the California Western School of Law. The project was cofounded and run by a man named Justin Brooks, a defense attorney who'd made it his life's calling to see innocent people freed from prison. Since 1999, he'd helped exonerate more than twenty people with this nonprofit organization. It was inspiring to me to read his story, and to learn that he'd helped a whole bunch of people get out of prison based on *facts*—facts that were blatantly overlooked if not shoved under the table by unscrupulous lawyers and investigators looking for a conviction and not the truth.

I addressed my letter directly to Justin. I detailed the facts that I believed would catch his attention and potentially get me exonerated. I rewrote the letter multiple times, just to make sure it was perfect.

I sent it off.

I was told that the California Innocence Project receives hundreds, sometimes thousands of letters from prisoners each year, and only takes on three to four cases a year.

So I prayed. And prayed some more.

Then I waited.

While I was waiting, another prayer was answered: My points security classification was lowered. The prison system reassessed my points and decided to send me to a medium-security prison.

I was told early on that I could get moved out of maximum security within six months. Despite all my "good behavior," it took fourteen.

In February 2005, I boarded a prison bus headed for the California Rehabilitation Center in Norco, or CRC Norco. The facility was only an hour-and-a-half drive from Long Beach, which I hoped would make visitation a little easier on my mom.

The move definitely made things a little easier on *me*.

For the first time since I'd entered the adult system, I didn't feel like every minute of every day was a moment when shit could get crazy and I might wind up inadvertently getting in a riot, or stabbed or killed.

I could breathe a little.

I could focus.

It is amazing what you can accomplish when you have nothing but time on your hands and no distractions to stop you from what you want to do. And what I wanted to do most was win back my freedom. So instead of just waiting around for the California Innocence Project (CIP) to get back to me, I reached out to a whole bunch of other attorneys, just to see if anybody might be willing to take on my case, or at least help me make my own case to the courts that this conviction should be overturned.

I didn't hear back from most of them, but a couple of attorneys were kind enough to write back and wish me well.

Eventually, CIP wrote back with news. They told me they couldn't help me.

In order to overturn my conviction, they said, there would have to be "new evidence" that proved my innocence. The DNA wasn't considered "new evidence" because it was information that was available at the time I took my plea agreement, they explained. The only other way they could get a judge to reopen my case was if the "victim" in the case "recanted." In other words, they needed Tiana Miller to admit that she made the whole thing up.

I knew that wasn't going to happen.

I didn't let their rejection stop me. I was on a mission.

CRC had a full-blown law library. I spent hours and hours in that place, reading up on the California Penal Code with the same attention with which I read the dictionary and the Bible from cover to cover. Of course, the penal code is much longer than either of those books, which is a remarkable fact when you stop and think about it; it would take years to get through it all. So when I had a question, I found one of the fine legal minds among the Norco inmate population and asked them to point me the right way.

Right after I got the rejection letter from CIP, I spoke to one of the library workers, an older black man with dreadlocks, glasses, and a beard. Without giving him any details about my case, I asked him, "How would I go about appealing my case if I was wrongfully convicted?"

"Oh," he said, "you have to petition for what's called a 'writ of habeas corpus.'"

He took me directly to the stacks and pulled out the exact book I needed.

"Okay. Well, now I got to study what a writ of habeas corpus is," I said.

For the better part of the next year, I took a crash course in wrongful-conviction law, and how to overcome the incredibly high bar it takes to even get a case like mine heard in the Courts of Appeal of the state of California. I discovered that there were provisions for "ineffective counsel," or a lawyer who did a shitty job, and I put a brief together around that. I researched the grounds for newly discovered evidence, just in case CIP had it wrong, and I became an expert in that. Then I studied the importance of DNA in rape cases. Eventually I composed a petition for a writ of habeas corpus entirely on my own.

You would think a few months wasn't enough time to become legally up to speed to the point of filing a complicated case to the state appellate courts. But I had nothing else to do but wake up, study, write, study more, rewrite, then write some more, go to sleep, wake up, and do it all over again. Every day.

Actually, I take that back. I had time to learn how to play the drums.

I had never played the drums, or any instrument, in my life outside of prison. But CRC was one of the only prisons in

California with a music program. They had a makeshift music studio and a soundproof room that could accommodate a full band. I learned how to play drums from a fellow inmate over the course of 2005—my fourth year behind bars.

I even joined a prison band that played a mix of classic rock, reggae, and soul. We would get paid our inmate pay rate of twenty-eight cents per hour to perform for graduations in the prison—from drug programs or high school equivalency, to college programs. We'd perform on holidays and Christmas, too.

It helped time pass, and was definitely an improvement compared to the other facilities I was in, but there wasn't one minute when it didn't feel like prison. It was just a calm enough place to allow me to "program"—a prison term for creating a daily schedule that keeps you focused and out of trouble.

But it was still prison.

Nobody got killed while I was there, but there were plenty of beatings. A few riots. There were fights all the time. The alarm went off at least once a day. At *least* once. That alarm would go off and I'd see ten officers run by with their batons out. And there's this hidden rule, this understanding, that when the alarm sounds, you get down on the floor and out of the way. If not, you'll be met with a violent strike from one of those batons as guards sprint to the altercation.

And they have all the right in the world to take you down because the code says "if you're not down, you're part of the problem."

I never got hit by a guard. I never got into a confrontation with a guard. They would cuss me out for no reason. They did that to everyone. They would come at you crazy, just waiting for you to say something so they could handcuff you, take you to a room, beat the shit out of you, then put you in the hole and let your body heal; so when you get out of the hole and you try to complain about getting beat, they can say, "Well, where are your marks and bruises?" Yeah. They know how to get you. They know how to *get* you.

When word got around that a black inmate who had just been housed in our dorm was moved from another dorm for stealing shampoo from a Mexican inmate, one of us blacks had to dole out the discipline. The rep for the blacks made the decision that I would be one of the guys to discipline him. I had no choice in the matter. If I didn't stay behind and go along with it, I would face punishment myself. The beating only lasted one minute, but we beat that guy to a pulp. Those were the rules. A thief while in prison is one of the worst things you can be in prison. Someone being disciplined was a normal occurrence. The COs would even be told in advance. They knew when it was going to happen and they looked the other way.

"Just don't make it so bad that we have to do any paperwork," they said.

I spent a lot of prison time biting my tongue, staying in my lane, keeping my head down, staying out of the way. And I learned to savor whatever good times I found.

A lot of those times were in the band. There were even a couple of times when we loaded our equipment onto the back of a flatbed truck and they hauled us over to play an outdoor concert for the women's prison next door. We weren't allowed to get off that flatbed under any circumstance, but it was still fun, watching all those women prisoners dancing around and nodding their heads to us playing Bob Marley's "No Woman,

No Cry" and "Get Up, Stand Up." We played classic rock like the Eagles' "Hotel California," and some Earth, Wind & Fire, and all kinds of different genres. Playing music was almost as much of a stress release as walking out under the stars had been back at CMC.

But the sweetest music of all was the sound of those type-writer keys as I put the final touches to my petition for a writ of habeas corpus in mid-2006. With clarity and conviction, I was able to articulate the grounds for my exoneration on three counts: ineffective counsel; newly discovered evidence (which was, in fact, the DNA, which I argued was "new" because it was never entered into evidence during my 2002 proceedings); and perjury, based on Tiana Miller's inconsistent statements.

I sealed the petition in a brown manila envelope, mailed it off, and waited.

August 29 marked the start of the one-year countdown to my release date. Full of prayer, mediation, and patience, I watched another Thanksgiving come and go, and another Christmas come and go, and another New Year's come and go . . . until one day in early 2007, I received a piece of legal mail—from the Courts of Appeal of the state of California.

FIFTEEN

Countdown

I did it. On my very first try.

Not only did the appeals court accept my petition for a writ of habeas corpus, but they also went ahead and scheduled a hearing on my case. They ordered me to be brought to court to "show cause"—similar to the preliminary hearing in my original case, in which Tiana was allowed to take the stand. Except here I would get an opportunity to show them the glaring errors that were made in my case. If I were able to show cause, that could lead to a retrial, or better yet, allow me to skip directly to an exoneration hearing.

I was ecstatic. I'd read that almost all petitions for habeas corpus were rejected, even those filed by top-notch, expensive attorneys. So I was overjoyed. I just couldn't let it show, not too much anyway. I still didn't want anyone to know the real reason why I'd been incarcerated. But I called my mom, first chance I got.

A year earlier, my mom had met a man who would become her new husband. They married and she moved to Wisconsin—but she still managed to come visit me all the time.

I'd gotten used to people moving on with their lives, so I said to her, "Mom, don't feel obligated to be here every other weekend. You just got married. Do your thing." But she wasn't having any of that. She didn't listen. She found a way to fly back to California as often as possible. My mom is amazing. I can't say that enough. She always, *always* put her kids first.

Once my release date was in sight, she wanted me to have a home to come to, so she told her husband that she needed to move back to Long Beach. He agreed it was a good idea. So they set up a plan for her to move back and for him to eventually follow her.

She moved back into an apartment complex she had lived in before she moved to Wisconsin, on Ocean Boulevard. That meant that once I was out, once I was on parole, she would be there. I often thought of how life would be without the family support I had, having a home to go to versus homelessness or some halfway house. I was thankful. Most people in prison go home to nothing and no one.

That wasn't me. I had my mom.

"I'm getting a hearing, Mom. I'm going back to court!" I said to her.

She cried. She'd been through the ups and downs as many times as I had. She'd experienced that feeling of hope that this was all going to get turned around and fixed; the little light of hope that would shine so bright on the day of a court hearing, only to get stomped out again and again.

"Brian, I know your hopes are up. I just don't want you doing anything to jeopardize your release. You're only a few months away. A few months! Shouldn't you wait until you're free before going back in front of another judge?"

"I'm proud of how hard you've been working," she said. She'd expressed again and again how thankful to God she was for all the reading and studying I'd been doing. She was so proud of me for creating and filing the petition all by myself. The fact that it worked, the fact that the court was listening to my cry for help—she was beyond proud of that.

She was just scared.

She had a right to be.

We'd learned how the justice system works, in the hardest way possible.

"Just share in this hope with me. At least a little," I said.

"I will," she said. "Of course I will."

I had no doubt.

I shared my good news with a few friends over the phone that day, too.

They were excited for me.

"This is it, man!" "You're doing it!" "You got this!" "That bitch is finally gonna get what's comin' to her once the truth comes out."

I'd read that Tiana and her mom reached a settlement with the school district back in 2005. We'd turned the corner into 2007 now and from what I understood, they hadn't received any money yet. It felt like there was some justice in that. For now. But when and if they did receive that settlement? The two of them were going to walk away with $1.5 million. One and a half million dollars for destroying my life. Supposedly half that money was going to their attorney, because they didn't have any money to pay him up front and he took the case on contingency. But that didn't make it any better. As far as I was concerned, their attorney was just as guilty as them for latching on to this case. If he'd done any research at all, if he'd had a shred of decency, if he'd so much as looked me in the eyes and seen the truth the way the school district attorney did when they sat down with me for the deposition, he'd have dropped this case and told that girl and her mom to get lost.

The more I read about the whole legal system, the more I understood that *decency* wasn't any part of the equation. Prosecutors, judges, defense attorneys, investigators—for far too many of them it seemed their profession was either just a job, a game, or a stepping-stone to something else. A judgeship. A political position. Some corporate job with a big fat salary. Anything but the truth and justice our system was supposed to be about. I wanted to believe that those who pursued law degrees and took on real cases didn't do so with some sort of malicious intent. There had to be those who went to law school hoping that maybe they'd be able to help someone, and maybe even improve our judicial system.

I don't know. But somehow, the system beat it out of them. They got jaded. They got broken. They gave up trying because the system pushed aside their ideals and exchanged them for a stark reality.

I don't know.

All I know is that after spending nearly five years behind bars, I laid just as much blame on the system itself as I did Tiana, if not more. Having established peace, prayer, and meditation as the foundation of my life, I no longer felt ill will toward her. It wasn't like I sat down one day and said, "Today, I'm going to forgive her." It just sort of happened over time. I simply realized that carrying around a bunch of hate didn't do anything to *her*. It just upset *me*. It caused me stress. It caused me all kinds of anxiety. It didn't do any good. Someday, maybe the truth would come out and maybe the system would find a way to punish her. But I knew for sure that it wasn't up to me to punish her. That wasn't my place.

That's God's place.

So I let that anger go.

To be honest, though, when I got news of the upcoming habeas corpus hearing, I didn't have very many people left to call with the good news. That's just the result of a lengthy prison sentence. Out of sight, out of mind. Friendships fade. Family loses touch. People move on with their lives and learn to live without you.

There are times when even the people you consider your lifeline, your *break* from the darkness—even *those* people sometimes fade way.

One of those lifelines was a girl. Back in high school she had had quite the crush on me. We flirted, maybe kissed once or twice, but our relationship never advanced past friends. When I was charged and arrested, she was one of the few friends who stood by me. She actually showed up for all of my early court dates. My mom recognized how caring she was, and the two of them developed a good relationship. Months into my incarceration, before I was to be tried as an adult, we spoke over the phone as we always did.

I asked her, "Why don't you just be my girlfriend?"

"All right," she answered. "I'll be your girl."

When I was convicted, she stayed by me. She answered my phone calls and wrote me every single day. Those letters were some of the things that I felt kept me going. She was always telling me how much she cared. She could never understand what I was going through. Nobody could. But in some way I felt like she was with me through it all.

Then I called her one day. "You are now being connected to this call" the programmed voice chimed in. This girl and I spoke almost every day. But on this day, she sounded different.

"What is it? Just tell me," I asked.

"You're going to be mad," she said.

"Just tell me."

"You're going to be mad. You're going to hate me. You're never gonna want to talk to me ever again."

"Whatever it is, just tell me."

So she explained.

It had been two and a half years, and she'd become lonesome. She had met a guy.

"And I'm pregnant."

"Really?" I said.

What else could I say?

That hit hard. In that moment I felt more alone than ever before.

"You promised me," I said. "You know, you made these promises to me. To be there. To be with me."

I regret that now. But then? It hurt.

Trusting people is hard. Believing in people is harder. Losing the people that you believed in and trusted? That can make you turn hard. Callous. It's what breaks people down. 'Cause in prison, a person's word is everything.

Having somebody I trusted, who showed up consistently and demonstrated they cared, and that I mattered to them— for her to just up and leave my life? That sucked.

In prison, you really have no power over anything on the outside. Maybe that's the case on the outside, too. But building a relationship from behind bars is nearly impossible. There's no way to be intimate, no way to spend time together or build memories. At the time I was angry, but after a few days, I looked at it as another opportunity to practice what I had been learning. Control my reaction. Be still. Let go of expectations. What else could I do? She met someone and obviously they liked each other. They stayed together. Eventually they would have another kid. So I don't blame her. I don't at all. I will always be thankful for all the love and dedication she showed me during that time.

I'd always thought about the future. I started to think about what might be next for me.

I wondered if I'd be able to go to college.

I knew I wouldn't be able to get into a prestigious college coming right out of prison, but I heard about some guys getting out and going to community college—and there was one community college where I thought I might have an in.

I wrote a letter to Jerry Jaso, the former head football coach at Long Beach Poly. He was a legend in his time at my old school. He was the coach who'd decided to call me up to varsity after my freshman season—but then he left. He saw the potential in me, but before I got a chance to play for him he took a job as head coach over at Long Beach City College.

I sent him a letter, and he wrote me back. He said he was happy to hear from me—and he wanted to help. He said that he remembered how talented I was, and that if I was still interested in playing football he might be able to secure a spot on the team. He sent me application forms and enrollment forms. He even sent over some of his playbook, so I could start to get up to speed with what his team was doing.

Then he wrote me a character letter to hand to the judge on

the day of my hearing—a glowing review of the human being I was, the human being he knew before I'd been locked up.

I told my mom about it a couple of days before the hearing.

"That's great, Brian, but look," she said. "I have something I need to tell you."

"What?"

"I can't be at the hearing. I can't miss work that day. I'm sorry. It's the end of the school year. It's just a busy time, and I can't—"

"Mom," I said, interrupting her. "It's okay. If you have to work, I understand. Please don't feel guilty about it."

I meant it. I was also pretty sure that she could have gotten out of work if she wanted. I was pretty sure that she was just too scared to show up in court again and face some awful decision that we didn't see coming. Especially since we were down to ninety days until my release.

"I'll call you as soon as I can after it's over," I said.

"Okay," she said. "I'll be praying for you."

I reread Coach Jaso's letter after I got off the phone.

I carried it with me as I made the necessary pre-court transfer back to county jail. I carried it with me as they put me in a holding cell in a courthouse I'd never seen, and then walked me into a courtroom where I stood inside a big Plexiglas box where the jury box should be.

I'll admit it was strange to look out into a courtroom and not see my mom. She was my rock. But then I noticed a face I barely recognized: my little brother. My little brother who wasn't so little anymore. He was nineteen now. *Nineteen.*

We just stared at each other. Staring, back and forth. I could hardly believe how big he 'was and how mature he looked.

He'd changed *so much*. And clearly I had, too. I was sure I looked very different to him. I knew he could see my prison tattoos. I didn't have any tattoos when I got arrested. Not one. I'm sure I looked as hard as I felt, too. But he just kept staring at me with a look of admiration that I didn't expect.

I thought he would have lost that a long time ago.

Our stares were interrupted by this strange man in a suit. He walked up to me and introduced himself as my "court-appointed attorney."

The court allowed me to write my own habeas corpus petition from prison, but I wasn't allowed to represent myself in court. I didn't have enough money for a lawyer, so the court appointed me an attorney and this was the first time I'd met him—a few minutes before the judge was scheduled to walk into the courtroom.

He was flipping through some paperwork as he spoke.

"We've got an order to show cause, I see," he said.

"Yeah," I responded.

"Well, I do want you to know that if you accept this order to show cause, if you go through with this, and if they grant you a retrial, that means that your entire situation restarts," he said.

"What do you mean?"

"That means that your deal is no longer your deal. Your plea bargain is no longer your plea. You don't go home when you're supposed to go home. You've got to stay in court to fight your case," he said.

"I've only got ninety days left," I said.

That's when he explained to me that if I went for a retrial, I wouldn't get out of prison in ninety days. I would stay locked up while the case was reheard. In order to overturn a verdict, I would have to go back to square one, opening myself up to a whole new outcome. And one possible outcome could be the very opposite of my intention. One possible outcome might include getting forty-one years to life in prison.

I was shocked and in disbelief.

There was *no way* I was going to give up my chance to walk out of prison in ninety days. So when a judge I'd never seen before walked into the courtroom a few minutes later and said, "I see we have an order to show cause. Mr. Banks, is that what we're doing here?" I stood up, secured in chains, leaned through the little bar in the Plexiglas, and replied, "Your honor, I want to apologize to you. I want to apologize to the court. I don't mean to waste anybody's time. I did file a writ of habeas corpus but I just realized that this would affect my current deal and my current parole date, and I only have ninety days left."

"So," he said, "are you wishing to withdraw this petition for writ of habeas corpus?"

"Yes, sir," I said.

The judge said, "Smart decision, Mr. Banks. Okay, it's withdrawn."

And that was it. The end of my self-designed attempt at habeas corpus.

I went back to CRC to finish the rest of my sentence. To count the ninety days, the 2,160 hours, the 129,000-plus minutes until my release on August 29—praying that nothing else would go wrong or get in the way. Remaining strong and being still. Listening to God. Staying out of the way. Dreaming about playing football again. Going to school again. Eating real food again. Trying to remember the kid I was in the letter I never got a chance to show the judge. Trying to convince myself that I could be patient enough to wait until I was out to contact the California Innocence Project again and show them my successful petition for a writ of habeas corpus and try to convince them, again, to take on my fight to prove my innocence.

I started thinking about hugging my mom on the outside.

Thinking about hugging my sister and brother.

Trying to imagine what it was going to feel like to live outside of a cage.

Trying to imagine what it was going to feel like to step into the world I'd left behind as a sixteen-year-old kid—now as a twenty-two-year-old man.

SIXTEEN

Transition

My last supper in prison, the night before my release, the night before my parole, a whole bunch of us got together for a spread.

It was a prison tradition.

On special occasions, inmates got together and threw whatever food they had in their possession on the table for a shared feast. But these foods wouldn't be eaten individually. They'd all get mixed up into a goulash to spread on bread and eat like a sandwich.

The essentials for a spread, the basics that you definitely need, include Top Ramen, Hot Cheetos, a spicy pickle, and hopefully some kind of sausages or pork rinds or maybe mackerel or something that you can chop up and use as protein, along with a boiled egg. You chop it all up together, and then you've got to have some bread to spread it on. And you know what? It's actually pretty good. The pickle gives it a zing. The Cheetos give it the crunch, as well as the spice. The noodles are the main ingredient, the foundation. That's what you get full off of, and it's definitely a crazy dish, but there's a camaraderie to how it all comes together. And this would be the last time I'd eat with the guys at that table.

After we ate, I put in one more good workout with the fellas—sit-ups, push-ups, squats, dips; we did what we could without a weight room. I had always maintained a workout regimen. Keeping the body just as sharp as the mind. I pushed a little harder that day. I was getting out! I was going to play football!

"You want this radio?" You can have this, you can have that. It felt like Christmas to some of the guys in that place, and it's surprising all the little things you can collect after two and a half years in one spot.

When it was lights-out, I couldn't sleep. I was too anxious. Too excited. But I closed my eyes and forced myself to sleep so that the morning would come faster.

They woke me at 5 a.m. and sent me to R&R. They put me in a cage with a couple of other guys and I sat there, and sat there, while they processed us. Discharge from prison is worse than discharge from a hospital. It takes forever. On that day, it took five solid hours. Five solid hours of waiting, with my knees bouncing up and down, my whole body itching to get out of that place.

When they finally called me up, they asked me all sorts of exit information questions. "Do you know where your parole office is located?"

"Yes."

"Do you know you've got twenty-four hours to report to him or he'll issue a warrant for your arrest?"

"Yes."

It went on and on, and then they put me back in the holding cell while they double-checked all my paperwork, recalculated my release date, even looked to see if I was wanted for any other charges. They were meticulous so they wouldn't let anyone out by mistake. Everybody told me the night before, "Just hope they got it right, man. Hope to God they don't kick you back."

After a certain point, they allowed us to change into our street clothes. My mom had sent clothes in for my release. It felt so good to put on some jeans—anything besides those prison-issued sweat pants would have felt good to me at that point.

During that process, one guy who was with us got kicked back. Something wasn't right in his paperwork, and they made him change out of his street clothes and back to his prison sweats.

No, no, no, I thought. I felt so bad for the guy.

I silently prayed to God that wouldn't happen to me. Eagerly I waited. And then finally I heard, "Banks. You're up."

They walked me out, through one open door that closed behind me, then another, and another, until we were outside, with only one double gate in the fences in front of us.

So close. So close.

A new feeling came running through my veins. *Freedom.*

I reached the last gate.

This was *real.*

I walked out of CRC on August 29 into the heat of the scorching Norco sun and saw my mom, my younger brother, and my cousin standing by my mom's car, waiting with big smiles on their faces. And when the final gate to that prison shut behind me for the very last time, I felt it. The sound of it rippled through me. I felt it in my soul.

I wasn't locked in anymore.

I was released.

We hugged and took pictures and I'm pretty sure I was smiling the biggest smile I'd ever had in my life. But as soon as we had a couple of poses complete, I said, "Let's get the hell out of here!"

I climbed into the passenger seat of the first car I'd been in for more than five years, opening and closing the door myself for the first time in all those years. My mom started driving as I stared into the passenger-side mirror—the one that says "Objects in Mirror Are Closer than They Appear"—and watched as the entrance to that facility got farther and farther away, until it disappeared from view.

"So," my mom said, "what do you want to eat on your first day out?"

I didn't even hesitate.

"McDonald's!" I said, and all three of them laughed. I don't know why I picked McDonald's. The word just popped out of my mouth. Maybe it just felt normal. At the drive-through I ordered a Double Quarter Pounder with cheese, large fries, and a Hi-C Orange, and as we drove off I realized why I picked it: This food took me right back to my childhood. That was what I ate when I was young. *McDonald's*. And I know it's terrible food, but at that point, in that moment, it was the best, most soulful, Thanksgiving, chef-made, grandma-cooked meal in the world. It was *heaven*.

It was a nice long drive from Norco back to Long Beach. I looked out at the landscape and the roads and the stores and saw my mom next to me and it was like I was in a dream. All the sights and sounds and smells and tastes we all take for granted. Every one of them, even sitting in traffic, felt good.

The first place we went to was to my mom's and brother's apartment. I was scared it would feel unfamiliar, and it did as we walked up to the door, approaching this place I'd never seen in my life. But as soon as we stepped inside, as soon as I saw some family pictures on the walls, it didn't feel foreign at all. It felt like home. In fact, it felt like the best home I'd ever walked into. It had two bedrooms, two bathrooms, a kitchen, and a living room, and it was near the beach.

"Damn," I said, "y'all doing it like this? This place is amazing!"

"Boy, this ain't nothing but a little apartment," my mom said.

To her, and maybe to most people, it was small. It was basic. To me it was the nicest apartment I'd ever seen.

My mom assumed I'd want to hang out and rest up for a while, but that was the *last* thing I wanted to do.

"Nah. I want to get started living!" I said. "First thing, I've got to go see my parole officer. I've got to get registered. Then I want to go straight to LBCC. Can you take me?"

"I've got to go back to work for a while," my mom said.

"I'll take you," my brother said.

"Well, let's go!"

My brother and I jumped in his car, which would have been my car back in the day, and headed off to meet my parole officer for the first time. He was surprisingly chill. There really weren't a lot of rules I had to follow, other than I had to register as a sex offender. There was no hiding it; that bothered me. It made me angry. But compared to being locked up, even that seemed like a breeze. He told me, "No drugs. Get a job or go to school, and stay out of trouble." Those were the guidelines. And I had to return every two weeks to meet with a psychologist or counselor, he said, who was going to ask me some questions in something called a mandatory counselor meeting.

"All right," I said.

"See you in a couple weeks," he said. And that was it.

We jumped back in the car and went straight to Long Beach City College, straight to the football field. They were expecting me. I met half the team and the coaches and then got my gear right away. They were working out, so they had me start going over film right then and there. They were planning on getting me right in the game, and they had a game scheduled for that Friday. It was crazy—in the best way possible. I could hardly believe I was actually there, talking about football, and getting ready to play football. I couldn't remember ever feeling so happy. How was it even possible that I was in prison in the morning and part of a college football team in the afternoon?

After setting things up with the coaches, I went over to the registrar and enrolled in my classes and got everything arranged to go back to school. Then me and my brother just kind of hung out on campus. I was running into people left and right from back in the day. They looked at me as if they had seen a ghost. It was like people couldn't even believe it. They didn't know I was home and they were surprised when I told them, "I'm going to be going to school here."

That day, that first day out, walking across the City College campus in the sunshine, I started to remember what freedom felt like. That sense of freedom that we all take for granted.

That night, I walked out of my mom's beautiful apartment and went over to the beach. I sat on the sand, listened to the waves, and looked up at the moon. For five whole years I had only seen it from behind walls and barbed-wire fences. I thought about that night in prison, the first night I had seen the moon and stars after nearly two years, and how much I wished back then that I was free.

And now I was.

• ◆ •

When I first got home, everybody was glad to see me: cousins, uncles, aunts, Mom, Dad: "He's home! He's home! He's home!" But within a couple of days everyone was back to work, taking care of bills and errands and their everyday day-to-day. It was like, "We're happy that you're home but now we've got to get back to life."

But there was nothing like seeing that smile on my mother's face. The level of happiness was different for her. I was her baby, her child. My family missed me, but not like Mom. They had no need to stress about it on a daily basis. They didn't give up a home, sell a car, and return home empty-handed. I was out of sight and out of mind for so long that in a way they all got used to me not being around.

It's tough to digest, that their lives just went on without me. It was hard to try to make sense of where I fit in, and whether or not I really mattered.

A couple days after being home, a homegirl of mine and her sister picked me up to go to the mall. I needed clothes. My mom gave me a couple hundred bucks and I had two hundred dollars in gate money that they gave me when I got out of prison. I was planning to buy a couple of pairs of jeans and some shirts, so we drove over to Lakewood and walked into a few stores. There were so many people there. There was so much movement. People were walking by, bumping me in the shoulder, not saying "Excuse me." I hadn't seen any little kids in forever and they were all over the place, running all around. The stores were packed and the clothes racks were really closed in tight. I began to panic. I couldn't breathe. My heart started racing. I turned around and walked out and sat down on a bench in the middle of the mall walkway and my friends followed me out.

"Hey, what's going on?"

"I just need a moment. I just need a moment. It's just a lot right now," I said.

I put my head in my hands and tried to catch my breath.

I had been caged for more than five years, and nothing ever changed in prison. I looked around that mall and watched my friends and I realized that during my time away, everything in the real world had *completely* changed. The cars looked different. The way people dressed looked different. The Internet was different. When I left, cell phones were not really a big thing. There had been little small ones around, like Nokias, but now everyone had iPhones and Sidekicks, and all kinds of other stuff. It was a whole new world—and I didn't feel like I was a part of it.

I told my friends I had to leave. They said they understood. We made a plan to come back in a couple of days.

Transitioning was going to be harder than I thought.

Back at home my brother was hanging with a friend.

"This the homey," my brother said, but all I could think while shaking his hand was *Who is this? Where you from? Is this dude bad business? I don't know if I can trust him.* Looking straight into this man's eyes, I sized him up as I had done with everyone else I'd encountered over those five long years.

222

When he left, my brother asked me, "You good, bro? What's up with you?"

I guess I came off completely standoffish. But I just wasn't used to the attention. In prison, you don't *want* attention. When people you don't know stare at you in prison it means you brought the wrong attention to yourself, or someone is plotting. I had trouble wrapping my head around the fact that out here, people look at you for lots of reasons. There was a lot of love and understanding coming my way from family and friends, but I had to remind myself that their looks were out of that love. That basic human interaction, the pleasure of making eye contact with other people, even people you love, had been taken from me.

When we went out to a restaurant or anyplace in public, I would scan the room, choose who I thought would be my biggest worry in a fight, and plot how I'd take them down. It was just instinct now. When we sat down, I'd sit with my back against the wall so no one could sneak up on me, and face the door so I could see who was coming in and out. I counted how many people were in the room.

"Boy, you're so paranoid," Mom said to me one night. "Is something wrong?"

I tried to explain it to her. "In prison you had to be three steps ahead at all times," I said. "Three steps ahead of everything. You cannot slip. You had to be able to walk into a yard of five or six hundred people and always be three steps ahead."

She told me to snap out of it. I tried. I kept telling myself, *Okay, I am home now. Don't trip, you're home now. I'm free!* But mentally? I wasn't free. I was still in prison.

One of the only places I felt like I was fully busting out of prison was on the football field. I *destroyed* people on that field. A man with no fear, I would run down the field on kick-off like a wild man. Smashing into guys, knocking off their helmets, putting people out of the game. No fear. None. It was a breath of fresh air to be running full speed again without worrying about the block gun, or the M16. To have that physical contact, to be able to go heads-up with guys without an alarm going off and ten guards running down the hall with their sticks drawn. I felt like a piece of me was given back by being able to play again.

I came in halfway through the season and played five games before it ended. I did pretty well, too. I was productive with the team. I was going to school and had good grades for my first semester. I was thinking, *Wow, what a great introduction back. One more season and I should hopefully be able to secure a partial scholarship and move on from here.*

I was five years behind my peers, but I could still play the game. Plus, I was better at school than ever. Two years at City College, I thought, and I could transfer to a four-year school.

Okay. I'm doing this. I'm following a plan. I'm off to a good start.

● ◆ ●

My biweekly parole meetings were nothing but a quick check-in, and the mandatory counseling meetings were a joke. They had me answer the same questionnaire every time: "How do you feel? Do you want to harm yourself? Do you want to harm other people? Is there anything you want to talk about?" I couldn't help but wonder about people who really did commit crimes. There was no rehabilitation in these meetings. No actual counseling went on. And what went on behind prison walls had men more messed up coming out than they had been going in.

I didn't have time to worry about anybody else, though. I had to stay on my path.

Right at the end of football season, I met a girl on campus. I hadn't paid any attention to most of the girls there. Most of them to me were too young for where I was mentally and emotionally. That, and the fear I lived in daily of another girl accusing me of something I didn't do. But this girl was different. When I first saw her, she was in scrubs, like, nurse scrubs. She was walking across the campus one way and I passed by her walking the opposite way and we made eye contact. I smiled; so did she. I stopped and turned around, and she did the same. We both smiled again. I walked over to her and we began talking. The next thing you know, we exchanged numbers.

We hung out once, and the very next day I invited her over to my mom's apartment. I was really nervous, but I had to tell her my story. I was more afraid of *not* telling her. I didn't want her to hear it from somebody else and think I was trying to hide it or something. So I pulled out all my paperwork and showed her the inconsistencies, and the DNA results, and my appeal for a writ of habeas corpus that I had filed.

She didn't doubt me at all.

"I believe you," she said. "Don't worry about it."

She was the first person besides my mom to put an arm around me and say, "Hey, it's gonna be all right. I got your back."

I fell in love right away.

She was about five foot nine, a light-skinned sistah. She wore reading glasses. Her Afrocentric state of mind matched

her love for African culture, African art, and African history—
I loved it.

It turned out she was ten years older than me, but age was
of no concern on both our ends. I had what she called an "old
soul." She fell in love with me, she said, because I "wasn't like
other guys." I was emotionally on a different level than most
men she'd come across.

It felt good to be acknowledged. To be admired. To be
wanted.

She liked how I took my time with her. It's when you've
had everything taken away from you that you learn to value
all that you receive.

Feeling the touch of a woman again was transcendent. I
relished it. I longed for affection after five years of solitude.
All those nights of not having someone there to comfort me,
or to tell me everything was going to be all right; not having companionship or someone empathetic to my cries. I was
alone. Cold. Isolated. Empty. But with her? I felt warm again.
The touch of her skin. The way she pulled me in. Trusted me.
Let me love her. Let me explore. Let me discover. Let me lie
back while she worked magic on me, in a way I was sure only
a more experienced woman could. All that adolescent fooling
around, the memories of what it felt like to get close to a girl
as a teenager, they were nothing compared to the togetherness,
the oneness this woman made me feel. It wasn't just bodies
rubbing against each other. She showed me the power of bond-
ing, of deep spiritual togetherness and loyalty.

She was everything I needed, and more.

And I would need her more than I realized.

SEVENTEEN

Chain, Chain, Chain

Just after we finished the football season, I got a call from a new parole officer.

His energy wasn't chill at all.

Straight to the point, he notified me of a mandatory special meeting. I arrived a little early. Sitting in a waiting room of a parole office always felt demoralizing. Every visit felt like a step back into prison. The nondescript building in Compton, the attitudes of the parole officers, the other parolees I saw there. Normally I'd meet with my parole officer one-on-one, but for this special meeting a group of us were called in.

This new parole officer was a ballbuster who spoke at us with disgust, as if he hated us, hated his job, maybe even hated some of himself. He knew he had the power to throw any one of us back in prison based on his word alone, and he let us know it, too.

"For those of you who haven't been reading the newspaper, I'm here to inform you that the law has changed, and for you, the new law goes into effect today," he said. "Per the state of California, all you sex offenders' days of walking around freely and openly wherever and whenever you want are over. From this day forward, you will be wearing a GPS monitor," he said, holding up a black plastic device on a black rubber strap. "This is a GPS monitoring device, and once it goes on, it does not come off. If it comes off, we get notified. We come find you. We arrest you. We haul your ass up to County and you get thrown back in prison."

I slouched back in my seat. This could not be happening.

"If you stray from your home or place of work, we will be notified, we will find you, and throw your ass in County. If you're out past your curfew, we will be notified, and we will find you, and we'll haul your ass in. You cannot live within two thousand feet of a school, park, or anyplace else where children are present. And I know a lot of you have lived by the spirit of the law already, and we haven't caught up to you. Well, those days are done.

"Now I'm going to call you up one at a time. When you come up, put your right foot up on the chair and lift your pant leg up," he said.

We followed orders. One by one we were called to the front and fitted with an ankle bracelet. I looked around the room but kept to myself. This was nuts. This was crazy. This could not be happening. I put my foot up on the chair and tried pleading with him, "Hey, I'm enrolled at Long Beach City College. I play football. I'll be able to take this off for games, right?"

"Are you hard of hearing, boy?" he said. "You cannot take it off for any reason. So stop thinking about football and focus on getting a job." He said it loud enough that everybody else heard him. It was humiliating. It was dehumanizing to get that thing put on my ankle. I felt like I'd been tagged like some animal.

"The device needs to be charged every twelve hours," he

said to the group. "You plug it into the wall and wait till the red light turns green. If you're at work and it runs out of battery, we will be notified, and we will *what*?"

Everyone responded, "Haul our ass in."

"Haul your ass in. That's right."

"What do we do when we take a shower?" somebody asked.

"You can take a shower with it but you cannot not submerge the device in water. Meaning no baths, no hot tubs, no swimming."

"How long does it take to charge?" someone else asked.

"Supposedly sixty to ninety minutes. I don't know. Just wait for the light. Got it?"

So we're supposed to tether ourselves to a wall for three hours a day?

Right then and there I was back in prison.

All that I had been mentally and emotionally processing since my release from prison resurfaced. Once again, my roller coaster took a plunge.

There was no way I could play football with that device on my ankle. There was no way I could handle my school schedule or live any kind of a normal life having to tether myself to an electrical outlet twice a day.

Without football, there was no way I could receive a scholarship. No way I could transfer to a four-year school. My whole plan, my dreams, were once again shut down.

There was no point in going on. I knew at that moment I was dropping out of school.

I gave up.

From that day forward, whenever I went outside, all I could

think about was how embarrassing it was to have that thing on my ankle, and how I didn't want anyone to see it. In order to hide it, I had to wear sweats or jeans every day, no matter how hot it was, and my mind fixated on that thing.

The first thing I did when I woke up in the morning was charge it, and it took an hour and a half to two hours. I had to sit there with the thing plugged into the wall and wait for the red light to turn green. When I left the house, even on a good day, those rare days when I could kind of forget about everything I had been through, I had to rush back to beat a curfew and plug it back into the wall for another hour and a half to two hours and wait for the light to turn green.

When I first got out of prison, my parole officer didn't even give me a curfew. I could live wherever I wanted to, and stay out as long as I wanted to. But with the tracking device they added a whole new set of rules that made life nearly impossible. I couldn't live within two thousand feet of any school or park. There are a lot of schools and parks just in Long Beach. I couldn't go to places where kids frequented. That meant I couldn't go into schools. I couldn't go to the beach unless it was during school hours or late at night when children wouldn't be present. I couldn't go to amusement parks or fairs because I was a registered sex offender. I couldn't even think about going to Chuck E. Cheese or anything like that. It was a blanket system for all registered sex offenders. Regardless of the sex crime, the punishment was the same.

I wasn't some pedophile. I wasn't a rapist. I wasn't *anything*! Yet they forced me to live like I was. An outcast. A criminal. A monster.

How could I get a job if I couldn't go anywhere?

They destroyed any chance I had of living a normal life, and yet they expected me to be normal. To not act out. To *simply* find a job and readapt back into society with no help or resources.

Any break from the rules, any slip-up, and I'd go back to prison. When I talked to the parole officer, it seemed like every question I asked only brought more bad news, including the news that I would have to keep that thing on my ankle *for the full five years I was on parole.*

It hit me hard.

I felt like I was dying again.

Like I was done.

I'd made it out of a cage only to be placed in another form of incarceration.

The hopelessness of it all consumed me. With no school, I found myself lying around the house at my mom's all the time. I quickly began to feel like a burden. As if I was more of a concern than a blessing. I was done stressing my mom out and living off her and seeing the pain in her face. Some nights I'd sit at the beach and watch the homeless people walking around and I'd think to myself, *That's going to be me one day.* I mentally prepared for that because somehow it seemed better than the alternative of continuing to be a burden for my mom.

I was so close to giving up and giving in—except I had one good thing still going on.

I had the comfort of my girl.

"I love you," she said. "I care about you. I'm here. I've got your back."

Her words kept me going.

We started to share space and time with each other almost

every day, which took my mind off my problems. Sometimes the parole officer would give me approval to spend the night at her apartment, but when he didn't I would see her until just before my curfew at midnight, then I'd leave, go back to my mom's to charge up and sleep for while, then jump back out to see her as soon as the curfew lifted at 4 a.m.

After a month and a half of talking and dating and seeing each other every day, she asked me to move into her apartment.

I had to figure out how to file the paperwork I needed in order to make the move, and then wait until it got approved. Once approved, I'd have to reregister as a sex offender in her city, Hawthorne—but once that was taken care of, I moved in.

It wasn't easy. She was there to witness every moment of my transition.

I had recurring nightmares, but one dream in particular haunted me most nights. It was the day I was supposed to be paroled and released from prison, but they weren't letting me out, and I was frantically going all over the prison, telling prison guards and workers, "I'm supposed to be getting out to-day. I'm supposed to be getting out. They're not letting me out. They're not letting me out!" I'd be covered in sweat, my heart pounding and racing in my chest. When I'd finally wake up she was there to calm me down. It was a lot for a girlfriend to take in. It was a lot for anyone to take in. But she tried her best to be there, knowing there was no one else stepping up to the plate.

In that state, it seemed like everything kept setting me off.

Only months removed from a six-year sentence, I often had flashbacks and unwanted reminders of where I once was. One day I was flipping through channels on TV and I stumbled across a show called *Locked Up*. The show focused on inmates and prison life that made everyone in that place look monstrous and scary, without addressing any of the realities of why people get sent to these prisons. It was so raw, I couldn't stand it. "What the fuck is this? What kind of fucking TV show is this? It's bullshit. Prison is not entertainment!" I was so pissed that a show had been made about the life I'd been forced to live.

But the worst part was stressing about work. I had no money, no job, and no chance at any independence. The only possible job I could have taken was a little warehouse job set up specifically for parolees. But I didn't want to be around parolees. I didn't want to be around ex-prisoners. That's not who I was; it wasn't who I needed to be around. I wasn't supposed to be there. I wasn't even supposed to *know* those guys. The last thing I wanted was to get out of prison but stay chained to its inhabitants, to spend my days around that same institutionalized mentality. I wanted to be far, far away from anybody and anything that had to do with where I'd just left.

I refused to take on jobs that were for parolees. It had nothing to do with being better than the next man. I just wanted better for myself. I needed better influences, needed positive visuals of success.

I had a friend who helped me get some under-the-table work on rare occasions, but besides that—nothing. Not being able to provide for myself or my girlfriend made it difficult to quiet my mind. Standing in line at the grocery story and having to watch my girl pull her wallet out to pay for me every time was demoralizing. It was embarrassing. Not only was I stripped of hopes of any future, but I felt like less than a man. Like a child. As if I were there with my mom paying for me.

Ultimately, the two of us didn't make it. I still had too much I needed to figure out in my own life before I would be able to make a relationship work. Looking back on it, I wonder if I was truly in love with that girl, or if maybe I was allowing her to fill a void in my heart. Either way, it ended. And that hurt.

In those first two years, readapting back into society but not being able to do so fully, it felt like I went from one form of institutionalization to another. How is it even possible to make sense of the minute-by-minute, hour-by-hour, day-by-day, waiting for seven whole years, and on top of that to realize that all of my dreams, all of my hopes, and all semblance of a normal life would still be on hold for another three?

In a lot of ways, it was harder than being in prison. Behind those bars and walls, you know the world is passing you by but you don't see it. Now it was like I was in a glass cage where I could see everything but couldn't touch it. I could watch people succeed. I could watch people fail. All I could do was watch them living their lives, even those who weren't taking the opportunities that I would have taken, knowing I couldn't do any of it.

In prison, I prayed to survive so I could get my life back. So I could live again. But this wasn't living. This was a nightmare. I was barely existing. I was labeled a "sex offender." My name, photo, address, and the details of my crime were all listed publicly on a website, for anyone to read. That was harder for me to deal with than almost anything.

I was afraid of people looking at me as if I were a monster even though I wasn't.

At night a tsunami of "Why me?" moments brought flooding tears that I could not control. And the days weren't any better. During the days I went to countless interviews. I was applying for any kind of work. To be a janitor. To do construction. Warehouse jobs. Packing boxes. Anything. I walked into every store and onto every job site I could find and they all said a version of the same thing: "We'd love to hire you, but we can't hire you with that"—"that" being my status as a registered sex offender—or "Man, I already know they're gonna say no, but I'll talk to the boss because you have a great personality." I tried to explain it over and over but they would just shake their heads. Some believed me, or *wanted* to believe me, but most people weren't even willing to listen. All they could see was "sex offender" attached to my name. To them, I wasn't a guy with a high school diploma who needed a job, who needed a chance, who would work harder than anyone they had just for that *chance*. I was a monster. A felon. A criminal. There was no chance in hell anyone would hire me.

I eventually found a job working in a warehouse for a clothing line in Irvine. A few months later they began laying off all their recent hires. Once again, I had no job. But I did meet a girl. Our first date was at the beach. I didn't have any money so I couldn't take her to get food or anything. I was broke. So I said, "Meet me at the beach?" We met that first day right in front of my mom's place for maybe four or five hours, just talking, laughing, vibing. I knew I liked her. I knew I wanted to date her. I knew I had to tell her. So the next day I did.

"I gotta tell you something. I don't know how you're gonna take it. You probably ain't gonna wanna be around me."

"Well, whatever it is, just tell me and we'll figure it out," she said.

It was nighttime when she came out to see me. We walked

up and down the beach in the moonlight for what felt like hours, until I finally explained my story. She wasn't quick to say, "I believe you." She wore a concerned look on her face; her body language had changed. I quickly chimed in: "Look, I know it all sounds crazy, but if you'd come up to my place, my mother's place, I can show you everything I'm telling you now. My mother herself can vouch for me. Meet her, and we can sit down and go over all my paperwork together. Whatever questions you have, I'll answer."

She was at a loss for words. After reading through my case file, she couldn't believe I had gone through all that I did.

We connected, and I fell in love a little too easily all over again.

I constantly wanted to be around her. She constantly wanted to be around me. She was living in Hollywood and worked as an administrator in downtown Los Angeles. She would get off work and drive out to Long Beach every day, or I would wait for her to get off work and I'd catch two Metrolink trains to get all the way up to Hollywood just to see her.

After a few months of dating she whispered, "I want you here. Just stay."

So I did. I moved in. I registered as a sex offender with my new address and we lived right there in the middle of all the madness on Hollywood and Hudson until eventually she bought a condo in Burbank. I registered once again, and I transferred my parole over to the Burbank office, which meant that I didn't have to deal with the PO from hell who first put the ankle monitor on me any longer. I was finally out of his hair, and he was out of mine.

I still had the monitor. I was still being tracked. I still couldn't hold down a job.

But for a moment, for a few moments of my hellish crazy life, I could almost breathe again.

Then one day in the middle of another blur of sifting through job postings online, exhausted, I took a break and opened Facebook.

Facebook definitely helped me early on, reconnecting with old friends from my high school, middle school, and even elementary days. I scrolled through my newsfeed for a while just to see what was going on in the world, and then I noticed a little red dot above the friend request tab. A little red dot indicating that I had a friend request.

I clicked the tab and a box dropped down.

And that's when the world stood still.

"You have 1 new friend request," the message said.

"From Tiana Miller."

EIGHTEEN

Contact

I slammed my laptop shut and slid it across the bed and went reeling back like I'd just seen the devil itself.

My heart began to beat just as hard as it did nine years ago when I saw Tiana walk out of Poly High with those police officers. Just as loud as it did every time I stepped into the courtroom to face the judge, just as fast as it did each time I had to walk into a new prison and face unknown demons. I was completely blindsided. I couldn't believe what I saw.

I sat there on the edge of the bed, staring out of the bedroom window, fixated on nothing. It was all a blur. I began having flashbacks of experiences over the years, the pain and heartache. Time stopped in that moment.

This has to be a joke. It's not her. It can't be her. Who would play such a sick joke? Who would make up a fake account just to do this to me? There's no way it can be her.

I opened the laptop again and looked at the profile picture on the friend request. It was her. She looked older. But it was *her*.

I began weighing my options. Part of me wanted to say to her all the things I'd bottled up over the last nine years. To scream, yell, and more.

I started to feel the rage I'd learned to redirect. The desire for revenge. I could feel it gnaw at my gut—but I knew that wasn't the way.

Making any contact with that girl meant risking my freedom. She'd been given the label of "victim" and me the "offender." So me making any contact with her was an automatic violation of my parole conditions.

I felt lost. I had no direction. But over the years I'd come to learn that in times like these, I had to be still in order to receive.

I dropped to my knees between the window and bed and prayed.

"God, I don't know what's going on right now, but I'm asking you to please help me. Help me play my cards right. Amen."

I unclasped my hands, stood to my feet, and before I could straighten my stance completely I knew what I had to do.

I didn't accept the friend request. Instead I sent her a direct message.

"Why would you friend request me?"

She wrote back immediately.

"I was hoping we could let bygones be bygones," she said.

Her exact words rang though my head. "*I was hoping we could let bygones be bygones. Let bygones be bygones . . .*" *She is hoping we can let bygones be bygones?*

What kind of crazy fucking shit is this?

A part of me still didn't believe it was her.

"Call me on this number," I wrote.

Not three seconds later, the phone rang.

This isn't happening.

I answered.

"Hello?"

"Hey, Brian."

It was *her*! It was her voice. It had been almost nine years, but that voice of hers was burned into my ears.

I didn't know what to say. I went blank. I held the phone to my ear in silence for a minute. Then another. And another. She didn't say anything, either. I could only hear noise in the background on her side.

"So," I said, breaking the silence, "what's going on? Why are you friend-requesting me?"

"Well," she said, "I was on Facebook, and I was looking for friends from back in the day from school. And I happened to come across your page. And, you know, you look good."

I look good?

"I was looking at your pictures," she said, "and you've grown up. You're looking *good*. And I asked my friend, would it be crazy if I reached out to you? But she was like, 'Nah, it should be cool because, you know, it's been so much time that passed by.' So, you know, I thought I'd hit you up and see what you've been up to. Did you look at my pictures? How you think I look?"

I was too in shock to respond. I just stayed quiet.

"I'd love to see you," she said. "Let's hang out. If you want, we can hang out tonight. You're up in the Valley somewhere, right? I can borrow a car, or I'll catch the bus and come and see you. And then, you know, let's hang out. I'd love to see you."

Am I in a twilight zone right now? This can't be life.

Of course I didn't look at any of her pictures. I didn't want to look at Tiana Miller ever again if I could help it. But I was listening to this voice, and it was her, and she was propositioning me. Complimenting me on how I've grown. Laughing, and flirting.

This is so sickening, I thought. *This is so fucked up!*

And then I started thinking, *She's trying to set me up. She's either trying to get me to meet up with her and have some thugs push the line on me, maybe even try to kill me. Or she wants to meet, have the police or my parole officer there, and then, boom, I'm back in prison on a violation. So there's no way that's going to happen.*

"You know," I said, "let me get back to you on that."

And then I just couldn't help myself.

"You know, I lost my life," I said. "I lost a lot of time. I lost my chance to play football—"

"Why are you trying to talk about all that? If that's what you wanna talk about, I'll just get off the phone right now," she said.

This girl is crazy, I thought. *But I don't want her to hang up.*

"All right, well, we ain't gonna talk about that. You know, I just want you to know it's been hard for me."

And she said, "Well, you know, I really wanna hang out with you. Let's hang out."

My mind abruptly diverted to another thought: the California Innocence Project, and their response to my request for representation.

The only way to make a case for my exoneration was if the "the *witness were to recant her statement.*"

I could see those words on the letter from CIP's cofounder Justin Brooks so clearly, it's almost like they were projected on the wall in front of me.

I had to play this right. I couldn't be sloppy. This was divine intervention, not coincidence, and I knew I needed to play chess, not checkers.

I closed my eyes. I dug deep. And I found the words.

"Well, you know," I said, "if you could help me get my life back, I'll be down to hang out."

"Oh," she said. "What you need me to do?"

I paused for a moment

"I'm really not sure. I just know it's you who can make this right. Let me think about it, and I'll be in touch with you."

"Okay, well, let me know because I wanna see you. I really wanna see you."

"Okay," I said. "I'll call you back."

We hung up.

I couldn't breathe.

I felt like I'd just been touched on the arm by my rapist. I was scared. My mind and body were exhausted. And all the trauma I'd ever endured over the years consumed me all at once.

Tiana was synonymous with prison. Her name was the seed that planted the darkness I'd crawled out of and vowed never to go back to. Ever, ever, ever. *I'm not going back to prison.*

I couldn't sleep. I couldn't eat. I kept shaking and holding back tears.

She knew. She knew what she did all this time and now she contacts me to "hang out"?

It had to be a trap. I had to get three steps ahead. I had to be ready. I had to figure this thing out. How to protect myself. How to stay safe. *I'm not going back to prison.*

One thought consumed me at first: *No way. No contact. I got less than a year to go on my parole. I can't risk it. I can't.*

I can't walk away from this!

God, I prayed, *she practically admitted it on the phone. She didn't say the words, but she said she was willing to help. What do I do with that?*

The next morning I received a text from Tiana, and three more by midday. Then a few more by the end of the night. And the same, every day, for a week. "I wanna see you." "I wanna see you." "I'll catch the bus." "I'll catch the metro." "Let's meet halfway." "Let's go out." "Take me out somewhere." "Let's kick it." "Let's hang out." "Whatever I gotta do to meet you. I'm coming. I wanna see you." "You wanna meet today?" "You wanna meet later on tomorrow?" "Wanna meet tonight?" "Just tell me." "What's your address?" "What's your address?"

I kept thinking, *This is a straight-up setup*. What else could it be? So I ignored her. I barely responded. Until one day she texted me, "Well, looks like you don't wanna hang out with me. So if you don't wanna hang out with me, then maybe I'll change my mind about helping you."

I had to do something now. This was it, the last chance. I knew I needed to make a move.

A friend of mine put me in touch with a private investigator, and I told him, "I want to meet this girl, and I need everything recorded just in case I'm being set up or she's planning to try to say something else happened that didn't really happen."

"Well," he said, "why don't you just do it here at my office? I've got some camera stuff that we could set up and we can go from there."

"Cool. I appreciate the help."

Then I texted her: "Hey, still want to meet? If you want to you can come visit me here at the office tomorrow during my lunch break at my job."

It wasn't my job. I had no job. The address I gave her was for the office of the private investigation firm. His business was so new, he didn't even have his name on the door yet. It was perfect. I sent the message and then I waited.

Ten minutes later, Tiana responded: "Okay. I'll be there. No problem. I'll be there."

Holy shit. What am I doing?

That night, I got no sleep again. I couldn't stop thinking of how it would be to see her. To be in her presence. I kept telling myself: *Control how you respond. Be still. Let the camera be your eyes. Let the recorder be your ears. Ask the questions you want to ask, then just fade out. Don't listen. Don't look. Just be numb no matter what she says. Be still.*

I went over and over it in my head all night long.

The next day I arrived at the investigators office and we began placing surveillance equipment around the room. Awaiting her arrival, while watching the PI place cameras and recording devices in the most obvious places and move about the room as if he was less experienced at this than I was, nervous wasn't even the word. The investigator was set to listen in from the office next door. His wife would listen in from the hallway. I wanted her there. The footage had to show clearly that Tiana and I weren't alone.

Then we waited. And waited. At one point, I thought she wasn't coming.

"This has got to be a setup. Something's not right here," I said. But as soon as my doubt surfaced, so did she. Looking out of the window from the second floor, we watched her walk up from the parking lot. And it hit me.

This is really happening.

My heart started racing. My body began to sweat.

"I don't know if I can do this, man. I don't know," I said.

"Calm down. You're doing the right thing," the investigator said.

I heard her knock at the door. I let her in.

"Hey," she said with a friendly smile.

Tiana Miller was standing less than a foot away from me, smiling at me.

I faked a smile back. "Hey, what's up?" I said.

She tried to give me a friendly hug but I took a step back and shook her hand instead.

I just shook hands with the devil, I thought. *Be cool, Brian. You can do this!*

We walked into the office. I motioned my hand toward a chair for her to sit in. I sat in a chair beside it. The vibe was horrific. She started talking about lost time. She said, "I've got three kids now."

"Are you married?" I asked.

"Nah," she said, laughing while explaining that her kids have three different daddies.

She started going on and on about dealing with some legal issue with her kids, as if I would feel sorry for her or something.

Then I tried to explain to her all the stuff that I'd experienced since being wrongfully incarcerated. I told her about my prison experience. I told her about what I lost. I told her how hard it'd been and how I couldn't find any work. And all of it seemed to go in one ear and out the other.

"Oh man, that's crazy," she said.

No empathy. No remorse. None.

Instead, she acted like she'd been the victim of her own lies.

"Well, you know, I've been through a lot of shit, too, since all of this has been happening. You know all these bitches been hating on me because, you know, I got that money from the lawsuit. And I was out here buying new clothes and cars and stuff, and everybody was hating on me, trying to get money outta my pockets. And the courts had me going to see a psychologist and that was getting on my nerves because they were forcing me to go see them."

Do not react. Do not react. DNR, man. DNR!

I kept nodding like I cared, knowing the cameras were capturing it all. But the whole time I kept thinking about the additional holes in her story now, which any professional should have seen the whole time they spoke to her. Here she was sitting here complaining to *me* about the fact that the courts were making it mandatory for her to seek help for a crime that allegedly took place and she was "sick of doing all that shit."

I told her I'd lost my life, and she told me about all the money she spent.

In my mind, in all the practicing I'd done for this moment in my head, I imagined I would just ask her straight up whether or not she really believed that I raped her, just to see how she responded. But in the actual moment, as I sat there listening, something told me not to. Something told me I needed to let her speak. I just kept listening, and occasionally talking, wanting her to feel comfortable. My only hope was that the cameras were working. That the audio was being recorded. Eerily enough, her only focus seemed to be on when she might be able to see me again.

"Would you mind talking to my lawyer, to see what would be the best way of going about this?" I asked her.

"Oh no," she said. "I ain't talking to no lawyers. If you want me to talk to a lawyer or the DA or some judge or anything, police officer, you can forget it. I ain't got time for that because I already know they're going to want me to pay back all the money that I got for the lawsuit. And that will take a long time."

"That will take a long time."

"I don't want to talk to nobody," she said.

I could see she was freaking out, so I stepped back a bit.

"Well, how about this? How about we speak to this investigator that I know? He's not a lawyer. He's not a cop. He's just a private investigator. But he can advise us on the best way to go about you helping me in this situation."

She thought about it for a few seconds and said, "Okay. I'll do that."

• ◆ •

The next day, she showed up. Same office. Same time. We talked for about five minutes, and then the investigator came in and joined us.

"Hey, thanks for coming," I said. "Have a seat."

I started things off by saying, "We were hoping you could help us," but then he jumped in and started talking about all kinds of stuff. Just shooting the breeze! I don't know if he was nervous or what, but he was all over the place. I kept thinking, *Dude, come back. Stay on subject here.*

Eventually he got to why we were all there. He said, "Look, I'm not judging you. You know, I remember being a teenager, and my hormones raging. So I do have to ask, you know, just so we can have this part clear: Did Brian rape you?"

248

"You want me to say it now?" she said.

"Well, yeah, you know, I just want to know."

"No, he didn't rape me," she said.

Do not react. Stay cool. Stay cool.

"Well, did he kidnap you?"

"No," she said. "He didn't kidnap me."

"So what happened?"

"Well, we were just being young and curious, and one thing led to another. And then all these adults got involved, and it just got worse, worse, and worse."

I wanted to stand up and yell, "We got you! We got you, bitch!"

I wanted to say, "Get the fuck outta here! Get outta my face!" But I remained calm and treated her words like they were nothing new.

I stayed still.

Real still.

When she finally left, when we were sure she'd exited the building, *then* we celebrated. The PI and his wife started yelling and screaming inside his office. He was super pumped, this being one of his first investigative cases, and he knew it was a big one. He grabbed the pen camera he'd picked up in a spy store, rushed it over to his computer, injected it into the USB slot, and began the downloading process. As the files began to load, his attention quickly turned to lawsuits and how much money could be made. I could see dollar signs in his eyes as he spoke with excitement. I didn't care about money one bit. I just wanted my life back.

Distracted by the thought of money, he reached for the pen still in the computer's USB portal and pulled it out.

The computer buzzed and flickered.

"Wow, that was loud," he said.

His complete focus was now the computer screen. Slowly he placed the pen back into the USB portal. His face grew worrisome; his eyes stopped blinking.

"Did they download? Did they *download*?" I asked.

"Ummm," he said. "Hold on. Something happened. I—"

I walked around the desk and looked at the pen camera's file list on the screen.

It was empty.

"Holy shit," I said. "Is it gone? Did you erase it?"

"Something happened, yeah, I just, I'm sorry, I don't know—"

His wife came over and the three of us each tried plugging and replugging the pen camera into the USB portal—and it was wiped.

All the footage. Gone.

I inhaled and exhaled deeply, staying calm. "Just try one more time," I said.

The folder was empty.

He hung his head and began to cry.

"I'm so sorry. I'm so sorry," he cried.

His wife began to cry.

And so did I.

I flopped and fell back in my seat and flashed back to everything that had just happened—the one-in-a-billion probability of what had just happened. And the fact that it was *gone*. All lost. All gone.

This can't be life.

Fuck.

NINETEEN

Hope and Harassment

The private investigator jumped to his feet. He grabbed his cell phone and stepped into the hallway. As I sat there slouched in my chair, I could overhear him on the phone, repeating his story about how he'd wiped the files from the hard drive. After an hour of phone calls he returned to the office with a somewhat hopeful look on his face. He'd been told about a company out in Hollywood that did great work recovering digital files.

We hopped into the car and took the camera pen to them. And waited. Two days. *Two days.* I spent those hours replaying her words in my head over and over again. Words I thought I'd never hear. Those simple words, "No. He did not rape me. No. He did not kidnap me."

Where were these words four years ago when they strapped me to a GPS tracking device and labeled me a sex offender? Where were these words when a judge served me up a six-year prison sentence?

Hoping for the best but fearing the worst, all I could do was pray.

Forty-eight hours or so later the call finally came in. They were able to retrieve 60 percent of the footage.

What if that 60 percent is just the first day's tape? What if

*her saying those words, the most important part of the foot-
age, was the other 40 percent?*

But it wasn't. It was exactly what we needed. The whole
second day's tape was there. It was damaged; the video quality
was subpar and there was a loud buzzing sound throughout
the video. But it was there. It was *there*.

What is meant to be will be.

We made multiple copies of the footage on CDs and flash
drives, and I took a couple of them with me. There was no one
else I trusted with this footage. At home I grabbed my laptop
and began searching for help. I had done the impossible. I cap-
tured absolute proof of my innocence. A recantation from the
accuser herself. I knew that what had to be done next, only an
attorney could do. So I began searching.

I found a listing online for California's top one hundred
criminal lawyers, then tracked down emails and office numbers. A name on the list stood out to me: Cofounder and director of the California Innocence Project Justin Brooks.

I didn't get through to Brooks himself, but I did manage
to get through to Kim Hernandez, the program's director. She
was kind enough to listen.

The call was brief, but I was able to quickly walk her
through all that had happened.

"I have her on tape," I said.

She put me on hold for a few minutes.

She picked up the phone and said, "Okay. We'd like to see
it. Can you come meet us?"

I couldn't go all the way to San Diego with the ankle monitor on, not without setting off alarms, so we agreed to meet
halfway just a couple of days later, in Irvine.

Kim Hernandez and Alissa Bjerkhoel from CIP showed up to meet me at the grocery store we'd picked. Hernandez was the office manager who reviewed cases that came into the office, and Bjerkhoel was a staff attorney. We sat at these little tables outside the store. I popped open the laptop and played them the video. It was a little hard to see in the daylight, and the loud buzzing sound made it difficult to hear on the little laptop speakers. But none of that mattered. They saw it all. They heard it all.

They looked at each other, silent, in shock, and then Kim said, "Brian, do you mind if we make a copy of this and take it with us?"

"You can have this copy," I said. "I made a few."

"Great. We're going to take this back to the office and show Justin."

"So does this mean I don't have to look for a lawyer anymore, that you'll take my case?"

"You don't have to search for an attorney anymore," Kim said. "We're going to take on your case."

They made the decision right then and there.

I felt like I was going to explode—but I kept my cool. I kept my composure.

"Thank you so much. I really appreciate this. You won't regret it, I promise you," I said. "Thank you, thank you, thank you." We shook hands and I hugged them both. I walked to the parking lot and got in my car—and it all hit me at once. I yelled loud and long at the top of my lungs. My hands were banging the steering wheel. "Aaaaaaah!" I'm sure people outside could see the car shaking in the parking lot and wondered what was going on in there, but I didn't care. I was *full* of joy. Full of *tears* of joy.

I started calling everyone. My girlfriend, my best friends, my brother: "They finally took my case! They took my case! I'm going to get my *life* back."

I waited until after-school hours to call my mom and tell her what happened. I hadn't told her one word about any of it before that moment, and instead of reacting joyfully, she was afraid. The fear of losing again outweighed any hope of winning.

"Are you out of your mind?" she asked me. "Are you crazy?"

"Mom, we got her recanting the accusation on *tape*!"

"I don't know about this. I don't know. I just don't know," she kept saying.

She had seen too much go the other way. She had gone to court too many times thinking I was about to be freed, and instead seen me locked away for longer and longer periods of time. She was terrified that the district attorney or my parole officer or the judge would take the fact that I was in the same room as Tiana and use it against me, to put me back in prison regardless of anything Tiana said on that tape.

"Mom," I said, "I'm not alone. The California Innocence Project is taking my case. They're the best. They're like angels. This is what they do!"

"I don't know, Brian. I just don't know," she said.

The California Innocence Project got to work right away. One of their attorneys, Michael Semanchik, began the investigation, first by calling Tiana to see if they could get her to back up her recantation a second time. In the meantime, another attorney, Audrey McGinn, started collecting all sorts of information from me. She was impressed that I had so much information and knowledge at my fingertips. They got right to work formulating my appeal. They started digging into the case and found all of the same inconsistencies that I had found within Tiana's statements (along with a few more she'd made during her case with the school district), as well as the indisputable DNA findings, and came up with a whole list of reasons they could file an appeal.

It was beyond validating to have a team of professional lawyers look into my case, *believe* in me, and see fully what I went through, for the first time ever.

I kept asking them all kinds of questions, furthering my understanding of the law and the court system every step of the way, but the biggest question I had was "When will this be done?"

"Be patient. This kind of thing can take years. It could take a while," they told me.

At that time, the district attorney and the courts had basically no time constraints on when they had to respond to an appeal like mine. That meant you could quickly file an appeal that could then sit there for a year, two, even three years—and at the end of all that waiting, more than likely the court will just respond back with a no.

The California Innocence Project didn't want that to happen, and they had been fighting to change the law on response time long before I ever met with them. They asked me to be patient in part because they did not want to turn my appeal in until this new law passed—and within a few months, it did. Once that law passed, they entered my appeal, and the communication started back and forth between the appellate office and the California Innocence Project.

They kept me involved at every step. No closed doors. No secret deals.

We were about six months into it before I met the co-founder, Justin Brooks, in person. It was awe-inspiring to meet a man who was taking on the system and trying to use the law for good. And he was damn good at it. He made a positive impact on many people's lives. I had a lot of respect for this man, and he seemed just as impressed by me. He was blown away that I'd filed my own appeal for a writ of habeas corpus from prison, and that the court had given me a cause hearing.

I met with Justin at the CIP office at California Western School of Law in San Diego. My parole officer let me out of Los Angeles for a day to meet my lawyers. As Justin walked me through the office I saw that the walls were lined with pictures of people they had released from prison. He told me the stories of innocent people who had served ten, twenty, even thirty years in prison! I wasn't alone.

Not long after my visit I got a call from Audrey McGinn, a staff attorney at CIP.

"Hey, Brian," she said.

"What's up?"

"Well, I'm looking over these recruiting letters that you sent us, and I notice you had a bunch of them from Nebraska. You know, my dad's an alum from Nebraska. Have you ever thought about playing football if you get exonerated and get your life back?"

"Oh, wow. No. Hell no. I'm not thinking about football. I haven't thought about playing football in a few years now."

"Okay, I was just wondering. If you think about it and change your mind I can probably get you on the team. He knows everybody."

I didn't even know how to process that bit of information.

"Okay. Yeah. Thanks," I said. "I appreciate the offer."

The whole rest of that day, all I could think about was football.

Man, it would be dope if I was to play and make a comeback and go to school while I'm doing it. I started to feel my old dreams awaken, and I could not stop thinking about them.

But then I did some math, and the dream dimmed. I realized that I started my college football tenure when I first got out of prison—I officially played for Long Beach City College—and in college, you only have a five-year eligibility to play Division 1 football. After five years from your start date, unless due to injury, you can't play college ball anymore. So when they started fighting my case, this was 2011; I had started playing college ball August 29, 2007, the day I got out. That meant that by the time I was exonerated, if by some miracle that happened, it would be 2012. My five-year tenure for college football would be over.

I decided not to let that stop me.

Instead, I turned that dimmed dream into something brighter: *If I can't play college ball, then I'm shooting for the stars. I'm going to try out for the NFL.*

Within a few days I was in touch with an old friend of mine I hadn't seen since high school. Marcus Hobbs and I went to middle school together and ran into each other throughout our high school days. He had transitioned his life to focus on body building, health, and training.

"Hey, man," I told him. "I know this is going to sound crazy, but I think I may be playing football again. I'm real close to getting my life back. Proving my innocence. And when that happens I'm taking a shot at the NFL. I was hoping you'd train me."

"You sure that's what you want to do?" he asked, double-checking what he'd just heard. I nodded.

"Cool, man. You know I've always believed in you, and I know you didn't do that shit."

"Yeah," I said.

"Okay. So show up to the gym when you're ready."

I showed up a couple days later and started training with him at a gym called Metroflex Gym Long Beach. I was introduced to Chris Albert, co-owner of the gym at the time. Marcus explained the situation to him. I had lost a lot of time, I had no money for a membership, no money to pay for training. But I was determined. Chris and Marcus never charged me a dime. I started getting in shape and losing weight, and it was rough. I was in the worst shape of my life. The first several workouts had me throwing up. Soreness, exhaustion, cramps. Halfway through my workouts I'd be done.

But I kept at it. And every day it got a little bit easier. I got a little bit stronger. As I trained daily in the gym, and CIP worked on my case, I was assigned to a new parole officer, a Filipino guy who was actually pretty cool. Now I felt like I had a little more space to think about the future. I was still broke, still had no job, and that eventually became a serious issue between me and my girlfriend. After a year of her paying for just about everything, neither her pockets nor my pride could take it anymore. We agreed it would be best if I found somewhere else to live until things were sorted out with my case.

I reached out to the same friend who put me on to the private investigator, the one who helped record Tiana's recantation. He was more than happy to allow me to stay at his home. Being a registered sex offender, anywhere I lived I had to register with the city's police department. So after I got the approval from parole and registered with the neighborhood of Signal Hill, which was back within Long Beach city limits, I moved in. I was twenty minutes away from the gym now by bus. I started training every day, waking up at 5 a.m. for 6 a.m. sessions and coming back to the gym at midday for another.

The move worked. And me and my girl were back on solid terms.

A few weeks later, just before December, I stopped in to visit her at her condo in Burbank. We were hanging out in the middle of the day when we heard a hard knock on the door. I opened it to find a detective standing there, a white guy, with two other cops just behind him.

"Hey," I said, "what's going on?"

"Are you Brian Banks?"

"I am Brian Banks."

"All right, man, we're having some discrepancies here and I need to talk to you about them."

"Okay," I said. "What's up?"

"Where do you live?"

"I live in Signal Hill."

"Okay. What's the address?"

I gave him the address.

"Okay," he said. "Well, the problem is this: we still have you as being registered here in Burbank."

"Okay, well, I did everything I was supposed to do," I said.

I'd moved a number of times by this point. I knew the routine. I knew I had followed it. "I went over and registered," I said.

"Right, but you're supposed to *un*register; that's part of your parole conditions."

"Unregister? That's the first I've heard of that. I didn't know. My apologies. I didn't know that. What do I need to do?"

"Well, first, we're going to search this house," he said.

That was weird. I would find out later from my friends at California Innocence Project that it was probably illegal. But I didn't think I had a choice. "Okay," I said.

The detective and two officers came into my girl's condo and turned the place upside down. After they finished wrecking the condo, he said, "All right, everything's cool. I'm going to need you to come down to Burbank Police Department so we can get you deregistered. You can follow us."

I apologized to my girlfriend. I told her to just leave it. I'd clean everything up when I got back. I told her I loved her. I hopped into the car. I followed him over to the office. I unregistered as a sex offender in the city of Burbank. I signed the paperwork and he said, "All right, man, don't worry about it. We got it squared away now. You're good to go."

I had never unregistered anywhere else. I had never been told to unregister. It had never been a problem. I thought it was pretty messed-up how they came in and tossed my girlfriend's condo the way they did. It pissed me off. I'd come to accept the fact that the system is messed up. Things happen that shouldn't happen. But that didn't mean the people around me had to experience it. I didn't complain, though. As long as I was out of prison, as long as I was working toward my exoneration, as long as I had less than a year to go before that ankle monitor came off, I was happy. I didn't want to ruffle any feathers. I just wanted to get out of there.

"Okay, thank you," I said. "Happy holidays."

Then one night just before New Year's Eve, I made my way to my girl's house as usual. Workouts had me beat. My body ached. My girl said, "Lay on the floor. Let me walk on your back."

I stretched out on the hardwood floor and she started walking on me. It was better than any sports massage, having her bare feet on my back. We shared our day with each other, laughed, and began planning our New Year's Eve, when all of a sudden there was a hard knock on the door.

Boom, boom, boom!

I opened up the door and was met by two police officers I'd never seen before.

"Are you Brian Banks?"

"Yeah, I'm Brian Banks."

"Hey, would you mind putting some shoes on and stepping outside so we could talk to you?"

"What do y'all want to talk to me about?"

"We'll tell you. Just let's get you outside first, then we'll talk to you about it."

"Okay. Give me a second," I said.

After I closed the main door to go put some clothes on, I walked to the bedroom in silence, my girl following behind me. We didn't say a word; we just looked at each other. We knew something wasn't right. For them to show up at night like this, the day before New Year's Eve. Something was wrong.

Shoes on, I gave my girl a hug and kiss, took a deep breath, and stepped outside. Immediately an officer said, "Why don't you turn around for me and put your hands against the wall?" They began searching me. And then the handcuffs. I looked out as they turned me around and saw there were five police cars in the alley, and six police cars on the other side of the street. They sent the whole force!

"What is going *on*?" I asked.

I pushed the panic down. I tried not to worry that someone had called the cops trying to frame me up for something I didn't do. Again. I tried not to give in to the idea that this had something to do with me having put myself in the same room with my "victim," and that somehow that got back to my parole officer. But all of those thoughts and all of that panic tied my stomach up in a knot.

"The detective needs to talk to you really quickly, so he wanted us to come and get you," the officer said, as if it was no big deal that all those other cops were there.

"Why couldn't he just come up here and talk to me? Why couldn't you just ask me to come in?"

"Well, I don't know, he just asked us to come and get you so he could talk to you and that's all the information I have."

Do not react.

"All right, cool," I said, doing everything I could not to show my fear.

They put me in the car and we got on the freeway—headed away from the precinct.

"Where are we going?"

"We're taking you down to County," he said.

"LA County?"

"No. Glendale," he said.

I'm going back to jail.

This cannot be happening again.

I was used to nightmares by now. They were expected. When you're a number in the system, they can pull up on you anyplace, anytime. All parolees know, "You got no voice. You got no choice." Parole is supposed to be about reform, but it's one of the biggest frauds there is. It's people exerting power and control, and you never know when they're going to come for you. You just try to keep your head down, which I thought I'd done.

I was so sick of the kidnappings.

God, this is not happening.

As it all set in, my mind and heart began to race, and my hands began to sweat.

"I thought you just said he wanted to talk to me?"

"Look, man, I don't have anything to do with this," the officer said. "He wanted us to process you and he's going to come talk to you at some point."

"What are my charges? Why am I going to County? What's going on?"

The officer didn't talk to me after that. Not a word.

When I got to Glendale County Jail, they started processing me like any other inmate, and I kept asking everybody to please look at their paperwork. "Why am I here? What are the charges?"

All anyone said is, "We don't know."

I was stressed and infuriated. I could not *believe* I was back in jail. And my mom? Once they let me make a phone call, she lost it. My girlfriend lost it. We all lost it.

This wasn't right.

They put me in solitary confinement—for four days.

No detective ever came to talk to me.

No one told me what my charges were.

Parole violation?

Made-up charges?

Tormented.

Again.

Caged.

Again.

Imprisoned without being told what my charge was.

Solitary confinement?

How does anyone believe we are "free" in this country? How dare we call this a system of justice!

What a joke.

Left in a cell with nothing but my thoughts. My thoughts. My *thoughts*.

For *four days*.

On the third day I was finally told what put me in jail. The charge:

"Failure to deregister."

Failure to deregister.

A charge based on paperwork? Paperwork that I'd already gone and filled out?

It made no sense.

How did this *help* anyone? How did this *serve* anyone? How did arresting me do anything other than hurt *me*? Is that what this was about? Hurting me? Punishing me more than I'd already been punished?

Who was behind this? Was this just a detective with nothing better to do than harass a parolee who'd managed to stay out of trouble? Or was it something else?

After four days, they dragged me out of the jail, chained me, and placed me in a line of other inmates headed to court. Oddly enough, one of the transporting officers was the detective whom I'd been waiting to speak to, the same one who had asked the officers to arrest me, the very same detective that searched and trashed my girl's place.

"I thought you were going to come talk to me?" I said.

"Yeah, I've just been tied up with stuff."

I've been in solitary for four days, but you were "tied up"?

"What's going on, man? Why is this happening? I took care of everything. You know I took care of everything."

"Yeah, I know you took care of everything. I don't know why they still wanted to detain you," he said.

He said "they," but I didn't know who "they" was.

So I asked: "Who? Who are *they*? Who told you to detain me?"

I got no answer, but he said, "You know, more than likely they're gonna kick you. They're gonna let you go. You're going to appear in front of the judge. The judge is gonna see that you took care of your deregistering paperwork, and they'll kick you."

I didn't reply. All I could do was stare at this man past his eyes and deep into his soul as if trying to truly understand evil.

When I got to the courthouse, California Innocence Project lawyers Mike Semanchik and Raquel Cohen were there. They pulled me into one of the small interview rooms, and I broke down.

"Guys, you got to get me out of here. I'm freaking out. I'm losing it, you know? I can't be in here, I can't. Please, whatever you do, don't leave me in here. Please. Just make sure I get out."

In the courtroom, my case was called to the stand, and the DA went into full-on attack mode. He started in with "I'm pursuing this case, which carries a three-year sentence and a felony strike, doubling the sentencing time to six years"

Six years.

In prison.

For failing to deregister when I registered.

The judge—an older, white judge—listened to the DA, and he listened to my attorneys as they explained that I had registered as ordered under my parole, and that they didn't understand what the problem was since my girlfriend was in Burbank and I spent significant amounts of time at her residence.

As he sat there, listening and looking at the paperwork, the judge did not look happy.

I assumed he was unhappy with *me*.

When he finally spoke, he said, "So, you mean to tell me that Mr. Banks *did* register in Burbank. And that he *did* register in the new city of Signal Hill. So he's doing everything that he's supposed to do, and he's here now because he didn't *un*register in Burbank? So, you are basically saying that he's over-registered? Is that what's going on here? You're telling me that he is over-registered?"

The DA was silent.

"Wouldn't that be a good thing that he's registering at multiple police departments, and we know where he is and he's doing what he's supposed to do?" he said, looking directly at the DA.

"I just don't understand this," the judge said. "This doesn't make sense."

Right! I thought. *This doesn't make any sense!*

I was so grateful that a judge—any judge—finally admitted

that something about my case and the way this whole system was working made no sense.

Mike and Raquel explained to the judge that I was in court for another case, and they shared as much as they could about the status of my appeal, but the DA was relentless. He insisted, "We're going through with this."

Later I would learn the term "malicious hostile prosecution." Looking back, I think that term most definitely applied.

"Well, I guess by law I can't just throw the case out, but I'm going to release him on his own recognizance," the judge said. He looked over at me and asked, "Mr. Banks, do you promise to show up to court on your next court date?"

"Yes, sir," I responded.

"All right. No bail. Released on his own recognizance. This is ridiculous."

They let me out from court right there, but not before setting a court date to come back to face a whole new charge, and a whole new felony strike, with the possibility of facing another six years in prison.

Six years.

I'd already learned the hard way that anyone who thinks that can't happen is wrong. No matter how ridiculous a charge seems, no matter how much proof of innocence there is—whatever it is—in this so-called justice system, the worst-case scenario happens. It happens all the time.

Just because I didn't do anything wrong didn't mean I wouldn't pay for it.

I knew that.

I left that courtroom relieved, but terrified.

I prayed to make it all go away.

The judge set the court date for my "failure to deregister" case: May 25, 2012.

That was one day after the hearing date that the appellate court finally set for the California Innocence Project's case seeking my exoneration.

That meant I began 2012 not with a party or some hopeful new rear's resolution. I began 2012 with the soul-crushing realization that in less than five months I might gain my freedom— my *real* freedom, my exoneration, the clearing of my name—or I might be thrown back into prison one day later. For six more years of my life.

TWENTY

The Day

I kept training, every day, trying to keep my mind focused on the future. Trying to believe that the "failure to deregister" case would simply disappear once I was exonerated. But the California Innocence Project reminded me my exoneration wasn't a sure thing. There were many reasons we could lose this appeal. The justice system doesn't like to admit that it makes mistakes. The system isn't designed to backtrack. The district attorney's office had too much to lose if the public decided they put too many innocent people behind bars. The whole system would fall apart if people lost faith in it, right? So the pressure was on us. The only way to make sure my case was heard properly was to get the DA's office on board before we ever set foot in a courtroom.

I had no idea how to do that.

A few weeks later I got a call from Justin. He had a plan.

"Hey, Banks. Are you able to get up here to LA Court? The lead DA, Brent Ferreira, is here sitting in another case that we're fighting. If you can put some nice clothes on and get up here as soon as possible that would be great! I'm going to try to get you in the room with this guy," he said.

I got dressed and got there just in time to listen to the judge rule in a hearing that was taking place for another California Innocence Project case. I was sitting in the back of the courtroom in the audience box, watching another guy fight for his innocence. I could see his face. A hopeless man, hoping. He would drop his head and pray, moving uncomfortably in his chains. He watched as the lawyers went back and forth and then listened to the judge rule.

They lost.

The guy was to remain behind bars.

I could see the anguish on his face. The courtroom fell silent. No one seemed happy. The lawyers were really let down.

I couldn't help but think, *What if that happens to me?*

We were filing out of the courtroom when Justin reached over to me and said, "Hey, the lead DA said he's got ten minutes. Let's go."

I followed Justin, District Attorney Ferreira, and his lead detective out of the courtroom and into a small interview room just off to the left. They asked me to tell my story, from beginning to the end. They asked question after question. I answered him. Justin explained what the California Innocence Project was working on and what they'd been trying to do. And by the end of that conversation, the DA's office agreed to pursue a joint investigation of the case.

It was crazy. We had the lead DA's attention, and he'd agreed to investigate with us!

"They never do this," Justin told me on the way out of the courthouse. "Never."

The DA almost never meets in person with someone fighting for their freedom, because that person is usually in prison. I was in a unique position because I was out, and the DA was nice enough to sit with me, all due to the solid reputation of Justin and the California Innocence Project.

Just a few days after that meeting, the lead detective for the DA called Tiana Miller. Tiana responded, "Fuck you. Catch me if you can. I'm not coming to court. You all can kiss my ass. I'm done with this shit. I'm not coming back to court!"

She hung up. Then she disappeared. The detective sent officers out to look for her, but she was nowhere to be found. The DA's office couldn't find her. Their detectives couldn't find her. We couldn't find her.

I thought her foul mouth and disappearing act might help our case. I thought her actions would make it clear to the DA that this girl was hiding something and had no respect for law enforcement. But I was wrong.

Her disappearance was actually going to make our case more difficult, Justin explained.

The DA wanted to get her confession themselves. They needed to hear it from her.

Without that, there was now a chance that the DA would simply drop the investigation, and worse, that they would have no choice but to *fight* us in court—in which case, Justin said, we might well lose.

"What can we do? How can we fight this? We can't get this close and then lose," I said.

Justin explained that one option was to take the recantation video to the media—to go public with her confession. But he was also apprehensive.

Going public meant risking my freedom. If and when someone from the parole office saw this video, they'd see me sitting right next to her. A serious violation of parole. Coming in contact with the victim would mean an automatic two-year prison sentence.

Was it worth the risk?

I had a really tough decision to make.

Do I risk my freedom by going public about this? I didn't even have a year left on my parole. *Do I risk two years in prison and fighting my case from behind bars?* My parole was set to end August 29. But if we went public it could create pressure to draw out Tiana and her mom, and it could also put pressure on the DA's office to do the right thing.

I prayed hard. I had done so much these years to make sure I would never go back to prison. Ever. What if I made the wrong decision, which meant I was choosing that very thing?

I sat still, and contemplated.

I closed my eyes and focused on my breathing. I let the stress of it all fade away. And I listened.

What became clear was that in order for me to move forward, I might first need to be pulled back. I had to face my fear of going back to prison head-on. I never wanted to go back to that place, behind those walls. But I knew that in order for me to secure my freedom, for me to bring truth to a story full of lies, I would have to take the chance.

This woman had recanted. It was no accident. I had the video. The lawyers were fighting my case. This was God clearly saying "enough." This was God saying "Get up!" This was God saying "Now, now is the time. You're ready."

I called Justin: "Let's do it."

"Okay," he said. "I'll make the call."

From that moment on, I started mentally preparing myself

to fight the rest of the case from behind bars. I had a feeling in my heart, based on all that I had been through, that as soon as the video aired I was going straight back to prison. Back to a cage.

Justin reached out to Randy Paige, a reporter with CBS Los Angeles. He shared my story with him, as well as the video of Tiana recanting.

"I can make something out of this and really bring attention to it," he said.

Randy started putting a news segment together, and to give the piece some weight, in order to move beyond just the opinion of the CIP and myself, he found a former lead district attorney, played the recantation video for him, and got the former DA on the record saying, "I would have never pursued this case. I would have never tried him as an adult. And this case should be thrown out right now."

That blew me away. This man was the highest-ranking official to ever take a look at my case, and he said it shouldn't have been pursued. The validation of that. The resonance of that in my heart—it shook me.

I hoped and prayed that it would shake others, too.

On the news one night, a preview of the story aired. My phone lit up with texts and calls from friends and family. I started promoting it online to get people to tune in. More and more people reached out. It seemed like the whole city of Long Beach and maybe all of Southern California was planning to tune in.

After it aired, my phone blew up again. All of my social media, too. People I hadn't heard from in years were like, "I knew it, I knew it, I knew it! Bro, I knew it!"

The thing is, most people didn't know any details about my case. They just knew I got taken off the streets. But Randy Paige's news report was wrapped tight, and the public response was huge. The newspapers picked it up the next day. All sorts of other reporters called the California Innocence Project looking to get details and interviews. We didn't want any more publicity, though. What we hoped was that the district attorney's office would take it seriously, with or without getting Tiana on the record or into the courtroom. The public pressure was on now—and one of their own, the former lead DA, had said, "You should throw this out right now."

For one night, I felt redeemed. I cannot explain the feeling of validation that came from having so many people finally hear the truth and believe after ten long years when it seemed like no one would listen. It was crazy—until, just as I expected, the following morning, my old hard-ass parole officer called.

He was in charge of overseeing registered sex offenders for all of Los Angeles County now.

"Get to my office, ASAP," he said. He hung up the phone without another word.

This was it.

I called Justin.

"He called me. They want me to come in. I think I'm going to County," I told him.

"All right, we're going to call them. We're going to start talking to them and see what we can do right away," Justin told me reassuringly, but I'd been here too many times before. I knew the drill. I went to that office arrest-ready. I wore shitty clothes. I was ready.

I walked into the nondescript office building where the Compton parole office was located thinking, *This is it.*

I walked in confidently knowing my truth, knowing that all of Long Beach knew my truth, but also knowing better than anyone that the truth had never mattered to the system before. So why should it matter now?

I saw a couple of cops walking into the parole office just before I did. I wondered if they were headed to the second floor to get me, but they turned into another office. I entered the waiting room and checked in. They didn't call me for a while so I just sat there. Waiting. Waiting and thinking, *This is it.*

I sat there in a daze. All of it, from day one, kept replaying in my head. I prayed silently to God. Pleading. Praying for anything, for any *way*, to make this stop. To not be sent back to prison. Praying that the video reached the right people. Praying that the lawyers would be able to do something to make this stop before they locked me up. Praying for God to take care of my mom. Praying that the DA found Tiana and that the case would move forward quickly. Praying to God to just help me stay calm.

Finally the parole officer called me back to his office. Right away he went off on a tirade.

"You know it's against your parole conditions to do this and you went and did it anyway. We can lock your ass up right *now* for this!"

All I could do was shake my head, looking down at the scuffed-up floor, sitting there thinking, *Here we go. This is it. I've already prepared for this. I already understand all of this.*

But then, he changed his beat.

"You know, if it wasn't for the supervisors seeing that news report last night, you'd be in jail right now. But they did see it. And I saw it. So this is what we're going to do: we're going to modify your parole conditions to say that you're not allowed to come in any contact with that girl—at all—unless it revolves around the court proceedings."

I felt my breath get punched back into my chest. I looked up with disbelief in my eyes. I might have even smiled involuntarily. Because I just plain couldn't believe it.

"Thank you," I said.

Thank you, God.

Right there, before I left, they modified my parole conditions. Something they *never do*. I signed and headed home.

They showed me love for the first time in ten years.

I found out later that Justin went to bat for me. Even as I was traveling down there and sitting in that waiting room, fully prepared to go to jail, he was on the phone with the DA and the parole officer.

"I'm his lawyer and I'm telling you he's innocent," Justin told them. "And I've got the evidence to prove it."

And it worked.

I walked out of there feeling like I could breathe again. The fresh air was beautiful.

The day was beautiful.

Next stop? The big day. My hearing at the appellate court.

The night before the hearing I stayed at my girlfriend's in Burbank. I barely slept.

When I woke up that morning, I put on some ambient space music and started getting dressed. I plugged the GPS into the wall to charge it, hopefully for the last time, but I was running late. We hopped into the car and drove to a friend's house, where I plugged it back in to finish charging it. We sat there for a bit, and we watched the news that morning.

"Brian Banks will be in court today to face the same judge he faced ten years ago, now asking to reverse his conviction. We'll be here live for it."

The story was all over the news.

The GPS light turned green.

"All right, let's go!"

We piled into the car and headed to the Long Beach courthouse. As we made our way, I looked out of the window and across the big blue sky thinking this could be the day where everything changes. *Everything.* On *this day.* I'd seen days that mattered before. I had days that changed my life forever. But mostly I had years and years of my life to think about and to hope for *this day.*

This day.

The day I might get my life back.

There were so many people there to support me. We all met outside the courthouse and then walked inside together. Courtroom workers, reporters, bailiffs, everyone was getting ready. Cameramen stood and sat in the jury box to the left—part of the courtroom that had always been empty through ten years of hearings.

I hugged and kissed my mother, then made my way to the defendant's table. And in my head the room just went silent. It felt like I was in that courtroom all by myself.

Images began to play before me. Every single thing that I had gone through in ten long years came flooding back in my mind. The arrest. Juvenile Hall. The prisons. My lawyer talking me into taking that plea. Institutionalization. Programming. Violence. Sentencing. Years lost. Getting out. Dreams crushed. The ankle bracelet. Being labeled a monster. The poverty. The Facebook friend request. The recantation. All of it. Ten years.

There was motion in the courtroom. A bailiff came out and whispered something to another bailiff. It was almost time. My heart started pounding. My leg began tapping a nervous tap. My hands followed suit. I was just tapping on the table.

Judge Mark Kim entered the courtroom, the very same judge who sentenced me to six years in prison.

Here we go.

My head was down. I couldn't really bring myself to look up.

"All right," the judge said. "So what's going on here? I really don't understand what's happening here today. Could somebody explain it to me? The girl didn't show up, correct?"

"Right, your honor," the district attorney said.

"So what's happening? What are we doing?"

"Judge, can we have a quick conversation at the bench?" he asked.

The lead DA, Brent Ferreira, along with assistant district attorney Ann Park, and Justin Brooks and Alissa Bjerkhoel from the California Innocence Project all approached the judge's bench. I just sat there, head down, praying. I didn't want to try to read their expressions or read their lips. I didn't want to get any kind of false hope. I just kept praying, *Please don't put this off. Please don't throw this out. Please let this end. Please free me. Please release me. This day. This day right now. Please, God. It has to be today. It has to be today. It's got to be today.*

Every second felt like forever. And then all of a sudden they turned around and came back to the tables, and Justin gave me a little nod.

I wanted to feel good about that.

I couldn't.

I knew: *It's not over till it's over.*

"Okay," the judge said, "it's my understanding that we are dealing with a writ of habeas corpus. What do you want to do?"

The lead DA, Brent Ferreira, stood up.

"The court wishes to concede in the matter of this case," he said, "and furthering penal code section . . ."

I didn't hear any words after the word *concede*.

My head hung even lower as it rocked in a nodding motion. The word *concede* rang in my ears like an explosion.

To "concede" in this case meant the DA wasn't going to fight our appeal.

To "concede" meant the district attorney's office agreed that everything we presented in our appeal was *true*.

The room felt even quieter as I waited on every word said in that moment.

I began involuntarily rocking back and forth in my chair.

"All right," the judge said. "Petition is granted. Motion."

He offered no apology.

No "I'm sorry for what you've been through."

No commentary at all.

Just "All right." His gavel never hit the mahogany; it was just over.

It was *over*.

I dropped my head into my arms on the table with my eyes as wide as they could be. As my heart raced and tears fell from my face, a surge of energy pulsated through my body. So much energy that my hands clenched into fists and every muscle in my body tightened to its max. I was more alive in that moment than I had ever been. But I was left with the bitter taste of "why?" Why it had to happen in the first place, why I had to struggle so long and hard for it to end so quick and easily. I started crying.

Thank you, God!

I had no control. I just cried.

Ten years.

I tried to get up but I couldn't move. I just kept crying. Justin and Alissa tried their best to console me. Eventually Justin leaned in and said, "You gotta get up, you gotta get up. We're done. Come on, buddy, let's get out of here."

All right, I thought. But I couldn't move. I wasn't ready.

I'm being restored.

I closed my eyes.

Get up, Brian. You've been released.

I hit the table with a closed fist. I stood up, and I felt *strong*. I felt renewed. I was free.

I hugged Alissa and Justin, and then turned around and went straight for Mom. She was crying hard. I hugged her and it felt like we hugged forever. We just hugged, and hugged, and hugged.

Ten years.

And then everybody, one by one, started to come up to me.

I embraced everyone. Everyone was hugging me. Justin and Alissa handed me a black Innocence Project sweatshirt that said INNOCENT in bold white letters. I pulled it over my shirt and tie. We all filed out of the courtroom together in celebration.

As we walked down the hallway, exiting the building, people who didn't even know us came up and said, "Congrats, man. Congrats!" They had heard the news. There were people everywhere all around us.

"Congrats, man. Congrats. It looks like everything went right!"

People started getting up and following us out of the courthouse. It was surreal. The crowd grew bigger and bigger. And all I kept thinking, all I kept praying, all I kept feeling with every cell in my body and with every step I took was, *Thank you, God. Thank you, God. Thank you, God!*

TWENTY-ONE

Back in the Game

As we exited the courthouse, the media was already set up outside. There were cameras from every local news station.

Lead district attorney Brent Ferreira and assistant DA Ann Park addressed the media first: "We feel like the right thing was done here. This man is innocent."

I stood tall and with confidence hearing those words come from them both. This was validation. "Innocent." And to know the world was watching and hearing it, too.

"He should have never been in jail," he said, "and we feel like we're on the right side of the law today."

It was my turn to speak. It had been ten years of people speaking to me, people speaking at me, people speaking for me. I stepped to the podium, and for the first time since the beginning, I spoke for me. And everyone listened. I looked both Brent and Ann in the eyes and thanked them.

"Thank you for doing the right thing. Thank you for being the right kind of DAs that we need."

It was important for me to thank them, for me to say that. For all district attorneys to hear.

Not only had I been released, but I was now free to speak my truth.

I shared some of my story with the media. What I'd lost. What I'd learned. How I prayed that my case would shine a light on the failures of our justice system, and that maybe it would inspire more people to take a look at cases the California Innocence Project was dealing with, of innocent people who'd been wrongly convicted and locked up, just like me.

And then came a question I had been waiting for. A question I had prepared for.

"So," the reporter said, "what's next?"

I leaned closer to the microphones placed around the podium, my eyes never leaving the crowd.

"I want to play football," I said. "I want to try out for the NFL."

I could tell none of the reporters really took me seriously.

Justin interjected: "This young man has been through so much. And he's been working out for an opportunity at the NFL. This guy deserves an opportunity."

Justin was a believer in me just as I believed in him. He'd seen the workouts, the sacrifices and commitment I put into training. "If there's any team out there that's willing to give me a shot, I guarantee you I will outwork anybody on your team," I said. "Call me."

The press stuck around. They all wanted to get their own individual interviews, so we did some one-on-one questions-and-answers and interviews with newspaper reporters. The Associated Press dropped a story online right away. A national story! It went everywhere. People were driving by, leaning out their windows, yelling, "Brian Banks!"

While we were still celebrating and doing interviews in front of the courthouse, more family and friends pulled up out of nowhere. My extended family started calling from Chicago.

We stayed there for almost two hours before breaking away to go back to a friend's house to celebrate. I still had more interviews to do as reporters showed up there. I'd finish one, then Justin would walk over to me with another reporter on the phone from some outlet on the other side of the country.

I thanked them all for sharing my story.

I thanked everybody.

I thanked my mom.

I thanked God.

The press wanted to know if I was bitter, if I was angry, if I wanted to see my accuser get punished.

I said "no" to all of it. I told them again and again, "That's not my concern right now. My focus is on my future. I've come out of this a more patient person, a stronger person, and I just want to move on with my life from here," I said.

Despite all this celebrating, I wasn't completely free. I still had the ankle monitor on. Although my conviction had been overturned, I was still a product of the system as a parolee. News of my exoneration hadn't made it up the entire chain of command. So until I was processed out of the system, the monitor remained on my leg.

I could have gotten mad at that. The court admitted that I was innocent. I never should have been locked up in the first place. I never should have been registering as a sex offender and wearing that GPS monitor to begin with. Yet the bracelet remained, since I could have faced more time if I removed it—on top of the time that I was still potentially facing when I went back to court in two days.

In my mind, that's criminal. It's unconstitutional. It's immoral.

But that's our system of justice.

That night, I just laughed it off.

"Yeah," I said when Justin told me to be patient. "I had this thing on for five years, so a few more minutes is nothing for me."

I didn't want to think about anything negative.

Not on this day.

This day was mine.

I spent the rest of that day and right on into the night doing interviews, speaking to every outlet I could to share my story far and wide, as long as the press would allow—all in the hopes that maybe it would do some good, for somebody, anybody who might be going through something like I'd been through. And it wasn't until after the last interview, a segment we taped at a television studio for *Good Day L.A.*, set to air the next morning, that my parole office finally called Justin and gave us the good news.

"You're good to go. It's over, BB. You can cut that ankle bracelet off," Justin said.

Somebody ran back in and grabbed us some scissors. "Cut it off!" Justin yelled as the cameras watched. I cut it off right there in the parking lot of *Good Day L.A.* After five years of wearing that monitor, it finally came off.

And we *celebrated*.

I looked up into the night sky, breathing big sighs of relief, before I called up my mom to share the good news.

It was all so surreal.

We thought we were all done when another news crew

caught us in the parking lot. The reporter had a football with her.

"So, are you going to play football now?" she asked.

I guess the word got out.

We stayed out there in the parking lot for a while, playing catch, throwing the football around. I threw it to Justin. We threw it to the reporter. We were all just making noise and having a good time in the parking lot like a bunch of kids without a care in the world.

Shortly after, we hopped in a car and made our way down to San Diego, where the California Innocence Project set me up with a hotel room for the next day full of interviews. It was a really nice hotel. I had never stayed in a hotel this nice before. I arrived to champagne bottles, a congratulatory gift basket, and more CIP attire. Blue shirts with California license plates that spell out "XONR8." My girlfriend and I jumped from bed to bed like kids, playing music, taking it all in.

The next morning I woke up early and we went through the press all day, connecting remotely with stations all over the country, including CNN in the morning and again in the evening, with dozens of other outlets in between.

No one coached me. No one prepared me. I just spoke from the heart, every time.

The thought that potentially millions of people were hearing my story, experiencing my truth, getting a look inside the justice system gone wrong—it felt like a breakthrough. Like I was standing on a mountaintop delivering a message that needed to be heard.

And when we finally wrapped, my phone rang.

"Hello?"

"Hi," a male voice on the other end of the line said. "I'm looking for a linebacker. Do you know where I can find one?"

I looked at the number. It was a 213 area code. I didn't recognize it.

"Yeah, you got the right number. Who is this?"

"It's me, man. Coach Carroll!"

My heart skipped.

"Hey, Coach. What's up? What's up, man?"

Pete Carroll wasn't coaching at USC anymore. While I'd been locked up and tethered down, he'd made his way back to the NFL. He'd coached the New England Patriots. He was now head coach for the Seattle Seahawks.

"It's so good to hear from you, my friend," he said. "I'm so happy you're free, and you're home, and everything's okay. I heard you've been working out."

I guess he saw some of the press I'd been doing.

"Yes, sir, I *have* been working out. Hoping to get an opportunity."

"Well, I'd love for you to come out here and try out for the team, if you want to."

I was stunned.

"I would absolutely love to," I said. "I would absolutely *love* to!"

He asked me if I was in shape, and with a big smile on my face, I could honestly say, "Yeah."

All that time I'd spent in the gym. All those workouts.

I didn't have a guarantee that any team *anywhere* would give me a shot, let alone the Seahawks. But I'd done the work anyway. I knew what I wanted, and what was required of me to be prepared for such an opportunity. I chose to do the work.

I just hoped I'd get to follow through on this opportunity.

The very next day I stepped back into a courtroom with my CIP attorneys to face the possibility that I'd be sent back to prison for another six years.

What a joke, I thought.

I was somehow peaceful about it. Somehow prepared. Knowing I'd been exonerated, knowing that I'd come through it all and made it out alive and cleared my name, I felt like I could make it through anything.

But, man—I really, *really* hoped this was going to go in my favor.

How could it not? I thought. *I've just been exonerated!*

I walked in feeling pumped up and ready. I'd faced enough wrong in my life. It was time for things to keep going *right*.

But after the bailiff said, "All rise," just seconds after that same judge sat down and said, "Be seated," the district attorney started up ready to put me away: "Your honor, we're prepared to move forward with this case. As a reminder, Brian Banks failed to deregister in the city of Burbank on—"

"Sir," the judge said, interrupting him, "where have you been for the last forty-eight hours?"

"Excuse me?" the DA said.

"This man has been all over the news in the last forty-eight hours. He was *exonerated*," the judge said. "What are we doing here?"

The DA looked flummoxed.

"I wasn't aware of that," he said. "I've been on vacation. Can I have a second? Let me step into the hallway and make a phone call."

"Yeah," the judge said. "Sure. Go ahead."

We waited while he stepped out, and I kept thinking, *What if we got a different judge today? One who didn't watch TV? What kind of a battle might this have been? Would I really be on my way to trial and possibly prison, and fighting this from behind bars? Again?*

Five minutes later, the DA walked back in, but before heading to his table he came to me in the audience box and said, "Mr. Banks, I just want to let you know, we're gonna handle this. I want to apologize to you. I'm so sorry. We're going to take care of this right now."

I didn't respond. I just shook my head at the ridiculousness of it all—and thanked God that the media had done its job when clearly nobody else had bothered to do theirs.

The DA went up in front of the judge and apologized. "We just missed this," he said.

The judge gave him a little piece of his mind and warned him not to waste the court's time in the future.

"Case dismissed," he said.

The gavel came down.

It was over.

And for the first time in five years, the threat of returning to prison—the constant threat that hung over my head, ready to drop with no notice and crush me without any warning—was gone. Just like that. *Gone.*

◆ ◆ ◆

Life kicked into overdrive in the next couple of days. First of all, Jay Leno called and invited me to come on *The Tonight*

Show to talk about my wrongful conviction. He'd seen me on the news and said he was moved by my story.

"Can I bring my mom?" I asked.

"Bring whoever you want! Whoever stood by you. I wanna meet 'em all. We'll bring everyone backstage after the show," he said.

I took him up on his offer. I brought my mom, and my dad, and all my lawyers and even the students who worked on my case from the California Innocence Project, and some other friends and family, too.

Jay talked to me for about ten minutes before we taped the show, and he told me he'd never had someone like me come on and talk about such a serious subject before then. It was normally actors, politicians, and comedians, but he really thought I had something important to talk about, and he appreciated how positive I was after going through all of that. He wanted America to hear what I had to say.

Sitting on that couch next to Julia Louis-Dreyfus, next to the desk on *The Tonight Show,* was crazy. It was incredible. And then afterward, he did what he said he would. There must have been twenty-five people stuffed into the greenroom backstage after the show when he came in. He brought my mom a huge bouquet of beautiful roses, gave me a powerful hug, and then posed for pictures with everybody. I never expected anything like that to happen to me in my life. And for it to happen because he was impressed with how "positive" I was after my experience—that really meant something.

The Tonight Show taped in Burbank, California, and once it was over, once I said good-bye to everyone, I went straight to the Burbank airport to board a flight up to Seattle for my tryout with Coach Carroll and the Seahawks.

I hadn't been on a plane since I was a little kid. I was nervous and excited about that, but mostly I was surprised by how grumpy everybody was at the airport. All around me were people angry and in a rush. It was funny to me. I was *happy* to take my shoes off for the Transportation Security Administration. This was nothing compared to getting processed in prison. I was happy just to be alive! To be free. And I was heading to an opportunity to be considered to play in the NFL. I enjoyed every single moment of that first flight. Justin helped orchestrate it and traveled with me to my tryout. He said, "You seem more excited to be going on a plane than you were to be on *The Tonight Show*!"

I arrived in Seattle a few hours later to the full-blown red-carpet treatment. A fancy car. Another beautiful hotel. They embraced me and treated me like family.

The morning before the tryout, they brought me in for a physical at the hospital, followed by a big breakfast at the training facility, followed by some free time sitting in a room where I could mentally prepare and get ready. I'd been training and working out for this opportunity for months at this point, so I *felt* ready—and I did great.

I performed so well that day, the team invited me back to minicamp, or what are called OTAs (organized team activities), which is like an unofficial training camp before training camp starts. I took part in all three days, training hard, working alongside some of the brightest players and coaches in the whole league—before they gave me the word that I wasn't going to make the team.

Coach Carroll brought me into his office, and he was honest with me. "You know what, Brian? To be honest, man, you're moving good, you look good. I just think that mentally, you've been away from the game so long, it's a lot to learn. I'm not really sure if this is for you. I know what you're trying to do. I can see how important this is to you. But you gotta understand, these other guys haven't missed a beat."

I was ten years behind. Ten *years*.

I got it. I respected everything he had to say. I was like, "Yeah, that makes sense. That makes sense."

It was a tough pill to swallow leaving the facility that day. I had worked so hard, put in so much work, been on such a positive wave, and then a riff. I was down for a couple of days. It hurt. I'd been riding so high since the day of my exoneration, it was a little like, "Damn, I really thought that they'd just bring me on and make this thing happen."

I called my sports agent to talk about it— Oh yeah! I had acquired an agent soon after my exoneration, too. Bruce Tollner with Rep One Sports in Irvine, one of the top agencies in the business. A good-spirited, religious man who'd seen my story on the news, Bruce tracked me down and offered his services, saying, "I want to represent you. Free of charge. I don't need anything from you. I just want to make sure you've got the right people behind you and are taken care of."

When the Seahawks didn't pick me up, I confided in Bruce, "Man, I don't know. Maybe I'm trying to do something that can't be done. I've been out of the game for a long time. Maybe it's over."

"I understand how you feel," he said. "But you know what? Just sleep on it. We'll talk tomorrow, and you can tell me what you want to do, and if you want to line up some more of these workouts, we can."

Before I had even made up my mind, Bruce called me the next day to let me know that another team had called. And then another. Then two more!

I said yes to all of them.

Within days I was training with Jay Glazer, an NFL sports insider and celebrity mixed martial arts trainer, and Travelle Gaines, a trainer to NBA and NFL stars and more, in the heart of Hollywood, where they trained some of the best NFL athletes (and the occasional celebrity). I was welcomed into a brotherhood of players during the off-season.

Between Jay Glazer's MMA program and Travelle's field conditioning and weight lifting, I was training three times a day. Jay was a huge motivator. He told me all the time that he was going to help me get my dreams back. "Just you wait," he said. "It's gonna happen!"

It was definitely a challenge at times. Most of the athletes I was training with were younger than me. At twenty-two, twenty-three, twenty-five, they were veterans of the game. And here I was, at twenty-seven, just getting started. I was the rookie. The new one. But my drive and determination helped make up for that. I began pushing and challenging the guys around me. Outworking some, while chasing after others. And along the way, friendships were formed.

We pushed each other.

Seven NFL teams offered me a tryout, all back to back. I went and tried out with Kansas City. I went to San Francisco for the 49ers, and they invited me back to their minicamp. I did their minicamp for three days, but they didn't sign me. KC didn't sign me, either. I went and tried out for the Philadelphia Eagles. I went back to San Diego and tried out for the Chargers. Minnesota. And last, I tried out for the Atlanta Falcons.

I learned something at every one of those camps. I paid attention to everything I did wrong and tried to correct course as quickly as I could. By the time I got to Atlanta, I had the best of all the tryouts I'd had. I knew it was my last shot. I told myself, *I'm gonna die on this field. I'm gonna give everything I've got! Whatever it takes! They're gonna know me after this.*

And sure enough, the Falcons coaches agreed. "Wow, we're impressed!"

There was just one problem: by that time, the regular season was only two weeks away.

"Unfortunately, it's just too close to the season for you to get up to speed," they told me. "And to be honest, we really don't want all of the media attention as we enter into the season."

As always, I kept a straight face.

"We want to sign ya, it just can't happen now, Banks. So let's reconvene. In the meantime, look into the CFL or UFL. Could be an opportunity to get some experience. Get you some reps, and on tape."

As the preseason approached and training camps began, the gym became silent as everyone made their way back to work, back to their respective teams.

I started to wonder if my football dreams were over, even though they never really got started.

At the last minute, I decided I'd take the advice from the Falcons and pursue the UFL.

The United Football League was a start-up independent

league that the founders hoped would turn out to be for football what minor-league baseball was to the major leagues.

I went and tried out for the Las Vegas Locomotives, and I *made it*. But the league was short-lived. The whole operation folded after four games. I never even got paid, and the owner of the league filed for bankruptcy.

Dreams don't come easy.

I'd overcome worse obstacles.

And I had learned patience in prison.

I left Las Vegas and headed back to California. No longer living in Signal Hill, and recently single, I made my way down to San Diego. Justin Brooks was kind enough to put me up at his house while I got back on my feet, and San Diego was the perfect place to do that.

I was amazed at how far my story had traveled. How many people knew about it. The fact that so many people were moved and affected by it. As I chased after my dreams, interview and public speaking requests continued to pour in, including a request to fly to New York City to appear on *The View*.

Justin would join me onstage, and my mother was in the audience. It was incredible. I had heard people refer to New York as the "greatest city in the world," but I never understood what that meant until I saw it in person. The subway and traffic, the skyscrapers, the sightseeing, and all of the things to see and do in the city. We walked all over Manhattan, just feeding off the energy and the scenery and the people.

We were standing in the crossroads of the world, in Times Square, when my phone rang. It was Jay Glazer.

"Hey, buddy! You remember I told you I was gonna help you to get your dreams back and one day it'll happen?" he said.

"Yeah."

"Well, congratulations. The Atlanta Falcons want to sign you!"

"You've got to be kidding me," I said.

"I am not playing. I just hung up with the GM, and they want to sign you. They want you to fly out there *right now*. All you need to do is pass a physical and you're signing!"

I started screaming right in the middle of Times Square. I thanked Jay for all of his help, for believing in me, and for going to bat for me. I hung up the phone and shared the news with my mom and Justin. For ten minutes we cheered and celebrated, then my phone rang again. It was the Falcons! They had called to deliver the good news, and to rebook my travel arrangements. Instead of heading home from New York in two more days, I was off that day to Atlanta. My mother made her way back home to Long Beach, and Justin back to San Diego.

It was déjà vu all over again. I went to my physical in the morning, was put through a small workout, then later was asked to wait in the team's clubhouse for word of my fate.

I sat there, watching ESPN on a big screen, when suddenly I received a text, then another, then seven more. My phone was ringing off the hook! But before I could unlock my phone to read the messages, it happened. It was like looking in a mirror. There, on the TV screen, was a picture of me and a caption that read "Brian Banks signs with the Falcons." The word was out before I even signed on the dotted line. This was real. It was happening.

"You ready?" a voice from behind me called out.

An assistant was sent down to escort me to Head Coach

Mike Smith's office. I stood up, adjusted my clothing, and replied, "I've been ready."

I didn't quit. I never gave in, nor gave up. And now I was here.

The assistant led me upstairs to the main office. I met with Coach Smith and Falcons general manager Thomas Dimitroff. From there I was went to a meeting room next door to officially sign on.

My agent was on the phone. He'd already gone over everything. We were good to go. I signed my contract. My NFL contract! I was officially a part of the Atlanta Falcons.

They gave me my number: 53.

My number. A jersey number, not a prison number.

Falcons staff took me on a tour of the entire facility while the messages and congratulatory emails silently piled up by the hundreds in my pocket.

I was brought into the locker room, where they fit me for my gear. Then they took me to my locker, which already had my name on it, up high with the rest: "Brian Banks 53."

I felt welcomed in, and I was honored.

I flew home feeling like I had a brand-new home waiting for me in Atlanta.

I would spend that spring and early summer training my ass off in preparation for summer training camp.

The thing is, signing with an NFL team isn't the same for all players. And it is definitely not always how you see it play out in the movies.. It didn't make me a millionaire. It's not like winning the lottery. My contract was a basic contract, which would pay me good money if I played in the regular season. But that was a long ways off. I would receive only a minimum salary during training camp later that summer. And at this point, I was still transitioning back into society's norms. There was a lot of fallout that I still had to deal with, and that fallout seemed to rear its head every day.

Amazingly, my first day of official training camp fell on my twenty-eighth birthday, July 24, 2013.

I'd spent my eighteenth birthday in prison. Now here I was, ten years later, starting training camp with the Atlanta Falcons.

In life, you never know where the waves will take you.

I thank God for helping me navigate the waters and giving me the strength to stay afloat all these years.

● ◆ ●

On August 8, 2013, I made my NFL debut in a preseason game against the Cincinnati Bengals.

I got a nice, fresh haircut that morning. I wore black dress pants, with a black buttoned-down long-sleeve shirt. Dress shoes, too. It wasn't flashy, but it was the best I had.

That afternoon, we all piled into buses and made our way to the stadium. The first game was a home game. It was pretty ironic—and pretty cool—that we were driving from the facility to the stadium under full police escort. I was still putting my life back together in ways that no one else on the team could even begin to understand.

The locker room was like any other on game day. Lots of energy, tons of excitement. But this time I was among superstars, lifelong athletes, players I grew up watching. Some were wearing headphones, hyping or relaxing themselves to their choice of music. Others listened to music from boom boxes that played in different sections of the locker room. High-fiving, dancing, studying the playbook just once more. And every few minutes, one player or another would come up to me and say, "Hey, man, proud of you, bro." "It's your day today, Banks!" "Hey, man, God bless you, bro." "I just wanna tell you, man, I'm inspired."

One by one, those players were coming up to *me*. I'm talking Matt Ryan, Tony Gonzalez, Julio Jones, some of the greatest players in the NFL.

As with tradition, those who wanted to take part in team prayer would gather together before taking the field. The room grew silent as we came together, some taking a knee, all of us hand in hand. The team's chaplain shared a few words before unexpectedly offering the floor to me.

I was honored.

I don't remember exactly what I said, but it was something along the lines of "Now is your time. Seize the opportunity. This is an opportunity few will get. So, be in the moment. Cherish today. I missed this opportunity the first time around. Had it taken away. I'm only getting a glimpse of what things should have been. You guys have an opportunity to make a career out of this, to feed your families playing the sport you love. Let nothing stand between you and your destiny, not only on the field, but in *life*."

I could see that a couple of guys were emotionally affected by my words. I know I was. I realized what an incredible moment this was, and I wanted them to feel it, too.

After my speech, we all took a knee and I prayed over the team, asking God to protect them, to give them strength, and to give us a good game. We filed out of the locker room and piled into the tunnel. I heard a few players say, "B! Lead us out!

I said, "No." I didn't want to lead the team out. "Nah, fellas. It's all good," I said.

This wasn't about taking the spotlight. I wasn't here to lead. I worked my way into the middle of the players. I wanted to be a *part* of the team. One of the few.

Part of me knew I wasn't here to stay. I hoped I'd stay. I'd worked my butt off. But these guy were ten years ahead of me. No matter how hard I tried, those ten years missed, ten years of struggle, had taken their toll.

I was okay with that. I had to be. I pushed myself to the absolute max. I did all that was required of me. I did the impossible. I beat the odds.

I flashed back for a moment to everything I'd learned in prison, going all the way back to Mr. Johnson's first teachings. *Who am I?* I was more than my circumstances. I was more than a football player. I was more than a part of a game. More than a player on somebody else's field.

When I was still, right there, observing all of my surroundings with minutes to go, I finally understood that my future would surpass all of this, that this was only part of the dream. That there was something more important in store for me. I just didn't know what it was yet.

For now, being present and in this moment was all that mattered. It was all that existed.

And then the time came. I was just seconds away from taking the field with the Atlanta Falcons in an NFL game.

We started rocking. Music boomed through the stadium and echoed down the tunnel, and we rocked back and forth, the energy magnified with each beat.

"B, let's go, baby!"

"Much respect, bro. This is your time!"

The crowd started to roar. I could feel it as much as I could hear it.

"All right, let's go!" someone yelled. We ran out of the tunnel as the pyrotechnic flames shot up into the air. I could feel the heat. The crowd was going crazy. I ran out onto the field in awe, looking back and forth, taking it all in, raising a fist in the air as we made our way to the fifty-yard line.

At the fifty, I took my helmet off and looked around at that crowd of tens of thousands in the Georgia Dome. I took a knee and started praying. *Thanking* God.

I couldn't stop myself from crying.

After a minute or so, I opened my eyes and noticed that there were cameras on the field. More than one of them was pointed right at me. I wiped away my tears, strapped my helmet back on, and hopped to my feet. "Here we go, baby. Let's go!"

But the tears of joy kept coming. During warm-ups before the game, I kept having to wipe my eyes. I just couldn't believe I was *there*. I couldn't stop flashing back. Comparing the now to the then.

• ◆ •

I didn't have the answers to why I went through it all. Why God chose me to endure such struggle. But I'd *made* it. I was *here*. I was unbroken. I had turned my dream into reality.

I didn't get into the game until the fourth quarter. But once I was in, I made the most of it. It didn't matter that the game was almost over. It didn't matter that this was a preseason game. I played like it was my Super Bowl.

I made three tackles in that one quarter, and whoever was running the sound in the Dome did something for me that they didn't do for the entire game: with each tackle I made, they rang a big loud bell.

I made my first tackle, and this big bell sound rang through the stadium.

Dong!

The crowd went wild.

Another tackle.

Dong!

Everybody went crazy again.

Another tackle.

Dong!

I looked out at that cheering crowd and I let that sound ring right through me.

• ◆ •

On August 30, 2013, after I'd played in four preseason games, the Falcons released me.

It wasn't much of a surprise.

As much as I wanted to make the team, my goal wasn't to lead the team, or to win a Super Bowl, or even to make a career out of football. It was to recapture a dream deferred. To play in the NFL. And I did that.

I set the bar of success at *my* level. I achieved what I said I'd do. And to do it after ten years of hell, ignoring the naysayers and defeating my own inner struggles, was success to me. No one could take that away.

So what was my dream now? Now that football was over.

I knew I had a message to share. I knew other men and women in my situation needed help. Laws needed to be changed. The California Innocence Project needed more support.

Would it be easy?

No.

Whatever life, whatever new dream I decided on would not get handed to me.

But that's life. And having a life is better than the alternative.

I'd been "released," and I took comfort in that word.

Because I'd been caged, because I'd been locked down, because I'd seen the worst of what can happen to a life when humans treat each other with anything less than the truth and honesty and equality with which we deserve to be treated, I learned to value the best of every little thing that life brings to us every day.

And that made me a better man.

I was free to start *my* life again. A life complete with new dreams, new loves, new direction, and new purpose—all backed by my understanding of God and my confidence in His creation: *me.*

An understanding that lifts you up.

An assurance that makes you fearless.

Yeah. You know what that is?

That's freedom.

True freedom.

I could not only dream of it now.

I was breathing it.

I was living it.

I *am* living it.

AFTERWORD

Closing Arguments

Football wasn't it for me.

Football wasn't my triumph.

I was *more* than football. I was *more* than some game. *More* than a player on somebody else's field. I had a more important future in store for me. I knew that. And thank God I knew that or I might have been crushed when I got the phone call releasing me from the Falcons.

Aside from football, I realized that what I truly want to do is to change the system. I want to help people like me who were imprisoned on false charges. And I want to lift people up—people from all walks of life—to teach them some of the lessons I went to hell and back to learn, so that maybe they won't have to endure so much pain in order to experience all the greatness that life has to offer.

At first I didn't know how I was going to accomplish any of that, or how I was going to make a living doing any of that— after all, we've all got bills to pay. But I put my trust in God. He'd led me this far. He'd brought me here. I knew He could get me to where He was telling me I ought to go.

Even before I played for the Falcons, I used what little celebrity I had gained and the press attention I'd earned from my exoneration to draw attention to other cases like mine in California. When I attended rallies, the news cameras showed up. And along with a bunch of other dedicated individuals, we managed to get a couple of people freed from their unjust imprisonments. One was Jason Puracal, who was sentenced to twenty-two years in a Nicaraguan prison for drug trafficking and money laundering, despite a complete lack of any evidence of those crimes. Another, Daniel Larsen, was convicted and served thirteen years of a twenty-eight-year sentence under California's three-strikes law for possession of a concealed weapon, despite overwhelming evidence that he wasn't carrying the knife police officers said he carried, and despite the fact that his trial lawyer failed to call any witnesses in his defense. (CIP found plenty of witnesses and gathered statements from them after his conviction, but it took eleven more years to finally get the case heard.)

It's hard to describe just how good it felt to know I'd played even a small role in helping to free those individuals.

And when it came to paying work, the NFL had more in store for me than I realized. After my career ended on the field, I started working with the NFL in a different capacity: First for the front office in New York City, in administration, and then simultaneously in the Officiating Department. I spent two years doing that before moving on to cohost a TV show on the Oxygen network: *Final Appeal* explored potential cases of wrongful conviction, spreading the word to hundreds of thousands of viewers about the injustices of our justice system, and working to reopen a few cases that had long been forgotten.

Then Hollywood came calling, and a director by the name of Tom Shadyac took on the task of bringing my story to the big screen. Tom was known for directing blockbuster comedies, from Jim Carrey's *Ace Ventura* and *Bruce Almighty* to Robin Williams's hit *Patch Adams*. But after suffering a nearly fatal accident in the desert, he'd reevaluated his life and decided to make films focused on big-picture *meaning* rather than just making big pictures. He turned my story into a compelling film starring Sherri Shepherd (from *The View*, and known primarily for comedy) as my mom, Greg Kinnear as CIP founder Justin Brooks, and an extraordinarily talented actor named Aldis Hodge as yours truly. I don't think we could have found a better cast if I'd asked the man above to do the hiring.

The film debuted at the Los Angeles Film Festival to standing ovations, and I learned that the film had found major distribution (through the film company Bleecker Street) just as I was finishing up writing this book—another opportunity that came my way, thanks be to God, to help spread my story and my message far and wide.

Walking red carpets at film festivals and seeing my name on the cover of a book—it's all surreal.

Surreal.

And honestly, I would trade it all if I could. Yeah, you read that right. I would happily give up all the attention and "fame" in a heartbeat if I could go back and relive my life without having suffered the consequences of someone else's false accusation; without suffering the consequences of being sent to prison and losing so much of my life, my hopes, and my dreams; without putting all of that pain and suffering on my family.

But there's no use crying about it. When it comes to the resilience of the human spirit, sometimes you've got to approach life with a zero-tolerance policy toward self-pity. When things go wrong, when the whole world seems against you, you have to stop and realize: This is your life now. This is where you are. So now what? It's up to you to make a choice with what you do with the situation. You can cry and complain, or you can get started making lemonade out of lemons, as the cliché says.

It's your choice. Just remember: nobody will work harder for you than you.

Think about when you were a kid and your parents demanded that you clean your room. You might have gone in there and thrown a tantrum for thirty minutes, but after that tantrum was over, guess what? The room still needed to be cleaned. Was anything gained by wasting that half hour of your life? If you hoped the outcome of the situation would change without you having to do anything, you were clearly mistaken. It's your room. Stop waiting for other people to clean it for you!

By eliminating self-pity and replacing it with self-empowerment, we have the ability to move forward.

I couldn't change what had happened to me. But I could change how I allowed it to affect me and what I chose to do moving forward.

And maybe this was God's plan.

Maybe you, after reading this book, will want to make a change. Maybe you'll want to see a change in the world, and will want to help make the changes we need to make in our justice system—before something like what happened to me happens to *you* or to someone you love.

The way things stand now, it is far too easy to make false accusations, to lie to investigators and lie in court with no consequences.

False accusers rarely serve time for their crimes, even while their victims suffer, go to prison, lose their jobs, and lose their names and reputations over the very lies those accusers tell.

That needs to change.

And please, do *not* twist what I'm saying here. I'm not saying that all accusations are false. In fact, I think statistics out there will show that the vast majority of accusations, especially those of a sexual nature, are absolutely true. People do not normally make these things up. Sexual assault is an abominable offense. But false accusations do exist. People lie. Men lie. Women lie. This isn't a sexist issue. This isn't a male-versus-female debate. There is nothing about my story—not one thing—that negates the empowerment of women. I support women. From my mom, to my sister, to the mother of my child and all the women who surround me, I love them and want to protect them.

I want *all* people to feel safe.

So this isn't about whether we "believe" accusers or not. Our justice system is supposed to function so that "belief" is removed from the equation.

Justice is supposed to be served through facts and evidence. "Truth and justice." They're supposed to go hand in hand. Yet we all know that people commit perjury in courtrooms all the time—in family courts as well as in criminal courts—and rarely do they get in any substantial trouble for the lies they tell, lies that hurt other people and corrupt and corrode the very idea of justice itself.

Why?

The system itself is to blame.

When someone gets up on a witness stand in the courtroom, they swear on a Bible to tell the truth, the whole truth, and nothing but the truth. But ask yourself this: How many of those people have ever read the Bible? How many are God-fearing individuals? What happens to the millions of people who don't read the Bible, don't believe in God, and don't fear any punishment from God for breaking that Bible-based oath?

I'll tell you what: those people lie with ease, and without consequence.

Why does the Bible play such a crucial role at the most critical junctures in our legal system?

What if instead of swearing on a Bible to tell the truth, the whole truth, "so help you, God," what if every witness was sworn "to tell the truth, the whole truth, and nothing but the truth or face an automatic sentence of thirty years in state prison."

Imagine how quickly the justice system would change. Imagine how quickly the *whole* system would change. Imagine if people were prosecuted for their lies!

And please note that I didn't say "persecuted." This isn't about *persecuting* anybody. This is about *prosecuting* people who commit the crimes of perjury and false accusation. Like I said, people lie. That's just a fact. Men, women, black, white, Hispanic, "other"—this isn't a gender issue, and it isn't a race issue, either. It's a *justice* issue. And right now, our justice system is broken.

So why don't we fix it?

Have you noticed that this issue of "truth and justice" keeps coming up again and again? From the political spectrum, to divorce cases, to all sorts of criminal cases, in movies, television, podcasts, social media—it's everywhere. And I believe this issue, all sides of this issue, are so prevalent in our society today and so widely covered in the media for one reason: because we need to listen.

It is our time now to stop complaining; to stop getting lost in the noise of what's broken; to look inside as a nation and consider what matters to us as people; to take a good long look at this issue and *do something about it.*

We all know there are false accusations in the world. We all know there are people sitting in prison who are innocent. And we all know that it's *wrong.* We also know there are lots of guilty people in the world who lie about the terrible things they've done and are somehow given a free pass to keep on lying, to lie without consequence.

In my opinion, *all* of that needs to end. And I'm not saying we need to take the Bible out of the equation. We just need to take it out of the courtroom. We need to bring back a sense of morality, a belief in something bigger than ourselves, a shared belief that lying is immoral. And we need to create new rules, new laws, and just consequences for those who lie—especially and specifically when it hurts other people.

Innocent people.

In my case, the statute of limitations for prosecuting my accuser was eight years. She was free and clear from being prosecuted for her lies before I ever had tangible proof that she was lying.

Does that make sense? To you? To *anyone*? That I should lose ten years of my life, ten years of unjust punishment for a crime I didn't commit, and yet she's the one protected under the law?

The only thing the system came after her for was the money: The school system successfully sued and won a judgment from the state against my accuser and her mother, demanding they return the money they received in the settlement after suing the

Long Beach City School District. Of course, as of this writing, they have yet to find her. They have yet to receive one cent.

None of it makes sense. And I understand there are reasons for statutes of limitations in some instances. How would society function if we were constantly prosecuting crimes from fifty or one hundred years ago? The courts are already clogged as it is.

But allowing liars to make false accusations without punishment is far worse, in my opinion, than the suffering that might be caused by clogging up some courtrooms.

And if we put concrete punishments for lying in place, concrete punishments for provable false accusations and perjury, I have a feeling that millions of currently unjust cases would suddenly go away. *Poof*. Our court systems would be far less clogged.

Will people ever stop lying? No. Of course not. But can we change the ability to lie without consequence in our court system, in our "justice" system?

Yes. Yes, we can. Of course we can!

Any step in the right direction would be just that, a step in the right direction.

It's time for all of us to accept our responsibility and to rejoice in our ability to *be* the change we want to see in the world. Through my story, and the stories of countless others, we are seeing the injustice highlighted like never before.

It's our time now to *fix* it.

So I hope you'll join me in whatever capacity you can to elect individuals who care about these issues; to support changes in laws that address these issues; and to help make sure that those in power stop running from and brushing aside our desperate cries for reform—when what they really need to do, once and for all, is to be still and listen.

ACKNOWLEDGMENTS

I want to take this moment to thank my mom, my brother and sister, my extended family, and all of those who believed in me and never gave up on me. And to those I promised I wouldn't take this second chance for granted: I have not let you down.

I want to thank the California Innocence Project, without whom this book might have a very different ending.

Thanks also to my literary agent, Jaidree Braddix; my editor, Peter Borland; the entire team at Atria Books; and my coauthor, Mark Dagostino (and his editorial assistant, Terry Taylor), for allowing my words and my story to shine.

Thanks especially to my loves: Vanessa and our baby, O'rion King Banks.

And of course, my Creator. Without You, there is no me.

WHAT SET ME FREE

Brian Banks

This reading group guide for What Set Me Free *includes an introduction, discussion questions, and ideas for enhancing your book club. The suggested questions are intended to help your reading group find new and interesting angles and topics for your discussion. We hope that these ideas will enrich your conversation and increase your enjoyment of the book.*

INTRODUCTION

At age sixteen, Brian Banks was a happy, popular high school junior—and a nationally recruited All-American football player, ranked eleventh in the nation as a linebacker. Before his seventeenth birthday, he was in jail, awaiting trial on charges of a heinous sexual assault he did not commit. Despite being innocent, Brian took a plea and was sentenced as an adult to six years in prison. Surrounded by darkness, Brian had an epiphany that would change his life. What follows is the story of a remarkable young man who is determined to prove his innocence and recapture the future that was taken from him, refusing to allow his circumstances to destroy him.

TOPICS & QUESTIONS FOR DISCUSSION

1. Mr. Johnson says to Brian, "Be in this world, but not of this world." How do those words impact Brian when he first hears them, and when he recalls them later? How do you think those words might apply to someone facing other challenges in life?

2. The National Association of Criminal Defense Lawyers (NACDL) reports that fewer than 3 percent of state and federal criminal cases go to trial, meaning 97 percent of cases are resolved by plea deals. Brian's own lawyer strongly encourages him to take the plea deal he's offered (pg. 82), even though Brian insists he is innocent. How does Brian's experience illustrate why so few cases go to trial? Do you think this is a fair system, and if not, how would you improve it?

3. In juvie, Brian encounters other minors who have been sentenced to thirty, forty, and even seventy-two years in prison (pg. 93). According to the Sentencing Project, twenty-one states have banned life sentences without the possibility of

parole for juveniles. Do you believe there should be a maximum punishment for juveniles? Should juveniles be allowed to be tried as adults?

4. Brian is given ten minutes to decide: face trial with the possibility of serving forty-one years to life, or take the plea bargain and go to jail for anywhere from ninety days to six years. Even though he knows he is innocent, he takes this deal (pg. 109). Do you think he made the right choice, given his circumstances? Would you have made the same choice in his situation? Why?

5. "The fact is, prison was a minute-by-minute, hour-by-hour existence. The only thoughts I had were about what I should and shouldn't be doing all the time" (pg. 133). How is Brian's mind-set changed by the harsh conditions of prison? In what ways do these conditions impose a mental imprisonment in addition to Brian's physical confinement?

6. When told by his evaluator that he can change his time served through good behavior, Brian thinks: *Good behavior. In a maximum-security prison. Do any of you people even know what prison is like?"* (pg. 170) After reading about Brian's experiences, in what ways do you think prisoners are set up to fail? Is the purpose of prison to punish or to rehabilitate, or something else?

7. When Brian is given the chance to read the complete file on his case, he is stunned to see how his interviews with investigators and psychologists were portrayed. Do you think the reports were biased because Brian was presumed to be guilty? How could the system have arrived at a more accurate evaluation of who Brian was and what he did?

8. Brian finds that life as a parolee presents a whole new set of challenges. What surprised you about his descriptions of the parole system? What do you think is the main purpose of the parole system? What sorts of resources would be useful to someone in Brian's position as they are attempting to rebuild their lives?

9. Brian develops a mantra as his time in prison drags on: *"For one that is free in the mind is free no matter their physical condition"* (pg. 185) Do you agree with this statement? What were your biggest takeaways from reading Brian's story?

10. Brian achieves something remarkable when he writes his own writ of habeas corpus from prison, has it accepted by the appeals court, and a hearing on his case is scheduled. Then, in court, he makes the sudden decision to withdraw his appeal. Why did he give up the chance to have his verdict overturned and to get a new trial? Would you have done the same thing under those circumstances?

11. One of the most surprising moments in Brian's story occurs when his accuser reaches out on Facebook with a "friend request." What do you think might

have motivated her to contact Brian? What did you think of the way Brian responded to this request? What would you have done in the same situation?

12. In the afterword, Brian says, "I'm not saying that all accusations are false. In fact, I think statistics out there will show the vast majority of accusations, especially those of a sexual nature, are absolutely true" (pg. 309). According to *The Cut*, only 5 percent of reported rape allegations are false, while 90 to 95 percent of assaults don't get reported to the police at all. Even though Brian's case is rare, what does it illustrate about flaws in the system of justice that hurt both the falsely accused and the victims of sexual assault? Can you think of examples of women who were assaulted and came forward to tell the truth, but did not get justice? In the judicial system, is it possible to treat those who have been accused of a crime as "innocent until proven guilty"? Should someone who is found to have made a false accusation be prosecuted?

13. Brian advocates "eliminating self-pity and replacing it with self-empowerment," because "nobody will work harder for you than you." Do you believe that to be true? What are some areas of your life where you might be able to make a positive change by changing your point of view?

ENHANCE YOUR BOOK CLUB

1. Brian Banks's story has been turned into a movie, *Brian Banks,* which will premiere nationwide on August 9, 2019. Take your book club to see the movie and discuss how the book and movie versions differ. What does the book focus on and show that the movie does not, and vice versa? What is most powerful about each version? Do the performances of the actors align with the vision you had of these people after reading the book?

2. *What Set Me Free* touches on many injustices in the current criminal justice system in America, such as prison overcrowding (pg. 127) and racial disparities in prison sentencing (pg. 94). Go to www.sentencingproject.org and look up some of the statistics they provide about the criminal justice system. What were you most surprised to learn that you didn't know previously? How does learning these statistics enhance your understanding of Brian's story? How does reading *What Set Me Free* make these statistics personal?

3. After his harrowing ordeal, Brian did not become bitter, but instead decided to turn his life into something positive. Think of three things you can do personally in the next year, such as donating to nonprofits, joining local organizations, or writing your congressional representative to help support criminal justice reform. With your book club, plan some dates to take action together.